This Is <u>Not</u> Propaganda

Adventures in the War
Against Reality

Peter Pomerantsev

FABER & FABER

First published in 2019
by Faber & Faber Limited
Bloomsbury House
74–77 Great Russell Street, London WC1B 3DA

Typeset by Ian Bahrami
Printed in England by CPI Group (UK) Ltd, Croydon CR0 4YY

A CIP record for this book
is available from the British Library

ISBN 978–0–571–33863–4

FSC
www.fsc.org
MIX
Paper from
responsible sources
FSC® C020471

6 8 10 9 7 5

Contents

Preface: 'Telegram!'   1

Part 1: Cities of Trolls   11
Part 2: Democracy at Sea   57
Part 3: The Most Amazing Information Warfare
         Blitzkrieg in History   107
Part 4: Soft Facts   153
Part 5: Pop-Up People   193
Part 6: The Future Starts Here   227

Acknowledgements   257
Notes   259

Preface: 'Telegram!'

He came out of the sea and was arrested on the beach: two men in suits standing over his clothes as he returned from his swim. They ordered him to get dressed quickly, pull his trousers over his wet trunks. On the drive the trunks were still wet, shrinking, turning cold, leaving a damp patch on his trousers and the back seat. He had to keep them on during the interrogation. There he was, trying to keep up a dignified facade, but all the time the dank trunks made him squirm. It struck him they had done it on purpose. They were well versed in this sort of thing, these mid-ranking KGB men: masters of the small-time humiliation, the micro-mind game.

Why had they arrested him here, he wondered, in Odessa, not where he lived, in Kiev? Then he realised: it was August and they wanted a few days by the seaside. In between interrogations, they would take him to the beach to go swimming themselves. One would sit with him while the other would bathe. On one of their visits to the beach an artist took out an easel and began to paint the three of them. The colonel and major grew nervous – they were KGB and weren't meant to have their images recorded during an operation. 'Go have a look at what he's drawing,' they ordered their prisoner. He went over and had a look. Now it was his turn to mess with them a little: 'He's not drawn a good likeness of me, but you're coming out very true to life.'

He had been detained for 'distributing copies of harmful literature to friends and acquaintances': books censored for telling the truth about the Soviet Gulag (Solzhenitsyn) or for being written by exiles (Nabokov). The case was recorded in the Chronicle of

Current Events. *The* Chronicle *was how Soviet dissidents docu-
mented suppressed facts about political arrests, interrogations,
searches, trials, beatings, abuses in prison. Information was
gathered via word of mouth or smuggled out of labour camps
in tiny self-made polythene capsules that were swallowed and
then shat out, their contents typed up and photographed in dark
rooms. It was then passed from person to person, hidden in the
pages of books and diplomatic pouches, until it could reach the
West and be delivered to Amnesty International or broadcast on
the BBC World Service, Voice of America or Radio Free Europe.
It was known for its curt style:*

*'He was questioned by KGB Colonel V. P. MEN'SHIKOV and
KGB Major V. N. MEL'GUNOV. He rejected all charges as base-
less and unproven. He refused to give evidence about his friends
and acquaintances. For all six days they were housed in the Hotel
New Moscow.'*

*When one interrogator would leave, the other would pull out
a book of chess puzzles and solve them, chewing on the end of a
pencil. At first the prisoner wondered if this was some clever mind
game, then he realised the man was just lazy, killing time at work.*

*After six days he was permitted to go back to Kiev, but the inves-
tigation continued. On the way home from work at the library,
the black car would pull up and take him for more interrogations.*

*During that time, life went on. His fiancée conceived. They
married. At the back of the reception lurked a KGB photographer.*

*He moved in with his wife's family, in a flat opposite Goloseevsky
Park, where his father-in-law had put up a palace of cages for
his dozens of canaries, an aviary of throbbing feathers darting
against the backdrop of the park. Every time the doorbell rang
he would start, scared it was the KGB, and would begin burning*

anything incriminating: letters, samizdat articles, lists of arrests. The canaries would beat their wings in a panic-stricken flutter. Each morning he rose at dawn, gently turned the Spidola radio to 'ON', pushed the dial to short-wave, wiggled and waved the antenna to dispel the fog of jamming, climbed on chairs and tables to get the best reception, steering the dial in an acoustic slalom between transmissions of East German pop and Soviet military bands, pressing his ear tight to the speaker and, through the hiss and crackle, making his way to the magical words: 'This is London'; 'This is Washington.' He was listening for news about arrests. He read the futurist poet Velimir Khlebnikov's 1921 essay 'Radio of the Future':

Radio will forge the unbroken chain of the global soul and fuse mankind.

The net closed around his circle. Grisha was taken to the woods and roughed up. Olga was accused of being a prostitute and, to make the point, was locked up in a VD clinic with actual prostitutes. Geli was taken to remand prison and refused treatment for so long that he went and died.

Everyone prepared for the worst. His mother-in-law taught him a secret code based on sausages: 'If I bring sausages sliced right to left, it means we've been able to get out news of your arrest to the West, and it's been broadcast on the radio. If I slice them left to right, it means we failed.'

'It sounds like something out of an old joke or a bad film, but it's nevertheless true,' he would write later. 'When the KGB come at dawn, and you mumble drowsily, "Who's there?" they often shout, "Telegram!" You proceed in semi-sleep, trying not to wake up too

much so you can still go back to a snug dream. "One moment,"
you moan, pull on the nearest trousers, dig out some change to
pay the messenger, open the door. And the most painful part is
not that they have come for you, or that they got you up so early,
but that you, like some small boy, fell for the lie about delivering
a telegram. You squeeze in your hot palm the suddenly sweaty
change, holding back tears of humiliation.'

At 08.00 a.m. on 30 September 1977, in between interroga-
tions, their child was born. My grandmother wanted me to be
called Pinhas, after her grandfather. My parents wanted Theodore.
I ended up being named Piotr, the first of several renegotiations
of my name.

———

Forty years have passed since my parents were pursued by the
KGB for pursuing the simple right to read, to write, to listen
to what they chose and to say what they wanted. Today, the
world they hoped for, in which censorship would fall like the
Berlin Wall, can seem much closer: we live in what academics
call an era of 'information abundance'. But the assumptions that
underlay the struggles for rights and freedoms in the twentieth
century – between citizens armed with truth and information
and regimes with their censors and secret police – have been
turned upside down. We now have more information than ever
before, but it hasn't brought only the benefits we expected.

More information was supposed to mean more freedom to
stand up to the powerful, but it's also given them new ways
to crush and silence dissent. More information was supposed
to mean a more informed debate, but we seem less capable

of deliberation than ever. More information was supposed to mean mutual understanding across borders, but it has also made possible new and more subtle forms of conflict and subversion. We live in a world of mass persuasion run amok, where the means of manipulation have gone forth and multiplied, a world of dark ads, psy-ops, hacks, bots, soft facts, deep fakes, fake news, ISIS, Putin, trolls, Trump . . .

Forty years after my father's detention and interrogation, I find myself following the palest of imprints of my parents' journey, though with none of their courage, risk or certainty. As I write this – and given the economic turbulence, this might not be the case when you read it – I run a programme in an institute at a London university that researches the newer breeds of influence campaigns, what might casually be referred to as 'propaganda', a term so fraught and fractured in its interpretation – defined by some as deception and by others as the neutral activity of propagation – that I avoid using it.

I should add that I'm not an academic, nor is this an academic work. I'm a lapsed television producer, and though I continue to write articles and sometimes present radio programmes, I now often find myself looking at my old media world askance, at times appalled by what we've wrought. In my research I meet Twitter revolutionaries and pop-up populists, trolls and elves, 'behavioural change' visionaries and info-war charlatans, jihadi fanboys, Identitarians, meta-politicians, truth cops and bot herders. Then I bring everything that I've learnt back to the hexagonal, concrete tower where my office has its temporary home and shape it into sensible Conclusions and Recommendations for neatly formatted reports and PowerPoint presentations, which diagnose and propose ways of remedying the flood of disinformation, 'fake news', 'information war' and the 'war on information'.

Remedying what, however? The neat little bullet points of my reports assume that there really is a coherent system that can be amended, that a few technical recommendations applied to new information technologies can fix everything. Yet the problems go far deeper. When, as part of my daily work, I present my findings to the representatives of the waning Liberal Democratic Order, the one formed in no little part out of the conflicts of the Cold War, I am struck by how lost they seem. Politicians no longer know what their parties represent; bureaucrats no longer know where power is located; billionaire foundations advocate for an 'open society' they can no longer quite define. Big words that once seemed swollen with meaning, words that previous generations were ready to sacrifice themselves for – 'democracy' and 'freedom', 'Europe' and 'the West' – have been so thoroughly left behind by life that they seem like empty husks in my hands, the last warmth and light draining out of them, or like computer files to which we have forgotten the password and can't access any more.

The very language we use to describe ourselves – 'left' and 'right', 'liberal' and 'conservative' – has been rendered near meaningless. And it's not just conflicts or elections that are affected. I can see people I have known my whole life slipping away from me on social media, reposting conspiracies from sources I have never heard of; Internet undercurrents pulling whole families apart, as if we never really knew each other, as if the algorithms know more about us than we do, as if we are becoming subsets of our own data, as if that data is rearranging our relations and identities with its own logic – or perhaps in order to serve the interests of someone we can't even see. The grand vessels of old media – the cathode-ray tubes of radios and televisions, the spines of books and the printing presses of newspapers that contained and controlled identity and meaning, who we were and how we talked to one another, how we explained the world to our children, how we spoke to our past, how we defined news and opinion, satire and seriousness, right and wrong, true, false, real, unreal – these vessels have cracked and burst, breaking up the old patterns of how what relates to whom, who speaks to whom and how, magnifying, shrinking, distorting all proportions, sending us spinning in disorientating spirals where words lose shared meanings. I hear the same phrases in Odessa, Manila, Mexico City, New Jersey: 'There is so much information, misinformation, so much of everything that I don't know what's true any more.' Often I hear the phrase 'I feel the world is moving beneath my feet.' I catch myself thinking, 'I feel that everything that I thought solid is now unsteady, liquid.'

This book explores the wreckage, searches what sparks of sense can be salvaged from it, rising from the dank corners of the Internet where trolls torture their victims, passing through the tussles over the stories that make sense of our societies, and ultimately trying to understand how we define ourselves.

Part 1 will take us from the Philippines to the Gulf of Finland, where we will learn how to break people with new information instruments, in ways more subtle than the old ones used by the KGB.

Part 2 will move from the western Balkans to Latin America and the European Union, where we will learn new ways to break whole resistance movements and their mythology.

Part 3 explores how one country can destroy another almost without touching it, blurring the contrast between war and peace, 'domestic' and 'international' – and where the most dangerous element may be the idea of 'information war' itself.

Part 4 will explore how the demand for a factual politics is reliant on a certain idea of progress and the future, and how the collapse of that idea of the future has made mass murder and abuse even more possible.

In Part 5 I will argue that in this flux, politics becomes a struggle to control the construction of identity. Everyone from religious extremists to pop-up populists wants to create new versions of 'the people' – even in Britain, a country where identity always seemed so fixed.

In Part 6 I will look for the future – in China and in Chernivtsi.

Throughout the book I will travel, some of the time through space, but not always. The physical and political maps delineating continents, countries and oceans, the maps I grew up with, can be less important than the new maps of information flows. These 'network maps' are generated by data scientists. They call the process 'surfacing'. One takes a keyword, a message, a narrative and casts it into the ever-expanding pool of the world's data. The data scientist then 'surfaces' the people, media outlets, social media accounts, bots, trolls and cyborgs pushing or interacting with those keywords, narratives and messages.

These network maps, which look like fields of pin mould or photographs of distant galaxies, show how outdated our geographic definitions are, revealing unexpected constellations where anyone from anywhere can influence everyone everywhere. Russian hackers run ads for Dubai hookers alongside anime memes supporting far-right parties in Germany. A 'rooted cosmopolitan' sitting at home in Scotland guides activists away from police during riots in Istanbul. ISIS publicity lurks behind links to iPhones . . .

Russia, with its social media squadrons, haunts these maps. Not because it is the force that can still move earth and heaven as it could in the Cold War, but because the Kremlin's rulers are particularly adept at gaming elements of this new age, or at the very least are good at getting everyone to talk about how good they are, which could be the most important trick of all. As I will explain, this is not entirely accidental: precisely because they had lost the Cold War, Russian spin doctors and media manipulators managed to adapt to the new world quicker than anyone in the thing once known as 'the West'. Between 2001 and 2010 I lived in Moscow and saw close up the same tactics of control and the same pathologies in public opinion which have since sprouted everywhere.

But as this book travels through information flows and across networks and countries it also looks back in time, to the story of my parents, to the Cold War. This is not a family memoir as such; rather, I am concerned with where my family's story intersects with my subject. This is in part to see how the ideals of the past have fallen apart in the present and what, if anything, can still be gleaned from them. When all is swirling I find myself instinctively looking back, searching for a connection with the past in order to find a way to think about the future.

But as I researched and wrote these sections of family history I was struck by something else: the extent to which our private thoughts, creative impulses and senses of self are shaped by information forces greater than ourselves. If there is one thing I've been impressed with while browsing the shelves in the spiral-shaped library of my university, it is that one has to look beyond just 'news' and 'politics' and also consider poetry, schools, the language of bureaucracy and leisure to understand, as French philosopher Jacques Ellul put it, the 'formation of men's attitudes'. This process is sometimes more evident in my family, because the dramas and ruptures of our lives makes it easier to see where those information forces, like vast weather systems, begin and end.

Part 1: Cities of Trolls

Freedom of speech versus censorship was one of the clearer confrontations of the twentieth century. After the Cold War, freedom of speech appeared to have emerged victorious in many places. But what if the powerful can use 'information abundance' to find new ways of stifling you, flipping the ideals of freedom of speech to crush dissent, while always leaving enough anonymity to be able to claim deniability?

The Disinformation Architecture

Consider the Philippines. In 1977, as my parents were experiencing the pleasures of the KGB, the Philippines was ruled by Colonel Ferdinand Marcos, a US-backed military dictator, under whose regime, a quick search of the Amnesty International website informs me, 3,257 political prisoners were killed, 35,000 tortured and 70,000 incarcerated. Marcos had a very theatrical philosophy of the role torture could play in pacifying society. Instead of being merely 'disappeared', 77 per cent of those killed were displayed by the side of roads as warnings to others. Victims might have their brains removed, for example, and their empty skulls stuffed with their underpants. Or they could be cut into pieces, so one would pass body parts on the way to market.[1]

Marcos's regime fell in 1986 in the face of mass protests, the US relinquishing its support and parts of the army defecting. Millions came out on the streets. It was meant to be a new day: an end to corruption, an end to the abuse of human rights. Marcos was exiled and lived out his last years in Hawaii.

Today Manila greets you with sudden gusts of rotting fish and popcorn smells, wafts of sewage and cooking oil, which leave you retching on the pavement. Actually, 'pavement' is the wrong word. There are few, in the sense of broad walkways where you can stroll. Instead, there are thin ledges that run along the rims of malls and skyscrapers, where you inch along beside the lava of traffic. Between the malls the city drops into deep troughs of slums, where at night the homeless sleep encased in silver foil, their feet sticking out, flopped over in alleys between bars boasting midget boxing and karaoke parlours where you can hire troupes of girls, in dresses so tight they cling to their thighs like pincers, to sing Korean pop songs with you.

During the day you negotiate the spaces between mall, slum and skyscraper along elevated networks of crowded narrow walkways that are suspended in mid-air, winding in between the multistorey motorways. You duck your head to miss the buttresses of flyovers, flinch from the barrage of honks and sirens below, suddenly finding yourself at eye level with a pumping train or eye to eye with the picture of a woman eating Spam on one of the colossal advertising billboards. The billboards are everywhere, separating slum from skyscraper. Between 1898 and 1946 the Philippines was under US administration (apart from the Japanese occupation between 1942 and 1945). US navy bases have been present ever since, and US military food has become a delicacy. On one poster a happy housewife feeds her handsome husband tuna chunks from a tin. Elsewhere a picture of a dripping, roasting ham sits over a steaming river in which street kids swim; behind them an electric sign flashes 'Jesus Will Save You'. This is a Catholic country: three hundred years of Spanish colonialism preceded America's fifty ('We had three hundred years of the Church and fifty years of Hollywood,' Filipinos joke). The malls have churches you can worship in and guards to keep out the poor. It's a city of twenty-two million with almost no notion of common public space. Inside, the malls are perfumed with overpowering air freshener: lavender in the cheaper ones with their fields of fast-food outlets; a lighter lemon scent in the more sophisticated. This makes them smell like toilets, so the odour of the latrine never leaves you, whether it's sewage outside or the malls inside.

Soon you start noticing the selfies. Everyone is at it: the sweaty guy in greasy flip-flops riding the metal canister of a public bus; the Chinese girls waiting for their cocktails in the malls. The Philippines has the world's highest use of selfies; the highest use of social media per capita; the highest use of text messages. Some put this down to the importance of family and personal connections as a means of getting by in the face of ineffective government. Nor are the selfies narcissistic necessarily: you trust people whose faces you can see.

And with the rise of social media the Philippines has become a capital for a new breed of digital-era manipulation.

I meet with 'P' in one of the oases of malls next to sky-blue-windowed skyscrapers. He insists I can't use his name, but you can tell he's torn, desperate for recognition for the campaigns he can't take credit for. He's in his early twenties, dressed as if he were a member of a Korean boy band, and whether he's talking about getting a president elected or his Instagram account registered with a blue tick (which denotes status), there's almost no change in his always heightened emotions.

'There's a happiness to me if I'm able to control the people. Maybe it's a bad thing. It satisfies my ego, something deeper in me . . . It's like becoming a god in the digital side,' he exclaims. But it doesn't sound creepy, more like someone playing the role of the baddie in a musical farce.

He began his online career at the age of fifteen, creating an anonymous page that encouraged people to speak about their romantic experiences. 'Tell me about your worst break-up,' he would ask. 'What was your hottest date?' He shows me one of his Facebook groups: it has more than three million members.

While still at school he created new groups, each one with a different profile: one dedicated to joy, for example, another to mental strength. He was only sixteen when he began to be approached by corporations who would ask him to sneak in some mentions of their products. He honed his technique. For a week he would get a community to talk about 'love', for example, who they cared about the most. Then he would move the conversation to fear for your loved ones, the fear of losing someone. Then he would slide in a product: take this medicine and it will help extend the lives of loved ones.

He claims that by the age of twenty he had fifteen million followers across all the platforms. The modest middle-class boy from the provinces could suddenly afford his own condo in a Manila skyscraper.

After advertising, his next challenge was politics. At that point, political PR was all about getting journalists to write what you wanted. What if you could shape the whole conversation through social media?

He pitched his approach to several parties, but the only candidate who would take P on was Rodrigo Duterte, an outsider who looked to social media as a new route to victory. One of Duterte's main selling points as a candidate was busting drug crime. He even boasted of driving around on a motorcycle and shooting drug dealers while he was mayor of Davao City, down in the deep south of the country. At the time, P was already in college, attending lectures on the 'Little Albert' experiment from the 1920s, in which a toddler was exposed to frightening sounds whenever he saw a white rat, leading to him being afraid of all furry animals.[2] P says this inspired him to try something similar with Duterte.

First, he created a series of Facebook groups in different cities. They were innocuous enough, just discussion boards of what was on in town. The trick was to put them in the local dialect, of which there are hundreds in the Philippines. After six months, each group had in the region of 100,000 members. Then his administrators would start posting one local crime story per day, every day, to coincide with peak Internet traffic. The crime stories were real enough, but then P's people would write comments that connected the crime to drugs: 'They say the killer was a drug dealer,' or 'This one was a victim of a pusher.' After a month they dropped in two stories per day; a month later, three per day.

Drug crime became a hot topic, and Duterte drew ahead in the polls. P says this is when he fell out with the other PR people in the team and quit to join another candidate. This one was running on economic competence rather than fear. P claims he managed to get his rating up by more than five points, but it was too late to turn the tide and Duterte was elected president. Now he sees any number of PR people taking the credit for Duterte, and it riles him.

The trouble with interviewing anyone who works in this world is that they always tend to amplify their impact. It comes with the profession. Did P 'create' Duterte? Of course not. There would have been many factors that drove the conversation about drug crime, not least Duterte's own pronouncements. Nor was busting drug crime Duterte's only selling point: I have talked to supporters of his who were attracted by the image of a provincial fighting the elites of 'Imperial Manila' and the prim

Catholic Church establishment. But P's account of digital influence does echo some academic studies.

In 'Architects of Networked Disinformation', Dr Jonathan Corpus Ong of the University of Massachusetts and Dr Jason Cabañes of Leeds University spent twelve months interviewing the protagonists of what Ong called Manila's 'disinformation architecture', which was made use of by every party in the country.[3] At the top were what he described as the 'chief architects' of the system. They came from advertising and PR firms, lived in sleek apartments in the skyscrapers and described their work in an almost mythical way, comparing themselves to characters from the hit HBO fantasy TV series *Game of Thrones* and video games. 'It's game over when you're found out,' they would tell Ong. They were proud they had made it to the top of their profession from modest beginnings. 'The disinformation architect', concludes Ong, 'denies responsibility or commitment to the broader public by narrating a personal project of self-empowerment instead.'

Below the architects came the 'influencers', online comedians who, in between posting the latest jokes, made fun of opposing politicians for a fee.

Down in the slums of the disinformation architecture were what Ong called the 'community-level fake account operators': call centres full of people working twenty-four-hour shifts, paid by the hour, with one person manning dozens of social media personas. They could be either someone who needed a little extra cash (students or nurses, for example) or campaign staff. Ong interviewed one operator, Rina, who had been forced into the work when she joined a mayoral campaign. She had signed on out of idealism and had been at the top of her class at university. Now she was told to create multiple online personalities (girls clad in bikinis worked best), make online friends, promote her candidate and smear the opposition. Rina was ashamed. She felt she sabotaged herself, bringing in only twenty Facebook followers, whereas her colleagues brought in hundreds.

Ong noted that no one, at any level in this business, ever described their activity as 'trolling' or producing 'fake news'. Everyone had their own 'denial strategies': the architects stressed it was merely a side hustle to their regular PR work and thus didn't define them, and anyway they weren't in charge of the whole political campaign; the community-level operators said someone else was leaving the really nasty, hateful comments. In any case this was the architecture of online influence, which would shift into a more aggressive gear when Duterte came to power.

Duterte had vowed to kill so many drug dealers it would fatten the fish in Manila Bay, and joked that he would sign a pardon to forgive himself. He boasted of having killed someone over a 'look', that the lives of drug dealers meant nothing to him. Now vigilante gangs and cops began to shoot anyone suspected of connections to the drug trade. No one knows exactly how many have been killed in the campaign. Human rights organisations estimate 12,000, opposition politicians 20,000, the government 4,200. At one point thirty-three were being killed a day. No one would check if the victims were actually guilty, and there were frequent reports of drugs being planted on the victims after they were dead. Fifty-four children were executed too. The alleys of Manila's slums filled up with corpses. Men on motorbikes would drive up and just shoot people in the head. The prisons became as crowded as battery chicken farms. A politician who pushed back against the killings, Senator Leila de Lima, suddenly found herself on trial: imprisoned drug lords were giving testimony that she was involved in their business. Online mobs bayed for her arrest. She was locked away pending a trial that never began: a prisoner of conscience, according to Amnesty International.[4] When the country's archbishop condemned the killings, the mobs turned on him. Next it would be the turn of the media: the so-called 'presstitutes' who dared to accuse the president of murder.

And the greatest presstitute the regime would target was Maria Ressa, the head of the news website Rappler. This was ironic, as it was Maria and Rappler who had inadvertently helped bring Duterte into power.

#Arrest MariaRessa!

After talking to Maria for a while, I noticed how uncomfortable she felt at being made the subject of the story. She was far too polite to tell me this herself straight away, but I noticed she was always turning our interview away from herself and towards the work of her journalists, the dramas of others. In her career she's always been the one who covers things: first as the head of the CNN bureaus in South East Asia, then as the head of news at the Philippines' largest television network, and ultimately as the creator and CEO of Rappler. And now it was not only me interviewing Maria in her office as she tried to swallow a rushed lunch of peanut butter and tinned sardine sandwiches (a Philippine speciality); there was also a documentary crew from the English-language version of the Qatari TV channel

Al Jazeera, who were following Maria around to document her battle with Duterte and disinformation.

The Al Jazeera crew asked whether they could film me interviewing Maria, and as they crouched in the corner with their huge cameras I felt increasingly ill at ease. I too am used to being the one who observes and edits, and whenever I become the subject of someone else's content, I find myself a little too aware of how I can be recut and recreated later. In my own time as a documentary producer I learnt the skill of making contributors feel significant, meaningful, maybe a touch immortal for a moment while I filmed them, knowing that later in the edit I would have the power to shape the material. The final story would be accurate, but there's oh-so-often a painful gap between a person's self-perception and the way they are portrayed, between the reality reconstructed in the edit and the one the subject feels is true. That day in Manila I consoled myself that I would be able to reassert narrative control by writing about the Al Jazeera crew in the book you are reading now.

So there we were, one set of journalists filming another sort of one interviewing a third. The job of journalists is to report information on reality, on where the action is. But, as Maria's own story showed, information itself is now where the action is.

Maria was originally from Manila, but when she was ten her mother had taken the family to the US, where Maria was the smallest, brownest girl in Elizabeth, New Jersey, and precocious enough to be the first in the family to go to university (Princeton). She returned to the Philippines on a Fulbright in 1986 to study political theatre, only to find she had landed in the middle of a revolution against Marcos, where the greatest political drama was playing out on the streets. She joined

CNN when it was just a minor US cable operation with grand ideas about becoming the first global news network. At CNN it was the on-screen reporter who was the most important, who decided which stories to cover, when and how. Maria wanted that authority, but she didn't like being on camera, not least because she'd suffered from eczema all her life, which meant she had to come up with a paraphernalia of make-up and camera tricks in order to disguise it. The camera, however, loved Maria: her lack of pretence and almost puppy-like enthusiasm; the big eyes brimming with curiosity.

Maria became the face of CNN in the region, narrating South East Asia's 'democratisation' in the 1990s, when, after Marcos, one authoritarian regime fell after another. It was tempting to see it all through the lens of Cold War victory, as many did, as a linear tale of ever-expanding freedom, which every new political turn was appearing to confirm. The terror attacks of 11 September 2001 shattered that simplistic story.

Maria was less surprised. She spoke local dialects fluently, knew how little 'democracy' was delivering in the unchangingly poor villages and slums. When she interviewed Al-Qaeda recruits and their families, what struck her was how normal their backgrounds were, how distant fundamentalist purity had originally been for most of them. Osama bin Laden's trick had been to take the very different grievances of very different groups and give them the illusion that if they united globally, they would achieve a better world, if only they could get rid of unbelievers. In 2005 Maria moved on from CNN. In retrospect, she realised it was just in time. The network was changing, reporters were being asked to express their feelings rather than just give the facts, making money was becoming a more obsessive motivation. Maria wanted to investigate terrorists, not star in some reality-show version of the news.

On 9 June 2008, when she was running the news side of the Philippines' largest television network, Maria was woken early in the morning by her star reporter, Ces Drilon: 'Maria, this is all my fault . . . We've been kidnapped. And they want money.'[5] Despite Maria's orders to the contrary, Drilon had chased an interview with Islamist insurgents and had been kidnapped, along with two cameramen, by Al-Qaeda affiliate Abu Sayyaf.

Over the next ten days Maria worked day and night to help coordinate the rescue effort, which ended after Drilon's family managed to get enough money to satisfy the kidnappers' demands.

After the hostages had been handed over, Maria began to research the identities of the kidnappers. She found that they were related to bin Laden through three degrees of association. This fitted in with a pattern she had observed since she began covering the growth of Al-Qaeda from Afghanistan into South East Asia. Ideologies spread through networks, and your fealty to them depended on where you stood inside the web. Instead of just studying ideas and socio-economic factors, one had to understand the interconnections between people to see why and how Al-Qaeda's ideology was spreading. The same jumble of personal and social issues could have quite a different expression if they came into contact with a different network. And Maria realised that these physical networks were quickly being replaced with social media.

In 2012 Maria created Rappler, the Philippines' first purely Internet-based news site. She wanted to put her insights into networks to good use. Rappler would not merely report on current affairs, but engage a greater online community that would organise crowdfunding for important causes. It would gather vital information to help victims caught in floods and storms find shelter and assistance. Rather than old-school hacks, Maria hired twenty-year-olds who knew more about social media. When you walk into Rappler's orange and glass open-plan office you notice how young and largely female the staff are, with a small band of older journalists overseeing them with a hint of matronly severity. In Manila they're known as 'the Rapplers'.

When Duterte began his social media-inspired presidential campaign, he and Rappler seemed perfect for each other. The TV networks didn't take him seriously. When Rappler held the Philippines' first Facebook presidential debate, he was the only candidate who bothered to turn up. It was a runaway success. A poll of Rappler's online community showed Duterte was ahead. His message – to vanquish drug crime – was catching on. Rappler reporters found themselves repeating his sound bites about the 'war on drugs'. Later, when Duterte went on his killing spree, they would regret using the term 'war'. It helped to normalise his actions: if this was a 'war', then casualties became more acceptable.

The trouble started with a wolf whistle. At a press conference Duterte whistled at a female reporter from a TV network. The Rappler reporter in the room asked him to apologise. Rappler's online community filled up with comments saying she should be more respectful of the president. 'Your mother's a whore,' they wrote. The Rapplers were taken aback. This language didn't sound like their community. They put it down to the vestiges of sexism: any time a woman held a man to account, she would be attacked.

Meanwhile, Duterte's language didn't let up in its coarseness.[6] He called the Pope and US presidents sons of whores; enquired whether a journalist he didn't like was asking tough questions because his wife's vagina was so smelly; bragged about having two mistresses; joked about how a good-looking hostage should have been raped by him when he was mayor, instead of by her kidnappers. On TV Duterte said he wanted to eat the livers of terrorists and season them with salt; that if his troops raped three women each, he would take the rape sentences for them.

I learnt a little about the linguistic context behind such statements when I visited the comedy clubs in Quezon City, the section of Manila where teenage prostitutes and ladyboys congregate by night next to the TV towers of national broadcasters. The comedians pick out victims in the audience and roast them, taunting them about the size of their penises or their weight – and this right in front of entire families, who all laugh along at their relatives' humiliation.

This is the language Duterte partially taps into with his incessant stream of dirty jokes. It's a use of humour he shares with a troupe of male leaders across the world. Russian president Vladimir Putin made his rhetorical mark by promising to whack terrorists 'while they are on the shitter'; US president Donald Trump boasted of grabbing women 'by the pussy'; Czech president Miloš Zeman called for 'pissing on the charred remains of Roma'; Brazilian president Jair Bolsonaro told a female politician she was 'too ugly' to be raped and that black activists should go 'back to the zoo';[7] while in Britain the anti-immigration politician Nigel Farage, his outsized mouth gaping in a braying laugh, poured down pints and belched out rude jokes about 'Chinkies'.

This toilet humour is used to show how 'anti-Establishment' they are, their supposedly 'anti-elitist' politics expressed via the rejection of established moral and linguistic norms.

When dirty jokes are used by the the weak to poke fun at the powerful, they can bring authority figures back down to earth, give the sense that their rules can be suspended.[8] That's why dirty jokes have often been suppressed. In 1938, for example, my paternal great-grandfather went down to the cafeteria of the Kharkiv mega-factory where he worked as an accountant, had a drink, told a wisecrack about the balls of the Head of the Presidium of the Supreme Soviet, and was speedily reported on and arrested, perishing in a labour camp on the Volga river.

But when such language is used consistently by men of real power to degrade those who are weaker, this humour grows into something menacing: it lays the linguistic path to humiliating victims in other ways as well, to a space where all norms disappear.

As Rappler began to report on Duterte's extrajudicial killings, the online threats became incessant. At one point there were ninety messages an hour: claims that Rappler was making up the deaths, that it was in the pay of Duterte's enemies, that it was all fake news. The messages were like an infestation of insects, swarming into the email in-boxes and descending like a scourge onto the site's community pages, which Rappler had curated with such care to enable what it hoped would be the Internet's 'wisdom of crowds'. Sometimes Rappler staff would check to see who was behind a rape threat: maybe it was an automated account? To their disappointment it would turn out to be a real person. People were enjoying this. Rappler journalists were shouted at in the malls: 'Hey, you – you're fake news! Shame on you!' Relatives would admonish them too.

Maria bore the brunt of the attacks. Some were so stupid they just bounced off her, like the memes of her dressed in a Nazi uniform, or comments such as 'Maria, you're a waste of sperm. Your mother should have aborted you!' Others got under her skin – literally. Her eczema had always been her weak spot. When the attackers started to taunt her about her skin condition, it would flare up without her having time to erect her psychological defences.

Her first instinct was to blame herself. Had she done something wrong? Misreported something? She checked all of Rappler's output over and over but could find nothing. The hashtag #ArrestMariaRessa began to trend, as did #UnfollowRappler. The government launched a case against her. One of Rappler's investors had been an American foundation, so the government charged the network with following foreign editorial instructions. Several of Rappler's board members resigned; advertising plummeted. Maria started to walk around town with bail money on her. The first trial against Rappler ended up in the appeals court, where it was settled. And then, when the worst was thought to be over for Rappler, Maria got wind that another case was being prepared against her.[9]

During all the attacks on Rappler, Maria's managing editor, Glenda Gloria, seemed to me to be the most serene person in the newsroom. Perhaps it's because she has seen it all before. Glenda remembers the Marcos years. In the 1980s she'd been a student journalist covering the regime's torture of opposition figures. Her boyfriend had been arrested for running a small independent printing press and had had electrodes connected to his balls. Torture sessions combined the psychological and the physical; the ultimate aim was not merely to brutalise but to break. Professor Alfred McCoy of the University of Wisconsin–Madison, who has studied the psychological torture techniques of the CIA and US client states during the Cold War, relates the story of Father Kangleon, a priest falsely accused of subversion and cooperating with Communists who was denied sleep and daylight for over two months. At the denouement of his interrogation he was blindfolded, led into a new cell and sat down on a stool. He could hear a series of people coming in. Then different voices taunted him in a pre-planned piece of theatre which, when I read it in 2018, almost anticipates the taunts of anonymous trolls on social media:[10]

'Father, what's the name of the sister you met with at Sacred Heart College? . . . You are fucking her? How does it feel?'

'For me he is not a priest. Yes, your kind is not worthy of respect of a priest.'

'OK, take off his shirt. Oh, look at that body. You look sexy. Even the women here think you are macho. You are a homosexual?'

After this, the interrogation became more physical:

'Let's see if you are that macho after one of my punches.' (A short jab was delivered below the ribs.)

'Hey, don't lean on the table. Place your arms beside you. That's it.' (Another jab.)

'Take the stool away.' (He stood up and was hit behind the head, he started to cower, then more blows . . .)

After he agreed to cooperate, Kangleon was taken to a TV station and forced to say on air that he had helped Communist insurgents, naming other clergy supposedly involved in the insurrection.

Under Marcos, remembers Glenda, the government had agents in every university, every farm, church, office. They would go around and tell your colleagues, your neighbours, your friends that you were a Communist – even if you were not – destroying your reputation with a whispering campaign before they came to arrest you. Marcos grouped the media into 'proper' journalists and 'Communists', so every critic was dismissed as a 'Commie'.

'The psychological warfare that Marcos mastered is very similar to what is happening now,' Glenda tells me. 'The difference is, Duterte doesn't have to use the military to attack the media. How is it made possible? With technology.'

After Marcos was overthrown, the new Filipino democracy was far from perfect: human rights abuses continued; journalists' lives, especially in the provinces, were cheap.[11] But unlike most of his predecessors, who tried to obfuscate the abuses under their rule, who at least pretended to abide by some rules, Duterte exults in his extrajudicial killings, celebrates his attacks on journalists. He is also rehabilitating Marcos. Duterte had his body exhumed and gave him a military burial with full honours. He formed a political alliance with his son, Ferdinand 'Bongbong' Marcos, who still controlled his father's old stronghold in the country's north. A drip of videos appeared online, absolving Marcos of his crimes in the 1970s, claiming it was just rogue elements in his army who had killed and tortured . . .

But even as an imprint of Marcos's media methods emerged, Glenda thought there was an important difference in its digital-era manifestation. Back then, you could see the enemy. There was a sort of predictability: they could kill you, or you could skip town, contact a lawyer, write to a human rights group, take up arms. You knew who the agents were, who was coming for you and why. There was something of a routine to it all.

But now? You couldn't see the enemy. You couldn't tell who you were really up against. They were anonymous, everywhere and nowhere. How could you fight an online mob? You couldn't even tell how many of them were real.

———

After several months of this onslaught, Maria and the Rapplers dedicated themselves to making sense of the attacks. They could now see a pattern to the chaos. First, their credibility had been attacked, then they had been intimidated. With their reputations undermined, the virtual attacks were turning into real arrest warrants. They wondered whether there was a design lurking behind it all.

First to catch their eye were the Korean pop stars.

They kept appearing in their online community, commenting on how great Bongbong Marcos and Duterte were. How likely was it that Korean pop stars would be interested in Filipino politics? When they checked out the comments the pop stars were making, they matched one another word for word: obviously fake accounts, most likely controlled from the same source.

Now that they had identified accounts that were clearly fake, they ran a program that could scour the Internet to see who else was using the same language. This took two months, but they found other accounts repeating the same phrases. These looked more realistic, claiming to be real Filipinos with real jobs. Maria and the Rapplers began researching each one individually, calling their purported places of employment. No one had heard of them. Altogether they found twenty-six well-disguised but fake accounts repeating the same messages at the same time and reaching an audience of three million.

The Rapplers breathed a collective sigh of psychological relief: here was something to hold onto. Now that they could see the design in the attacks, they could get a sense of firm reality. This wasn't their fault. Somebody was doing it to them.

They began to categorise every narrative the mobs were using to attack them. They listed dozens: that the media are corrupt; that Rappler should be boycotted; that Senator Leila de Lima should be arrested. They looked at the frequency with which each narrative would appear, a sort of heartbeat monitor of mentions. They found they would peak sharply before a political event: mentions of 'media corruption' could increase by several orders of magnitude prior to an election, for example; calls for de Lima to be arrested soared before the police came for her. How spontaneous could that really have been?

They built up what Maria calls her 'shark tank', a sort of Internet attack radar system that warns when fake stories are approaching, when a smear campaign is starting to be built. If the smear is an old one, Rappler can automatically send out ripostes, raising the alarm among its online supporters to defend the cause.

In February 2018 the Rapplers became aware of an unusual creature on the Filipino Internet. His name was @Ivan226622 and he was reposting articles frenetically: 1,518 pieces about Filipino politics in just one week. The cover photo was unremarkable enough: a Filipino man who claimed to be interested in computing. He had a video lecture created by an American university on the subject of 'Can You Trust the Press?' pinned permanently to his profile. Except when you looked up the 'university' in question, it turned out to be no academic institution, but rather a self-awarded accreditation used in videos produced by an American talk-show host.[12]

But what was even more unusual was @Ivan226622's activity prior to his appearance in the Philippines. Originally he had been posting frenetically about events in Iran first, then Syria. Then he switched his attention to Spain, posting hundreds of articles agitating for the independence of the Catalonia region. The articles he posted were from Spanish-language, Russian state media. A whole cohort of other accounts posted the same articles at the same time.

@Ivan226622's discovery in early 2018 came at a time when there was much talk in the news about perhaps the most infamous troll farm in the world: the Internet Research Agency (IRA) in St Petersburg, Russia, which gained great notoriety when it was revealed to have tried to influence the US presidential election in favour of Donald Trump. Attribution – knowing who is really behind an account – is always tricky, so these revelations about the IRA led to innocent people who just had interesting Internet habits also being accused of being 'Russian trolls'. @Ivan226622 disappeared soon after Rappler wrote about him, before anyone could work out who he really was.

But ever since Rodrigo Duterte had met, and got along with, President Putin, the Filipino government had started quoting Russian state media. Could @Ivan226622's brief appearance have been related? It was a little reminder that Rappler's experience was one front of a vast global phenomenon.

To Catch a Troll

Though it gained global notoriety for its American campaign, the IRA is more focused on attacking domestic opposition. In St Petersburg one young and rather fragile-looking woman, Lyudmilla Savchuk, had infiltrated the IRA as early as 2015, with the aim of gathering enough evidence to stop its work. I first bumped into her in Europe, then in the US, during her long, lonely campaign to stop the troll farm's operations.

Lyudmilla reminded me of other activists I'd encountered previously in Russia. As the state has destroyed so many civil society organisations, these activists can have very different professions: journalists, small-business owners, charity workers, or they can even move between jobs. When I look up Lyudmilla on Google I notice how Western journalists struggle to describe her: she's called by turns an environmentalist, a journalist, an Internet activist, a dissident . . . and in a way all of these are true.

'Ignore everything you read about me,' Lyudmilla tells me right away. She's upset about how some journalists defined her as a 'whistle-blower' from the troll farm, when she'd set out to go undercover there from the beginning.

'I suppose "whistle-blower" makes for more clicks,' she sighs.

Labelling Lyudmilla a 'whistle-blower' intimates she was one of 'them', a Kremlin troll. Lyudmilla can tell when people have read this erroneous description of her because they won't shake her hand, and she has to explain her story afresh.

Back in 2014 she was a TV reporter in the satellite town of Pushkin, covering stories about bureaucrats planning illegal construction projects in conservation areas. Soon she was helping organise protests to stop illegal builds in parks, and then stood for membership of the local council. Increasingly she noticed that activists were being smeared online, accused of being paid-for stooges, layabouts. There were already dribbles of information about a troll farm in the suburbs of St Petersburg, though no one knew about its scale or how it operated, and many were divided as to whether it was worth paying attention to at all. So what if you got trolled? The tougher activists thought it beneath them to respond. Lyudmilla felt differently. She thought that it was appalling that people whom she respected were being attacked.

Then, one day in January 2015, an old journalist colleague asked Lyudmilla if she wanted to join a project for the 'good of the motherland'. It dawned on Lyudmilla that she was referring to the troll farm. She was putting together a team for 'special projects' and needed good writers. Would Lyudmilla come for an interview?

Here was a chance to find out how the troll farm really worked. She hatched a plan with journalists from two of Russia's last independent newspapers, *Мой Раюон* and *Новая Газета*. She would infiltrate the troll farm, film and download evidence on how it worked, and they would publish it.

The office was in a four-storey new build with square pillars propping up the second floor, its narrow black-framed windows like long arrow slits. There were no signs on the door. The friend met Lyudmilla at the entrance and took her to see the manager. To Lyudmilla's surprise, it was someone she'd heard of before: a newspaper columnist. The farm didn't appear to be run by secret service guys or PR gurus, but former journalists. A couple of motivations quickly became obvious: she was being offered several times more than a regular media salary and steady work. The manager was uncertain about Lyudmilla, however: he knew of her investigative background. Lyudmilla's friend waved it off: 'Oh, come on, who here hasn't done that sort of work back in the past?!'

Inside the farm every floor was full of computers, crammed into thin lines and manned round the clock by changing shifts of employees with passes that clocked all arrival and departure times. Even smoking breaks were regulated.

The farm had its own hierarchy. The most looked down upon were the 'commenters', of which the lowest of the low were those who posted in the online comments sections of newspapers; a level up were those who left comments on social media. The more senior editors would instruct the commenters on which Russian opposition figures to attack, and they would spend their days accusing them of being CIA stooges, traitors, shills. Some of the commenters were not well educated and their written Russian could be imperfect, so a Russian-language teacher would come in to give them grammar lessons.

Lyudmilla was in another, more exclusive section. Her 'special project' involved the creation of a mystic healer, 'Cantadora', an expert in astrology, parapsychology and crystals. Cantadora was meant to be read by middle-class housewives who were not normally interested in politics. Lyudmilla's job was to drop in the odd bit of current affairs in between blog entries on star signs and romance. There were four, sometimes five people working on the profile. Lyudmilla liked Stas the most. He seemed utterly depressed by the work. Every day Lyudmilla, Stas and the other writers would be sent Word documents containing political articles and the 'conclusions' they were meant to draw from them: that the EU is just a vassal of the US, or that Ukraine, which Russia had invaded, was run by fascists. It was up to them to integrate these conclusions into Cantadora's blog. So Lyudmilla wrote, for example, how Cantadora had a sister who lived in Germany, and then related a nightmare in which she dreamt her sister was in a desert surrounded by deadly snakes, interpreting those snakes as US foreign policy endangering the EU. Some of the farm's work reached a level of granularity that stunned Lyudmilla. Two trolls would go on the comments sections of small, provincial newspapers and start chatting about the street they lived in, the weather, then casually recommend a piece about the nefarious West attacking Russia.

No one who worked at the farm described themselves as trolls. Instead, they talked about their work in the passive voice ('a piece was written', 'a comment was made'). Most treated the farm as if it was just another job, doing the minimum required and then clocking off. Many of them seemed pleasant enough young people, with open, pretty faces, and yet they didn't blink when asked to smear, degrade, insult and humiliate their victims. The ease with which victims were attacked, the scale at which the farm operated, it all stunned Lyudmilla. She kept herself going with the thought that her research would help stop all this. But it was proving hard to gather the necessary evidence. There were CCTV cameras in every corner, and she would have to flick her long, curly hair over her shoulder so that it covered her hand when she reached down to put a flash drive into her computer to download documents.

Who gave the farm instructions as to what to do? Was it the Kremlin? Or were they churned out inside the IRA? No one discussed this. The farm, other journalists had told her, was owned by one Evgeny Prigozhin. He relied on the regime for his official business: he provided catering services to the Kremlin. He had known President Putin personally since the 1990s and had served nine years in prison for robbery.[13] Later, it would transpire he also runs mercenaries who fight in the Kremlin's wars, from Ukraine to Syria.

There were moments when Lyudmilla could see that the farm was part of a much larger network. When the opposition politician Boris Nemtsov was murdered in February 2015, for instance, assassinated with a Makarov pistol on a bridge right underneath the towers and onion domes of Red Square, the farm's middle management suddenly started running into every office, giving the trolls direct instructions on what to post under which articles printed in mainstream Russian publications. The farm was working in rhythm with the whole government disinformation complex. No one had time to read the articles, but they knew exactly what to post. The trolls were told to spread confusion about who was behind the murder: was it the Ukrainians, the Chechens, the Americans? The IRA, an agency whose connection to the Kremlin was purposefully blurred, was in turn purposefully blurring the Kremlin's connection to a murder.

During the day Lyudmilla would see a fake reality being pumped out by the trolls. In the evening she would come home hoping to put the place behind her, only to hear relatives and acquaintances quote lines churned out by the farm repeated back at her. People who considered themselves hard-ened enough to withstand the barrage of television still seemed susceptible to social media messages which slithered into and enveloped your most personal online spaces, spun themselves into the texture of your life.

Lyudmilla spent two and a half months at the farm. Then, as planned, she gave the material to the newspapers. They pub-lished it as authored by 'Anonymous'. The next day she went back to work to find the commenters were busy undermining the credibility of the material she had provided to the media. 'No troll factories exist,' the trolls wrote, 'they are all fabrica-tions by paid-for journalists.' The management at the troll farm were already checking video cameras to find out who had been behind the leak. It was, she knew, only a matter of time before they worked out what she'd done.

Lyudmilla left the farm. She also decided to admit publicly that she was the one who had infiltrated it. She wanted to give interviews about what she had seen there, to campaign to have the place shut down; she couldn't do that as 'Anonymous'. She gave dozens of interviews. She gave talks across the world.

The farm now turned on her. There were comments and posts claiming she was a sexual deviant, a spy, a traitor. There were phone calls to her relatives saying that people were often killed for what she had done.

Lyudmilla tried to reach out to Stas, the co-author of the Cantadora blog whom she had liked, but he just sent her bitter messages full of swear words. This saddened her: she knew he hated the farm and hoped he'd understand her mission.

Lyudmilla had hoped that by unmasking the workings of the IRA she would cause so much outrage it would help stop its work, that she would shock people into seeing how they were being manipulated by it, shame those who worked there into resigning. Most of the people she had met at the farm were no monsters. They carried on working there because there was little social stigma linked to it.

But instead of an outcry she found that many people, including fellow activists, just shrugged at the revelations. This horrified her even more. Not only did the lies churned out by the farm become reality, but the very existence of it was seen as normal in itself.

At one point the death threats and abuse unnerved Lyudmilla so much she began to get anxiety attacks and went to see a psychotherapist. The psychotherapist listened to her patiently, nodded and then enquired why she wanted to fight the state this way – was she some kind of paid-for traitor? Lyudmilla, perturbed, visited another doctor. They said the same thing again. She felt as if the mindset promoted by the troll factory had literally penetrated into the country's subconscious. She had left the confines of the farm – only to find she was enveloped by it everywhere.

Then, in early 2018, the US Special Counsel Investigation found that the operations of the troll farm had stretched beyond Russia and deep into the US, creating thousands of fake accounts, groups and messages, while posing as genuine Americans: right-nationalist, gun-loving Americans who supported the election of Donald Trump; black civil rights campaigners who promoted the idea that his rivals weren't worth voting for. The activity continued after the 2016 election, as the farm tried to make Americans hate each other even more. Over thirty million Americans shared its content among their friends and families.[14]

Certainly, thought Lyudmilla, the US would punish the troll farm. She'd always noted how authors at the IRA would write screeds about how awful the West was through their troll personas, while dreaming of American holidays on their real-life walls. Even the most basic threat of a travel ban to the US, she reckoned, would be enough to put many off from working at the farm, undermine the sense that it was just another normal job.

She would be disappointed. The US Special Counsel opened cases against a few mid-level administrators for technicalities like using fake identities to open bank accounts, but not only did the farm not shut, it expanded to premises three times the size.

When I asked American government lawyers why sanctions couldn't be imposed on trolls, they answered that, firstly, it was hard to define whether the IRA worked directly for the Russian government, and therefore whether its actions constituted the operations of a 'hostile state'. And in any case, while the scale of the IRA's activities was spectacular, it was barely unique. Western PR companies were regularly caught running similar operations, using fake online personas for their clients. The American military had started a project called 'Earnest Voice' in 2011, which ran fake online accounts to counter terrorist messaging in the Middle East. It wasn't just the Russians who were using technology in this way.[15,16]

But even more importantly, I thought to myself, though one might not like what trolls write, lies are not illegal. In the 'marketplace of ideas', better information, the journalistic credo I had been raised with went, is the antidote to lies. After all, isn't freedom of expression exactly what democratic dissidents, such as my parents, had always fought for?

——

Camille François thought differently. She was a scholar of cyber-warfare at Harvard University and Google, and when she first read about Lyudmilla's research and heard Maria Ressa's story, she felt it fitted into a greater pattern which she had observed across the world: a new version of the old game of power versus dissent, freedom of speech versus censorship, but one that turned the old rules on their head. The previous methods of silencing and breaking people had become untenable; unlike in the Soviet Union, few regimes can prevent people from receiving or propagating information. However, the powerful had adapted, and now social media mobs and cyber-militias harassed, smeared and intimidated dissenting voices into silence, or undermined their reputation so that no one would listen to them. But because the connections between states and these mobs and militias were unclear, a regime could always claim that it had nothing to do with these campaigns, that they were merely private individuals exercising their freedom of speech.

What if, thought François, you could establish the connection between states and campaigns? Could one then hold them to account?

François had begun her Internet career supporting what were known as Internet 'pirates' in 1990s Paris: hackers who put copyrighted music, books and software online in the name of sharing all knowledge for free. François even advocated that people should give up their passwords so that everyone could access everyone else's Internet connections. Twenty years later, such idealism had given way to a realisation that the Internet was an increasingly dangerous place, and she became more preoccupied with Internet security. François had researched how states hack into the phones and computers of journalists and activists, especially in Latin America. Now she got back in touch with those victims and asked whether the hacks had been accompanied by online attacks. Almost everyone said they had been. Martha Roldós, an Ecuadorean politician who had swarms of online accounts threaten her, accusing her of killing her politician parents and of being a spy, perhaps put it most clearly:

> In the past I was denied my political rights, I had armed men outside my house pointing a gun at my daughter . . . but not cyber-harassment. Since I became a sponsor of investigative journalists, my time of cyber-harassment began.

Over the next three years, between 2015 and 2018, François put together a team of twenty researchers and a coalition of civil society groups who scoured Asia and the Middle East, the Americas and Europe to categorise what she was beginning to call 'state-sponsored trolling'. The research, part of which would later be published by the aptly named Institute for the Future,[17] defined several categories.

The most obvious were 'state-directed' campaigns, where the regime gave instructions on whom to target, how and when, though didn't necessarily take part in the campaign itself. This is the case in Venezuela, where the Maduro government has set up closed social media channels through which it directs enthusiasts on whom to attack, with what messages and when, but doesn't carry out the work itself.

For a modicum of deniability one could work through a youth movement. In Azerbaijan, for instance, there is Ireli, created 'to produce young people who can take an active part in the information war'. In practice this means sending online threats to critical journalists, like Arzu Geybulla: 'I've been called many things: a slut, a dog, a pig – you name it. These insults involved my ill mother and deceased father. She was a whore; he was a traitor who slept with an Armenian slut.'

More subtle was the situation in Bahrain, where, during protests in 2011, an Internet account suddenly popped up which showed close-up photographs of protesters, alongside their home addresses and personal phone numbers. There was even a link to a government hotline you could phone to report protesters directly to the regime. Who was behind the account? Nothing was ever proven, but after the government was told about its existence, they did nothing to stop it. Wasn't that enough, thought François, to hold them responsible? She classified this as a 'state-coordinated' campaign.

Another layer of deniability was to merely fuel attacks, but then take no part in their enactment. This is the case in Turkey, where columnists who are members of the ruling party incite mob attacks on anyone who dares criticise President Erdoğan. This sort of 'state-inspired' approach can also have its downsides: sometimes the columnists target the wrong person, and the president has to call off the attack by signalling he supports the victim.

These sorts of state-inspired campaigns have also become a feature in the US. The Institute for the Future report relates instances when the White House's social media team, websites that support the president and indeed the president himself have identified journalists, academics and opposition staffers as 'scum', 'slime' and 'enemies of the people'. The targets then receive vats of online vitriol, phone calls to their place of work demanding they are sacked, and death and rape threats.

This sort of activity led Freedom House, a Washington-based organisation that rates press freedom, to downgrade the US's standings in 2017: 'Fake news and aggressive trolling of journalists . . . contributed to a score decline in the United States' otherwise generally free environment.' Freedom House was created in 1941 as a tool with which to fight totalitarian regimes. It advocated for Soviet dissidents in the Cold War. Now it increasingly focuses on abuses of freedom inside the US (not for the first time: in the 1950s Freedom House also fought publicly against the anti-Communist witch-hunts of US Senator Joseph McCarthy).

Having established a scale of attribution, François began poring over legal documents. States had a legal obligation, enshrined in their UN commitments, to protect their citizens' fundamental rights. There was certainly nothing that defended a state's 'right' to use automated and fake personas to drown out, threaten and demean its critics.

The issue was no longer whether state-sponsored trolls had 'freedom of expression', but whether this was being abused to suppress the victims' human rights. This was censorship through noise. 'We observe the tactical move by states from an ideology of information scarcity to one of information abundance,' writes law professor Tim Wu, 'which sees speech itself as a censorial weapon.'[18]

It will need a landmark case to set a precedent so that a troll farm and the state that sponsors it are brought to justice. In the meantime Camille has put all her efforts into persuading the tech companies themselves. And to a certain extent she has succeeded. Between 2015 and 2018, social media companies like Facebook and Twitter at least began to admit that coordinated campaigns actually existed, began to take down offending accounts.

I was reading through François's research one morning at a Washington DC hotel, in the strange time lapse of jet lag where the usual logic of day and night is broken, and perhaps because time seemed to have lost its hold on me, unnatural exuberance took over. In this foolish hour it seemed to me François's vision was just around the corner. I started imagining a future where all the world's great powers and digital companies would promise to safeguard human rights online. Tech companies would protect dissidents by warning them when a campaign was building to target them, instantly taking down trolls, punishing them so they could never harass anyone again. States would no longer abuse 'freedom of speech' to crush those who speak truth to power; working for a troll farm could no longer be shrugged off as 'normal' . . .

Sauntering down to the cramped lobby of my hotel I snapped out of my reverie when I saw Maria Ressa. I hadn't seen her for three months and wondered whether the threats against Rappler had subsided. She showed me a text message she'd just received from Glenda Gloria. It contained an image of a thick file: a tax evasion charge against Maria personally, which carried a potential sentence of ten years in jail. Maria was leaving for the airport; she had a flight to catch to Singapore, before heading back to Manila. She managed to post bail, but a few months later there was another charge, this time accusing her of libel for a piece from 2012. I watched a Facebook live stream as she was arrested in the Rappler office, before being released again the next day. Rights groups condemned the charges as politically motivated.[19]

In between arrests and interrogations Maria received the 2018 Knight International Journalism Award, one of the world's most prestigious. 'Exponential lies on social media incite hate and stifle free speech,' said Maria as she collected her statuette. 'We battle impunity from the Philippine government and from Facebook. Why should you care? Our problems are fast becoming your problems. Boundaries around the world collapse and we can begin to see a kind of global playbook.'[20]

But despite all the international attention Maria's words mustered, the attacks and cases against her continued, as if someone was trying to say that freedom of speech, in the older sense of being able to shout about your cause to the wider world, was meaningless.

You will need to check for yourself whether Rappler's story has had a sad, happy or indeed any ending. But it was already clear when writing this in early 2019 that Maria was no longer just a reporter commentating on current history, but a symbol of how easily it could be undone. That was the paradox of the new media. It was meant to take us further into the future; instead, it has brought back the past – misogyny we had thought conquered, regimes thought laid to rest. The very form of social media scrambles time, place, proportion: terror attacks sit next to cat videos; the latest jokes surface next to old family photos. And the result is a sort of flattening, as if past and present are losing their relative perspective.

Whenever Lina would become stressed her psoriasis would flare up, her skin coming out in a red rash. She feared what would happen when the KGB hauled her in for questioning. Would she start itching like mad? How would she keep her composure? What if they threatened to take away her parents' jobs? How could she live with that? And who would feed Petya?

Esfir, her mother, calmed her down. She told her to forget about her parents – she only had a husband now and no one else. She needed to forget about her child: they would find wet nurses.

'The KGB will interrogate you so long the milk in your breasts will go sour with mastitis. They will swell, the ducts will block, burn and cover with abscesses. You will become feverish. So whenever you feel the need, get up, go to the wall of the interrogation room and squeeze the milk out of your breasts onto the walls.

'Make them feel ashamed and embarrassed.'

What shocked Lina is that her own straight-laced lawyer of a mother was describing how to resist the secret police so frankly, so directly. But though she never mentioned it, Esfir knew her fair share about arrests.

Back when she was still a student, in 1948, Esfir had been told by the dean of the law faculty to go work as a stenographer at the Kiev courthouse. She had a prodigious memory and there were rather a lot of trials at the time. Except they weren't really trials. They just brought in one person after the other and sentenced them, as if it were an assembly line. It was the time of Stalin's post-war purges of Ukrainian nationalists. After a while, Esfir got

47

to know which judge would give how many years: this one was a five-year guy, this one fifteen. If the judge was known for being particularly stern, in the seconds before the judgement was read out Esfir would stop typing, and everyone else who worked in the court would stop whatever they were doing and press their hands hard over their ears. They would see the judge move his mouth to utter the sentence and then the noise would start. A sound like the wind, rising to a gale of grief, a wail penetrating every part of you.

'Wooohoooooooooooo . . .'

It was the relatives of the sentenced, and it was the same every time.

And so Lina had been raised in a world where everyone did their best not to hear what was going on. She had spent her childhood among people speaking in the passive voice and whispers: 'X has been taken away'; 'Y has been disappeared'. (When she grew up she would always feel revulsion at the passive voice and whispers.) Or there was the time the dam holding the reservoir near the ravine at Babij Yar broke and a part of Kiev was flooded so violently that buildings and trams were swept away in the torrent. Some say hundreds died, others thousands. No one knows exactly: all news of the event was stifled by men 'from over there', all displays of public mourning barred. Esfir would say only that the 'the ground had wept'. This was a way of describing the unmentionable flood, which in turn invoked another unspoken catastrophe. Babij Yar was also where the Nazis shot thousands of Jews during the war, with help from local collaborators. Evasions were wrapped inside references to silences.

At university the first banned books began to come Lina's way. Here, finally, the unspoken was expressed. And here, in the little circle around my father-to-be, Igor, were people who said what they thought without whispering, without the passive voice, sharing banned texts that were printed on cheap paper, glued to pieces of card and then packed in shoeboxes.

One evening, a year before Igor's arrest, Lina had come home with a shoebox containing Solzhenitsyn's Gulag Archipelago. It was tucked under her arm as she turned to take off her raincoat, glanced in the hall mirror and in the reflection caught the look of Great-Grandmother Tsilya in the room opposite, staring at Lina with her one good eye. There must have been something in my mother's look that gave everything away immediately. 'Esfir!' Great-Grandmother screamed. 'The child has brought banned literature home.'

Esfir ran into my mother's room and leaned close over her. 'You think you're brave? Let me explain what they will do to you. They will take you down a long dark corridor. They will put you in a small cell. They will close the heavy door. And then they will turn the lock.'

And here Esfir made a noise with her throat like a great rusty thing turning over and over. It made my mother shrivel. Years afterwards she couldn't work out how Esfir had made that sound, what mix of guttural groans and throat movements one needs to communicate metal breaking willpower.

Mother took the shoebox out of the house that night. It was the first time her mother had spoken to her so directly of the other side of the Soviet reality: the prisons and false arrests and interrogation everyone knew about but never uttered.

'Maybe this is cruel of me, but I can think of no other word but betrayal when I think of those who were adults during my childhood and adolescence,' Igor would write later, in an essay called 'The Right to Read'.

I felt betrayed by my teachers. Not one spoke a single word of truth about the tragedy of my fatherland.

I feel as if I betrayed myself. Why did I believe the teachers and newspapers? Why did I take until my twenty-sixth year for my first public outcry in defence of my fellow citizens, mislaid behind bars, behind barbed wire, behind walls of psychiatric hospitals for their ability to think and express their words out loud?

I felt betrayed by my parents even though I loved them. At least at home they could have, for the sake of their sons, assumed some human dignity and honesty.

And it was books, only books that never betrayed me . . . I see all genuine literature as anti-Soviet. I feel any good book which acknowledges the human being, individuality, uniqueness is also anti-Soviet because the state dictatorship is directed against the human being as an individual.

Igor had seen his own father mangled by the contradictions of the Soviet experiment. Jacob Israelovich was a Bolshevik true believer who broke with his bourgeois, religious Odessan family, thinking he could build a just society free of anti-Semitism. He was made editor of the Dnipropetrovsk Youth Gazette *in 1941 and seemed all set for journalistic glory, until Stalin began a purge on Jews after the war. Jacob Israelovich was forced to take refuge with relatives in distant, dead-end Chernivtsi, a Ukrainian provincial town right on the border with Romania which had been a part of Austro-Hungary until the First World War, then became part of Romania, before annexation by Stalin in 1944. Even here he worked on the local newspaper – and had his first heart attack after he wrote an article about Yugoslav leader Marshal Tito that was deemed too soft, receiving 'a severe party reprimand for intentionally masking the nature of Tito's reactionary regime in Yugoslavia'. Jacob Israelovich was so outraged he wrote to* Pravda *in Moscow – violating party rules – defending his 'liberal' editorial. It was the only time Igor ever saw his father 'straighten his spine'.* Pravda *never replied.*

Jacob Israelovich died after another heart attack, when Igor was still a student. By that time Igor had already made up his mind about the regime. His turning point was 1968, when Soviet tanks rolled into Prague in an event everyone knew was an invasion, but were meant to pretend was 'brotherly help'.

In his first novella, Reading Faulkner, *written when he was twenty-seven, Igor played on motifs from his own life when his fictional narrator, a young writer, discovers his father's imperial, impersonal official writing and compares it with his own:*

This country has thrown off the chains of Capitalist Slavery! Bourgeois culture was always far from the people! Now it has revealed its true face: the face of the maidservant of monopolistic capital! Welcome the Socialist Sun! Let the Darkness be gone!

And:

Just a minute ago you were walking the street, breathing in air and breathing out words; now you have burst through to the page, now it will pour out, like wild berries you'd been carrying inside your jacket. Is there any joy greater than writing in the first person?

51

The novella is a celebration of the right and joy to define oneself. The narrator, inspired by reading the American modernist William Faulkner's novel The Sound and the Fury, *tries on different styles to describe his state of mind, Chernivtsi, his family. He writes in a punctuation-free stream of consciousness followed by brusque sentences, returns to a close reading of Faulkner's technique and then tries something new again, wonders whether the story of the 'I' starts with personal memories of parents (no), the first questions about ethnic identity (no), the moment when you fall in love and truly notice someone else for the first time (yes).*

I am in a room of music and smoke. My father's taut back. The awfulness of newspaper editorials; what ponderous words father has to juggle. Machine and Tractor Stations, Party Directive . . . Did Faulkner begin with this? No.

Midday, helmets of cupolas, steep steps, we're in T-shirts, six years old, in the cool close air of the church. From above a voice and a pock-marked face grunts: 'Out, Jewish runt.' Did Faulkner begin like this? No.

A girl, on the shore of you. How high the sky. How deep the kiss. We do not say 'you' to each other but 'I'. I swim far out into you: past – buoys, past – horizons; glancing back could not see the rim of the shore and was glad. Remember how ten Julys ago you went into the breath-taking Black Sea and were a warm current in it. But does Faulkner have anything to do with this? He does. He does!

'This admiration you have for William Faulkner,' Colonel Vilen (a shortened form of Vladimir Lenin) asked Igor during their first

interrogation, trying to find a way to get him to start talking, 'you do realise he is a bourgeois writer?'

'Actually he has been recently republished in the Soviet Union and proclaimed a Critic of the Bourgeois System,' Igor countered. The KGB men hadn't done their homework properly: Faulkner had recently been rubber-stamped. The line between 'acceptable' and 'unacceptable' authors was always shifting, depending on the political mood.

Igor's strategy was to refuse to talk about friends, family or colleagues, which meant the only thing left to discuss was books. The interrogations became literary conversations. The KGB would switch between seduction and intimidation.

'Cooperate with us! [As in report on your friends.] We have lots of writers whom we work with. We can help your career,' they would say with a smile, before suddenly changing the mood and slamming on the table the banned books they accused him of having proliferated.

'What criminal depths have you fallen to, Igor Jakovlevich?'

Vilen picked up one of the books. Aptly it was Invitation to a Beheading by Vladimir Nabokov, the nightmare story of a man in an unnamed country arrested for an unnamed crime. Vilen flicked through the book, shaking his head.

'You will get seven and five for this.'

The threat wasn't empty. Writers and literary critics in Kiev were getting the sentence all the time: seven in prison and five in exile in the Soviet hinterlands. In Moscow or St Petersburg you could keep Nabokov on the shelf with few repercussions. Here, where Soviet paranoia of Ukrainian insurrection ran deep, the rules were far more strict.

Igor denied ever having seen the books. 'Deny everything,' was the time-honoured tactic during interrogations, but at the same *time it hurt him to say it: books had never betrayed him, but now he had betrayed books. He found his mind wandering to all the other hard-to-find banned books that must be stored in the KGB cellars. It must be a literary gold mine!*

To keep his mind focused away from fear, he tried to human-ise his interrogators. What were they like when not performing the crass good cop/bad cop routine? In the corridor on the way to an interrogation he noticed the KGB had their own gazette pinned to the wall. He chuckled; it meant they too were forced to write for their company paper, the Dzerzhinetz, *named after Felix Dzerzhinsky, the founder of the original KGB, the Cheka. Did the crossword, he wondered, have a professional slant? These men followed some sort of invented professional ethic, which gave them the right to listen in to other people's conversations, record on a magnetic strip someone else's embraces, use those kisses for blackmail, to dictate which books you can and can't read. There seemed to be no dividing line between the precise, rational logic of their questions and the casual way they would then use violence. He noticed they didn't like being called KGB but preferred the old revolutionary term 'Chekist', as if that was more romantic, gave them a higher purpose. How did they inspire themselves to raid people's apartments, break their friends?*

The walks home after work were the worst. He listened for every car that drove past and prayed it wouldn't stop, would please keep going. He would pause for an age outside his own door, scared to open it and find out what was on the other side. In his poetry of the time, the joyful 'I' is replaced with the third per-son, as people around him are 'disappeared' like pieces of gram-mar. Sun-dappled days are replaced with cloying nights. Prison barracks loom out of the brown fog, and instead of lovers in the moonlight the secret police become your night-time companions. In one poem the author, some sort of unidentified animal himself, hides terrified from gangs of alley cats. He describes fear as a hedgehog that first raises its cute muzzle inside his chest and then unfolds its spiky spine to rip it to shreds.

'In October 1977 officials of the Kiev UKGB interrogated no less than sixteen acquaintances of POMERANTSEV, in an effort to obtain testimony relating to the charges,' states the Chronicle. *Of those interrogated only one broke and confessed that 'POMERANTSEV had circulated anti-Soviet fabrications of a defamatory nature, such as that a creative people cannot realise their potential in the USSR.'*

The KGB showed Igor the confession. When Igor confronted him, the snitch answered he had no desire to lie, even to the KGB: he was an honest person, wasn't he?

Walking down the street Esfir bumped into an old friend from law school who now worked 'over there'. 'The case against Igor is fixed. There's nothing you can do,' he told her. Igor wrote:

> The deed is done
> and arrest will follow
> in a month or so.
> But in the interval,
> even though everything is already determined
>   and predetermined,
> out of habit he thinks,
> weighs and calculates,
> as if he still had
> some kind
> of choice.

Part 2: Democracy at Sea

In the 1970s small bands of dissidents and non-conformists could barely dare to imagine how, just over a decade later, mass protests would swell across the world, from Moscow to Manila and Cape Town, and authoritarian regimes would be swept away, with millions of ordinary people on the street, pulling down the statues of dictators, storming the grim, large offices of the secret services that had oppressed them. The old order that Vilen represented seemed gone forever.

Those images of people-powered revolutions articulated the victory of 'democracy' over oppression, connected to a whole vocabulary passed down from the struggles of dissidents and civil rights movements.

But what if a cleverer sort of ruler could find other ways to undermine the dissidents, rid them of a clear enemy to fight, climb inside the images, ideas, stories of those great people-power protests and suck them dry from the inside, until they were devoid of meaning? Could one even use the same language and tactics as 'the democrats', but for opposite aims?

Waves of Democratisation

Srdja Popović is halfway through explaining to me how to bring down a dictator when he gets a call. It's a warning about a piece coming out tomorrow claiming he's connected to the CIA and is behind revolutions in the Middle East. The piece first appeared in an Istanbul daily and then reappeared on a minor Serbian-language website full of pro-Russian conspiracies. From there it moved to a site owned by Christian Orthodox patriots, and it would soon be featured on the front page of one of Serbia's largest tabloids, which, Srdja assumes, is publishing it because conspiracy theories sell rather than because the paper has it in for him personally.[1] After all, he makes for a good story. Recently Russian state TV camera crews turned up at his office among the monolithic Communist concrete cubes of New Belgrade, where it sits between a hairdressing salon and a pastry shop. They tried to force their way in. If they had hoped to find dozens of CIA operatives, they must have been disappointed. Srdja runs a permanent staff of four Serbs, who sit in a neat grey office which would look like an accountant's, were it not for the multiple posters of the clenched fist that is Srdja's logo. It's here they compile the step-by-step manuals for 'non-violent direct action campaigns', which are downloaded in their tens of thousands all across the world (the largest single location is Iran), organise workshops and schedule Srdja's online Harvard training courses, which allow activists everywhere to pass exams in how to overthrow dictators without firing a shot.

'Look at them widening the battlefield,' says Srdja, when he gets off the phone, 'copying the same messages even though they're not allies, attacking from different angles. It's as if they've been learning from me. And you know the funny thing? The two places we actually have never worked in are Russia and Turkey.'

He's worked pretty much everywhere else, though. As you read this Srdja might be in Asia or Latin America, Eastern Europe or the Middle East. Inside a meeting room in an unremarkable chain hotel studious-looking men and women of all ages – human rights lawyers and teachers, students and small-business people – will be sitting in a semi-circle of desks, in the middle of which stands Srdja: slim, dressed like a 1990s college kid in a hoodie even though he's in his forties, spinning and dipping his knees, then rising again as if he is trying to lift the mood in the room physically. He speaks in slightly Americanised English, his deep, rolled, Slavic 'r's giving every statement, even the most casual, an extra intensity. Everyone in the room already feels he is their closest comrade and that together they can change history. The students take copious notes, which they keep breaking away from as Srdja cracks another joke and they double up with laughter.

Srdja will often start his workshops with something seemingly light, like laughtivism: the use of humorous stunts in revolutionary campaigns. He might mention, for example, how Polish anti-Communist activists in the 1980s would go out on the streets with wheelbarrows filled with televisions during the Soviet news hour to express their rejection of state media.

Laughtivism, explains Srdja, fulfils a double role. The first is psychological: laughter removes the aura of impenetrability around an authoritarian leader. It also forces the regime into what Srdja calls a dilemma situation: if well-armed security services arrest activists for a jape, it can alienate parts of the population. Indeed, Srdja tells his workshops, activists should look to be arrested for doing something ridiculous. One thing you learn fast in Srdja's workshops: they may be 'non-violent', but that doesn't mean they are for the faint-hearted. Srdja's belief in non-violence doesn't come so much from pacifism as calculation. Regimes have the upper hand when it comes to physical force; what they can't deal with are massive, peaceful crowds out on the streets.

The archetypal protest movement Srdja refers back to is the one he led himself.[2] He dims the lights to show video archive from the time between the mid-1990s and 2000 when he ran the student group Otpor! in its attempt to overthrow Slobodan Milošević, the Yugoslav dictator who led the country into three wars with its neighbours and sponsored warlords who built concentration camps and slaughtered Muslim civilians. Milošević's media pumped out a version of the world in which Serbia was simultaneously on a 700-year-old mission to save Europe while also a benighted victim of the imperial West. Meanwhile, patriotic gangsters beat up opposition 'traitors' in the dark alleys of Belgrade and partied to a local mix of frenetically upbeat techno and folk music.

When Milošević's domineering wife announced she would rather see the protests end in bloodshed than her husband resign, Otpor! set up a blood transfusion station and delivered blood bags to the government: will the Miloševićs kindly leave now they've got their blood?

But such pranksterism is just the start. As Srdja's workshop moves on, the lessons become more strategic. He teaches the need to formulate a vision of the alternative political model you want to see; how to bring very different groups around a 'lowest common denominator'; how to find the weak spots in the adversary's 'pillars of power' and bring them over to your side.

Back in the final years of Milošević's Yugoslavia, Srdja and his partners developed a manifesto which argued that real patriotism meant peace with Serbia's neighbours and joining the 'international community' – the West, Europe. The world wasn't a conspiracy against Serbia. The student marches were full of the flags of many nations. This played to many Serbs' sense of self and history. Serbia had fought against the Nazis, had kept its distance from the Soviet Union: why shouldn't it be partnered with Western allies? It was a message that could resonate with miners and farmers, not just students.

Otpor! were making progress, but when, in 1999, NATO bombed Belgrade to try and curb Milošević's ethnic cleansing of Kosovo, Srdja feels it only helped reunite the people around the dictator. The bombs hit Milošević's TV complex, nicknamed the Bastille, but by that time its media monopoly was already broken. Srdja had B92, the banned radio station that broadcast from a friend's basement via the Internet – a technology the regime was only just starting to understand – and which offered a mix of punk rock and political discussion, forming an online network with small independent media throughout the land.

They had started winning over not only students and labour unions, but also one of the bastions of Milošević's regime: the police. Otpor! created street shows that rewarded the 'best policeman in Belgrade' with a prize, making the cops feel welcomed by the movement. When they saw polling that showed most of the country was now against Milošević but would never back city liberals like Srdja, Otpor! gritted their teeth and backed a patriotic academic as a unity candidate in the next election. Milošević cheated. Protests grew. Belgrade turned into a street party, the students joined by miners and farmers. Milošević sent the army onto the streets. Girls shone mirrors into the soldiers' faces so they could see their own reflections and remember their own humanity, put flowers into the barrels of their guns. The army refused to shoot. Milošević was overthrown and two years later was facing trial for war crimes in the Hague.

After 2000 Srdja's fame spread. He got requests from opposition groups in Zimbabwe and Belarus to train them. He realised that going round the world schooling protest movements could be a job. Together with another Otpor! founder, Slobo Djinović, he set up CANVAS: the Centre for Applied Non-Violent Actions and Strategies. He trained activists in Georgia, Ukraine and Iran, who would then take part in what became known as the 'colour revolutions' (Rose, Orange and Green respectively). Then came training for leaders in Egypt, Tunisia and Syria, who would go on to participate in what became known as the 'Arab Spring'.

Srdja, along with many political scientists, sees these movements as part of a greater historical process: successive 'waves of democratisation', with democracy defined as a mix of multiparty elections, plural media and independent institutions such as the judiciary. The first wave was the overthrow of authoritarian rule in South America, South Asia and South Africa in the late twentieth century, and the end of Soviet power in Eastern Europe – the Velvet Revolution in Czechoslovakia, the fall of the Berlin Wall, the Singing Revolution in the Baltic States, with their unforgettable images of millions pouring peacefully onto the streets in one great sea of anti-Soviet sentiment. The colour revolutions, argues Srdja, were the next wave, the Arab Spring the one after, swelled by the rise of social media.

Srdja sees himself as the connection between the first and later waves. Yugoslavia was both the last aftershock of the fall of the Soviet system and the first of the new 'democratisations'. For Srdja, the ultimate aim of his work is simple: if you give people more power over how their lives are run, democracy will be the better for it. Democracy's ultimate defenders are the citizens, aware and trained in how to keep their elected representatives accountable.

Over the years Srdja has become a bogeyman for authoritarian leaders. His manuals are required reading at the Russian, Belarusian and Iranian defence ministries. There are frequent stories about him in their state-controlled news. All this interest has a positive side effect for Srdja: the more the leaderships in Moscow or Tehran admonish him, the more clients he attracts.

Former Otpor! activists who have made good in business cover Srdja's office costs and salaries for his four staff. Opposition movements pay for him to train their activists. At other times a group like Greenpeace will pay for him to come and run courses there.

A significant proportion of his work comes from partnerships with organisations connected to what one might term the American 'democracy assistance complex', which emerged during the Cold War: US Congress-funded foundations like the National Democratic Institute (NDI), the International Republican Institute (IRI) and Freedom House. Their relationship with Srdja goes all the way back to the final days of the Milošević regime: it was the NDI that provided the polling which encouraged Srdja to unite behind a less urban, liberal leader. Other 'democracy assistance' foundations provided B92 with the technology to set up its Internet radio channels and helped train 30,000 election monitors for the 2000 elections, which Milošević tried to fix.

To their enemies these organisations are just a front for American imperialism and meddling. To their friends they are one of the few decent things American foreign policy produces, funding pro-democracy groups in places like the Middle East or Central Asia that fight the dictatorships American diplomacy makes friends with.

Srdja is irked by the suggestion that he trains activists only in countries that coincide with US foreign policy interests. 'President Mubarak of Egypt, who was overthrown by the Arab Spring, was one of largest recipients of American military and civil aid for decades, and I helped train activists there during his rule. And you know the only place CANVAS is officially blacklisted? United Arab Emirates – America's close ally. For me there are only two types of society: places where governments are afraid of the people, which we call "democracies"; and places where people are afraid of their autocratic governments. I don't care which dictator I'm empowering people to be free of.'

But lately a new generation of rulers have reinvented their tactics to undermine protest and nullify dissent. If once upon a time one could speak confidently about history's waves of democratisation flowing in a single current, now a great storm has broken out and you can't tell what's flowing in which direction.[3]

——

Srdja's first principle is to develop an alternative political vision and identity to that of the regime. This used to be straightforward: autocrat versus democrat, closed versus open. In Serbia it had meant joining the 'international community' instead of isolation.

But today's strongmen are not so stiff. Instead of hanging onto one single ideology they have learnt to speak with different tongues. Already in the early Putin years, for example, the Kremlin mixed overtures to Soviet greatness with Western reality shows and Western shopping. When the leadership embraces different identities so slickly, how is the opposition meant to find a space to project theirs?

But one doesn't need to go far from Srdja's original stomping grounds to see how things have changed.

In Serbia, where CANVAS hasn't run any workshops for over a decade, the new president is Milošević's old information minister, Aleksandar Vučić. He's begged forgiveness for his 'past mistakes'. If yesteryear he ran a media machine that saw the West as an implacable enemy surrounding Serbia, today he espouses integration with the EU and NATO. 'Reforms for all', is one of his slogans.[4]

Vučić has also swapped a dated form of media control for a more sophisticated one. In 1999 he would call in newspaper editors and threaten them if they didn't toe the line. Today there are dozens of media outlets, including many foreign ones. However, if a newspaper or television station wants to win government advertising or receive government funding, or if its owners want to win government contracts, then it ought to toe the government line.[5] It's similar to media in Erdoğan's Turkey or Orbán's Hungary: market-orientated in form, authoritarian in content. One of the premises of 'democratisation' was that a plural media based on free-market rules would help ensure democracy. It was always a tenuous idea. Tycoons with special interests often own the media in 'democracies', but now they can be utterly hollowed out from the inside.

And the Vučić the domestic media portray is somewhat different to the one who meets Western delegations. In the local tabloids he is still a good old Serbian nationalist, tussling with neighbours, lamenting the loss of territory after the war, while simultaneously promising to bring stability to the Balkans during summits in Brussels.[6]

All the while Serbia stagnates. At night, wrapped in the shawl of darkness, Belgrade emerges to play at glamour. Tall women in tight dresses and even taller men prowl low-lit bars and rows of restaurants at the base of grand squares with ambitious columns stretching towards the moon. Everywhere there's music: from the Gypsies on the street; from the boats-turned-clubs along the river. Only in the morning does the music fade and the light return, and you can see that the tops of the columns, now visible, are crumbling; that the buildings above the low line of restaurants are falling apart; that this city which used to rule south-eastern Europe feels like a haughty cliff slowly collapsing into the sea.

There are protests all the time: against corrupt construction projects; against suspicious election outcomes. But they can never quite connect and build up into a coherent story like they could in Otpor!'s day. If Vučić has a finger in all the alternatives, which one are protesters going to feed off? Pro-European? Vučić has Brussels in his pocket. Pro-free market? Vučić has incentivised business to stick with him. Anti-business? Perhaps, but that can end up slipping into resentful nationalism – which Vučić is fine with too.

Meanwhile, the pro-Vučić media dismiss protesters as paid stooges of foreign forces. This had been the case during Milošević's time too. The difference was that Milošević believed his own tall tales. During his many wars Milošević's media claimed that Otpor! were 'well-paid seduced students' run by the CIA. After the revolution, Srdja found that Milošević had sent secret service teams to Washington DC to look for Otpor!'s headquarters, when all the time it had been based in Srdja's parents' living room. Vučić uses conspiracies much more coolly, flirting with the West while loyal newspapers push stories about how 'Serbia is surrounded by the CIA' or how MI6 is plotting to murder Vučić. Conspiracy is piled upon conspiracy, a 'hidden hand' behind everything.

Conspiracy theories have long been used to maintain power: the Soviet leadership saw capitalist and counter-revolutionary conspiracies everywhere; the Nazis, Jewish ones. But those conspiracies were ultimately there to buttress an ideology, whether class warfare for Communists or race for Nazis. With today's regimes, which struggle to formulate a single ideology – indeed, which can't if they want to maintain power by sending different messages to different people – the idea that one lives in a world full of conspiracies becomes the world view itself. Conspiracy does not support the ideology; it replaces it. In Russia this is captured in the catchphrase of the country's most important current affairs presenter: 'A coincidence? I don't think so!' says

Dmitry Kiselev as he twirls between tall tales that dip into history, literature, oil prices and colour revolutions, which all return to the theme of how the world has it in for Russia.

And as a world view it grants those who subscribe to it certain pleasures: if all the world is a conspiracy, then your own failures are no longer all your fault. The fact that you achieved less than you hoped for, that your life is a mess – it's all the fault of the conspiracy.

More importantly, conspiracy is a way to maintain control. In a world where even the most authoritarian regimes struggle to impose censorship, one has to surround audiences with so much cynicism about anybody's motives, persuade them that behind every seemingly benign motivation is a nefarious, if impossible-to-prove, plot, that they lose faith in the possibility of an alternative, a tactic a renowned Russian media analyst called Vasily Gatov calls 'white jamming'.

And the end effect of this endless pile-up of conspiracies is that you, the little guy, can never change anything. For if you are living in a world where shadowy forces control everything, then what possible chance do you have of turning it around? In this murk it becomes best to rely on a strong hand to guide you. 'Trump is our last chance to save America,' is the message of his media hounds. Only Putin can 'raise Russia from its knees'.

'The problem we are facing today is less oppression, more lack of identity, apathy, division, no trust,' sighs Srdja. 'There are more tools to change things than before, but there's less will to do so.'

Permanent Revolution

I saw for myself how hard it was becoming to use the previous logic of protest when I had the privilege of attending one of Srdja's workshops in Mexico, where activists, journalists, academics and political strategists gathered (in a bland conference room in a chain hotel) to discuss how one could plan an anti-corruption movement.

Mexico had its great 'democratisation' moment at the same time as Belgrade: in 2000 seventy years of single-party rule by the Institutional Revolutionary Party (PRI) had ended and the country had become 'democratic'. Now the problem wasn't dictatorship – the country had real elections – but every new regime was just as corrupt, just as in league with the narco barons as the last, and with a media controlled by oligarchs who worked closely with the government.

Some of those at the workshop, especially those jaded by decades of working in Mexican politics, had little faith that anything could change. Mexicans had a hundred years of disappointment in revolutionary change. In the nineteenth century Mexico had fought a war of independence from Spain, only to be subjugated by its own dictators. At the start of the twentieth century it had been a hotbed of socialist utopian dreams, the country's fantasies projected onto the walls of Mexico City in mind-bending murals of a new society by revolutionary artists, but the result was seventy years of stagnation under the PRI. The only thing that would appeal now, the more cynical argued, was a strongman leader, even tougher than the gangsters, who would promise to clean everything up in the name of 'the people'.

When I slipped out of Srdja's workshop to meet those struggling to create protest movements in Mexico, I began to see how his ideas were being played out in a new, digital dimension.

———

When I first meet Alberto Escorcia he looks too tired to even be frightened any more. Someone's been ringing his doorbell, then running away again so he can't sleep at night, shining acid-green lasers into his bedroom, sending online death threats with his name spelt out in bullets – thousands of death threats every day so that his phone vibrates with alerts 24/7, having turned into some sort of psychological torture implement.

But there's no way Alberto can go offline. It's his livelihood. More than that, it's sort of his religion. 'I see the Internet in metaphysical terms,' he tells me, 'a war between love and fear. Which I can calculate through the algorithms.' There's something a little other-worldly about Alberto. He can spend months manually analysing linguistic patterns in thousands of social media posts in order to see connections. The sort of things others get machines to do he does himself.

But somehow, talking about the divinity of data doesn't seem such an unusual concept when you are in Mexico City. This is a city where religious drama is interwoven with everything, where the cocktail of mountain air and exhaust fumes makes the thin light shimmer and refract as if through stained glass, and where every year millions of pilgrims climb past rows of roses and limbless beggars to rise above the city and pray in the massive skirts of the Basilica of Our Lady of Guadalupe. There, the icons of Jesus are decorated with real hair so they seem at first glance to be sprouting, and the priests command vast congregations not to follow the ever more popular cult of Our Lady of Holy Death, the Lady of Shadows, Santa Muerte, the patron saint of the narcos, who carries a scythe and a globe at her great festival on the Day of the Dead, when the whole city dresses up in skeleton masks.

Alberto is a great admirer of Srdja Popović. He's never been to any of the workshops, but he and his friends would pore over Srdja's manuals as they planned their own protests, all united in their hate of the casual police beatings, drug hits, stuffed ballot boxes and rigged deals which enabled the awful chasm between the black-glass-fronted boutiques and security fences up in posh Polanco and the toothless, impoverished people sleeping in piles in the baroque squares, a difference not so much between rich and poor as between different eras.

Alberto and his friends started with pranks to provoke the police: after students were beaten by police, they went on silent marches and staged lie-ins where they stretched out supine on the street, blocking the road. Protest had started off as something personal for Alberto. In 2009 his family, along with other workers, had gone on hunger strike to save the Central Light and Power Company in his home town of Necaxa. Alberto, already a well-known blogger, helped amplify the protest to the nation. The workers won.

In the second decade of the twenty-first century, protest became a way of connecting to a greater world. This was the height of the Internet-powered 'third wave of democratisation', and Alberto was constantly in touch with partner movements in Spain and the US, who were in turn talking to others in Turkey and the Middle East. Alberto was simultaneously organising lie-ins in Mexico and pushing hashtags in Barcelona.

Dr Marcos Bastos, a Brazilian academic at London's City University, analysed twenty million tweets by these movements between 2009 and 2015, conducting twenty-one interviews, and described them as powered by 'rooted cosmopolitans'. A young woman unable to leave her home in Scotland as she had to look after her ageing relatives, for example, would watch live streams of protests in Istanbul and Cairo and guide protesters on how to avoid armed police. Discrete interests were pooled into something broader. A Swedish 'serial activist' told Bastos: 'I don't fight for class struggle, feminism, ecology or anarchism. My political reference is my mother. I need to persuade her. I'm fighting to reach out to the 99 per cent: public values like justice and freedom instead of private values.'[7]

But for all the excitement of the rooted cosmopolitans, Alberto found himself frustrated with the hit-and-miss nature of protests. Some caught on; others were a waste of time. At their meetings his co-organisers would blame the weather, the government . . . Their approach, as advocated by Srdja, was to gather different groups, establish the 'lowest common denominator' of mutual interests, then spread the message to what they hoped would be the right people. But how would they know which themes to choose? The way they approached it seemed unscientific, and Alberto sensed that rational political interests were only part of what was needed to make a protest work. People wanted to be part of something emotionally powerful. That's why they came to some protests and not to others. He sensed this instinctively, but he wanted to use data to turn his hunch into something practical.

Alberto started looking at Google searches in the periods leading up to protests. He found that interest in certain topics – gas prices, police shootings – would start to be visible online months before they became articulated reasons for protest. That meant one could anticipate the issues that would unite people in advance.

Then Alberto began to look at how social media messages travelled between people during successful protests. Protests grew as the communication between users increased online, forming a dense lattice of interconnections – what computer scientists know as 'capillarity'. Alberto read the tens of thousands of messages to see which ones generated the most connections. He went through every line individually, a painstaking process that took months. He found that every wave of protests had a certain amount of words that made the lattice of communication grow thicker, words that worked almost like magical magnets powering capillarity. This is what Alberto meant by 'love': the increasing interconnections that people looked for in a movement.

He realised that if he knew in advance which subjects brought people together, and which words strengthened the interconnections, he would be able to 'summon up' protests.

To show me, he opened up a laptop. In the centre of the screen was a vibrating ball of dots with lines in between, with new lines joining in between the dots all the time, the whole thing quivering, growing, thickening. This was a real-time representation of online conversation among protesters during Mexico's biggest-ever demonstrations in 2014, when hundreds of thousands came onto the streets after forty-three students were murdered by narcos and the government did nothing to investigate. Each dot was a person, each line a conversation between them, and the links grew with the mention of the words powering the movement.

As Alberto showed me the graphic representation, an actual march went by outside the cafe we were sitting in. This was how I'd always seen protests: images of passionate people, slogans, speeches, stories, history. Alberto saw them differently, as something more abstract: little throbbing lines and dots, individual words emanating power outside the linear logic of full sentences.[8]

From the top of the screen something new emerged: many darting little bat-like shapes. These did not connect with each other; instead, they descended separately on the ball, pecking away at it, pulling it apart. 'These', said Alberto, 'are the bots and cyborgs.'

The protesters weren't the only tech-savvy actors around. Already back in the elections of 2012 Mexico had become famous in computer science circles for the amount of automated social media personas – basically computer programs pretending to be people – used by the eventual winner, Enrique Peña Nieto. Known as 'peñabots', these were Twitter accounts that could be produced by the thousands and then programmed to push out pro-Peña Nieto messages. 'Bots' were usually pretty stupid: they just repeated the same message over and over. 'Cyborgs' were a step up: bots would push the original line, but when someone took the bait and interacted with it, a real human operator – a cyborg – would step in and guide the conversation.[9]

One time a cyborg had come to see Alberto. She was a student herself. PR companies close to the government would pay 'bot herders' like her to run over a hundred fake personas on social media. She said she felt guilty. But the pay was solid.

With the protests swelling, government bots and cyborgs were now repurposed to undermine them. Protesters suddenly found themselves being smeared as being paid by the opposition, as being anti-patriotic – all sorts of lies. Instinctively protesters started to respond, defending themselves online against their accusers. On Alberto's screen you could see the consequences. As the little bat-shaped bots pecked at the ball, the little nodes representing protesters would stop interacting with each other and instead turn outwards to engage with the attackers, and as they did so the thick lattice became thinner and the ball started to break apart into a shapeless, twitching mess.

At a moment of crisis for the protests Alberto had an idea. He knew the words that thickened the links between protesters. What if he could flood the Internet with them? He created a YouTube video. It was just a girl talking to camera, listing the reasons why the protests were important. But every word she said had been carefully scripted by Alberto, each one selected as a linguistic potion.

When the video went viral, protesters stopped being distracted by the cyborgs and began talking to each other again, repeating the words that brought them together. Alberto could see the quivering ball begin to coalesce again, the little bats pecking in vain.

'That's what I mean when I say the Internet is a great battle between love, interconnectedness on the one side, and fear, hate, disjointedness on the other,' he explains.

After the cyborgs came the sock puppets, social media accounts that embedded themselves within the protesters' online community and then manipulated it from the inside.

In 2017, when there were protests against a hike in gas prices, the sock puppets acted. Activists had been guiding protesters, helping them move around the city safely, avoiding the police and being beaten up. Now the sock puppets gave fake directions and pushed the protesters into the arms of the police. They spread fake stories that there had been violence and looting, posting photos of supermarkets with their windows broken – photos that had been taken of riots in other countries and relabelled as if they were in Mexico. Real criminals began to join the protests. This gave the police an excuse for violence.

And after the sock puppets came the online death threats against Alberto, the green laser beam shone into his apartment, his doorbell buzzing.

One takes such threats seriously in Mexico. During my visit Alberto asked me to meet him at the public gathering of Article 19, an international NGO that helps protect journalists (and which derives part of its funding from the democracy assistance complex, including Freedom House, the US State Department and European foreign ministries). At the Article 19 event the faces of murdered journalists were flashed up on the walls: eleven had been killed in the last year, with 99.75 per cent impunity for the perpetrators. The event was held in one of those russet-coloured colonial palaces in Mexico City where you are ushered into a cool courtyard of columns, arches and cloisters so tall and graceful they serve only to emphasise the sad context of the gathering.

As canapés were handed round, Ricardo Gonzales, one of the directors of Article 19, told me the story of a journalist from Reynosa, a city in the north-east.

In Reynosa the narcos controlled the local newspapers, which, like Soviet-era publications, talked only about how clean, peaceful and prosperous the city was, when the reality was drug shoot-outs, with locals getting caught in the crossfire of gun battles that officially did not exist. Then social media came and changed everything. A Twitter channel, Reynosa Follow, would give live updates on shootings. Reynosans warned each other where to avoid: 'Two gunmen on the corner of 3rd and 5th, take an alternative route . . .' Of course, everyone who contributed to the project did so anonymously, Ricardo explained. The narcos were offering money to anyone who would reveal the identity of those behind Reynosa Follow. They were particularly pissed off with an account named @La Felina, who had a picture of Catwoman as her avatar and who would even post photos of local narcos with demands for their arrest.

Then, one hot August day, a narco gang in Reynosa was caught up in a shoot-out and one of their men was hit and wounded. The narcos rushed him to the local hospital. Three doctors, two male and one female, were assigned to him. Nervous at being in a hospital too long, the narcos kidnapped the doctors and took them to a safe house to treat their wounded colleague – a common practice. They took the doctors' phones. When they checked the woman's, it opened up on @La Felina's Twitter account. It turned out this plump, fifty-something medic treating their comrade-in-arms was the person they had been looking for. A few hours later @La Felina tweeted:

FRIENDS AND FAMILY, MY REAL NAME IS MARÍA DEL ROSARIO FUENTES RUBIO. I AM A PHYSICIAN. TODAY MY LIFE HAS COME TO AN END.

DON'T MAKE THE SAME MISTAKE AS I DID, YOU WON'T GET ANYTHING OUT OF THIS. I REALISED THAT I FOUND

DEATH IN EXCHANGE FOR NOTHING. THEY ARE CLOSER
TO US THAN YOU THINK.

Her last two messages were photos: one of her looking
directly into the camera, the next of her lying on the floor with
her face blown off. They had live-tweeted her execution. Then
they replaced her Catwoman avatar with María del Rosario's
blown-off head.

The narcos like to show that information technology can't be
used to undermine them. One gang took a corpse and dressed
him up as a carnival figure made up of computer parts: a keyboard to replace his mouth, CD-ROMs instead of eyes. The narcos were good at symbolism.

Given this context, Alberto decided it would be wiser to spend
some time outside Mexico. He hid away in a nearby country.

At the next Mexican general election in 2017, the PRI lost to
Andrés Manuel López Obrador, otherwise known as AMLO.
Obrador promised to clean up corruption – but in his own way,
top-down. He had little time for civic movements. He spoke the
language of old-school state socialism and nationalism (though
he quickly reached an accord with oligarchs to protect their
assets). Alberto knew some of Obrador's strategists and felt it
was safe enough to return home. He liked the promises, but he
was wary too. 'Obrador also used bots in his campaign,' Alberto
told me. 'I will be watching him.' He felt the new government
had been able to capitalise on the hard work of protesters, but
would it listen to them when in power?

With the PRI out of power Alberto wanted to learn more
about his adversaries. He'd heard that a part had been played
by a campaign manager nicknamed Chochos, who was reputed

to run an army of online trolls, bots and cyborgs. Chochos's Facebook page was a grinning clown face.[10] He agreed to talk to Alberto over Skype, but refused to show his face.

Though they were on opposing sides of the digital barricades, Alberto and Chochos spoke like two mutually respectful professionals swapping notes. When my translator transcribed their conversation, she kept getting confused over who was who.

Alberto asked about the fake pictures of looted supermarkets that had been spread during the gas protests, which had encouraged them to turn violent.

Chochos said he knew precisely who was behind those. It was a nineteen-year-old, part of a Facebook group called the Scientific Sect. Whenever one of their fakes would go viral they would celebrate. The media might talk about 'organised cyber-criminals', about 'psychological warfare', but it was just a bunch of kids, teenagers, who wanted attention.

Alberto told him how people had started coming round to his flat, ringing his bell . . .

Chochos shrugged it off. The kids created avatars for themselves which were intimidating on social media. Now they were getting the online world confused with the real one, pushing their avatars into reality. It was still all a game. The thing with Twitter is you can be whoever you want to be – a woman, a troll, an activist. You can play both sides of an argument, and no one will know. They weren't, he insisted, actually violent.

'It's like a nightclub,' said Alberto. 'As soon as the lights go out you can be whoever you want.'

So had Alberto been frightened merely by pranksters? One could barely blame him for having fled abroad: violence was so casual in Mexico it would be careless to ignore cascades of death threats.

Alberto saw a greater problem. He still believed that the Internet could reveal a society's true needs and desires, demands for change lurking latent amid the fluctuations of search engines and algorithms. The tragedy of digital manipulation was not just that individuals were harassed and abused, but that people were once again being separated from their own reality. For seventy years Mexico had been a one-party state in which 'truth' had been dictated top-down. People had accepted the reality the regime imposed on them as normal. Today bots, trolls and cyborgs could create the simulation of a climate of opinion, of support or hate, which was more insidious, more all-enveloping than the old broadcast media. And this simulation would then become reinforced as people modified their behaviour to fall in line with what they thought was reality. In their analysis of the role of bots, researchers at the University of Oxford called this process 'manufacturing consensus'.[11]

It is not the case that one online account changes someone's mind; it's that en masse they create an ersatz normality. Over the decades there have been many studies showing how people modify their behaviour to fit in with what they think is the majority point of view. In 1974 a German political scientist and pollster called Elisabeth Noelle-Neumann looked into research that showed how people will go along with the majority opinion in order to fit in.[12] The need to belong is one of the deepest human inclinations, Noelle-Neumann argued, and people are motivated by fear of isolation; that is why exile, expulsion from the group, is one of the oldest forms of punishment.[13]

In the age of mass communication, media becomes the indicator by which people decide what the dominant public opinion is. Noelle-Neumann rather prettily describes the dynamic as a 'spiral of silence'. On one side are interpersonal connections, which push alternative opinions up the spiral; on the other are mass media, which push them down. At the bottom of the spiral lies the silence.

Noelle-Neumann defined two types of people who fight against the silence. The first are what she termed the 'hardcore', who feel so rejected by society they don't care what anyone thinks of them and revel in a lost, invented past.[14] The other type is the 'avant-garde': reformers and activists who do want people to listen to them despite all the setbacks. 'Those who belong to the avant-garde are committed to the future and thus by necessity, are also isolated; but their conviction that they are ahead of their time enables them to endure . . . The chance to change or mold public opinion is reserved to those who are not afraid of being isolated.'

The latter description seemed to fit Lyudmilla, Alberto and Srdja rather well.

'Dark days are coming, Peter,' Alberto told me when I was back in London. 'A new generation of bots and trolls are pushing us further and further into a world of pure simulation.'

Parodying Protest

While regimes have become adept at disrupting and dismaying protesters, the real art is to co-opt the tactics of Srdja Popović for authoritarian aims, to reverse-engineer 'how to bring down a dictator' in order to strengthen one – and thus to parody protest movements until they lose their power.

The Kremlin had started thinking about how to create their own variation on the colour revolutions almost the moment they took place. As early as 2004 the then chairman of the Duma Foreign Affairs Committee, Konstantin Kosachev, declared: '[Russia] cannot explain the purpose of its presence in the post-Soviet Union . . . The West is doing this under the banner of democratisation, and one gets the impression we are doing it only for the sake of ourselves . . . Our activeness is following too openly Russian interests. This is patriotic but not competitive.'[15]

Inside Russia the Kremlin created a 'patriotic youth movement' called Nashi (which literally means 'Ours'), one of whose stated aims was to stop any Srdja-style colour revolution from ever taking hold in Russia. In former Soviet republics the Kremlin developed networks of Russian cultural centres to serve diaspora populations, and in 2007, in Estonia, the world saw what a Kremlin-inspired version of 'colour' street protest might consist of.

———

'This one was shot, this one was disappeared – apparently killed – this one was deported.' Toomas Ilves, president of tiny Estonia, walked me down a long corridor in his Tallinn residence, pointing out portraits of the men who led the country during its first period of independence – between the fall of the Russian Empire in 1917 and its occupation by the Soviets during the Second World War, an occupation that continued until the fall of the USSR in 1991.

Ilves was dressed in his trademark tweeds and bow tie, a counterpoint to his mission to make Estonia the most digitally progressive country in Europe. Under his presidency the government declared Internet access a human right: citizens can vote, get medical prescriptions, deal with taxes and bank electronically, and pay for parking with a mobile phone. A new school programme required that all pupils learnt to code from the age of seven. This 'e-Stonia' project is practical – a search for an economic niche – but also symbolic, a way to tear the country away from its Soviet stereotype as Moscow's backward province. This was meant to have been sealed in 2004 with EU and NATO accession. But this sense of a smooth historical journey, from liberation from the Kremlin, through Internet-powered reforms and into the security of NATO and joining the club of liberal democracies in the EU, would soon be undermined.

Since Soviet times, every year on 9 May Russian nationalists and war veterans living in Estonia had gathered to celebrate Victory in the Second World War Day in the centre of Tallinn, at a statue known as the Bronze Soldier[16] – a large Aryan-looking hunk who commemorated Soviet victory over the Nazis. Around a third of Estonians are Russian, or at least primarily Russophone; the vast majority of these are descendants of Russians who were relocated from the Soviet Union after the Second World War, while thousands of Estonians were being deported to the Gulag. Between 1945 and 1991 the number of Russians in Estonia rose from 23,000 to 475,000. After 1991, some felt like second-class citizens in the new, independent Estonia. Why weren't prescriptions available in Russian? Why couldn't Russophone towns have street signs in Russian? Why did you have to take a language test to gain citizenship if you had been born in Soviet-occupied Estonia? Over 70 per cent watched Russian state media, easily available in Estonia, which claimed that the Soviet Union had never invaded Estonia in the first place, that Estonian Communist forces had invited them (in reality these had been Soviet agents). Russian politicians would suggest that Estonia was not a 'real country'. Russian historical TV dramas featured 'Estonian fascists' as the go-to baddie.[17]

When Russian nationalists and Soviet nostalgists would gather at the Bronze Soldier to sing Soviet songs and drape the statue with flags, Estonian right-nationalists began to organise counter-marches at the same spot. In 2006 one Estonian writer threatened to blow the statue up. In March 2007 the Estonian parliament voted to move the statue to a military cemetery – officially, for reasons of keeping the peace. But Russian politicians and media responded furiously. 'Estonian leaders collaborate with fascism!' said the mayor of Moscow. 'The situation is despicable,' said the foreign minister. The Russian media nicknamed the country 'eSStonia'. A vigilante group calling itself the Night Watch camped around the Bronze Soldier to protect it against removal.

On the night of 26 April, as the statue was about to be removed, ethnic Russian crowds started throwing bricks and bottles at the Estonian police. Riots broke out and there was mass looting. One man died. Russian media reported that he was killed by police (he was not), that Russians had been beaten to death at the ferry port (they had not), that Russians were tortured and fed psychotropic substances during interrogation (they were not).

The next day employees of the Estonian government, newspapers and banks arrived at work to find their computer systems down, crippled by a cyberattack known as 'denial of service', whereby so many requests are sent to an Internet address it crashes. e-Stonia had been taken offline. The whole country was paralysed by the combination of propaganda, cyberattacks and street riots.[18]

Who was behind the attack? The Estonian security services claimed to have observed meetings between the Night Watch vigilantes and staff at the Russian embassy. But ascertaining that the unrest had been coordinated by the Kremlin was a different matter. The Russian patriotic youth group, Nashi, took credit for the cyberattack, but claimed they had done it off their own bat; the government had had nothing to do with it. It was 'patriotic trolling', but the victim was a whole country.

For Ilves and his national security team the precise aim of the riots was something of a riddle. 'When Russian politicians make threats about being able to conquer Estonia, does that mean they would actually invade?' Ilves's former security adviser Iivi Masso said when I asked her about this. 'Are they just trying to demoralise us? Or do they want Western journalists to quote them, which will send a signal to the markets that we're unsafe, and thus send our investment climate plummeting? Sometimes we wonder whether the point of the attacks is only to make us sound paranoid and unreliable to our allies.'

What the attacks definitely signalled was that despite entry into NATO, Estonia could not just walk away from its former colonial master. The NATO alliance is predicated on a single phrase, contained in Article 5 of the treaty, which holds that a military attack on one member is an attack on all. For all the invocations of the idea of 'the West', its practical, geopolitical expression is Article 5 – a sentence, a promise. But what if that sentence was rendered meaningless? Russia could not risk a military war with NATO, but what if its attack was non-military and non-attributable?

After he completed his two terms as president of Estonia in 2016, Ilves moved to Palo Alto, California, where he was given a fellowship at Stanford University. Dressed, as ever, in his tweeds and bow tie he padded around in between the begonias, visiting the technology companies with their trays of jelly beans, where everyone wore trainers and rode around the brightly painted corridors on bicycles. These precocious computer-science geniuses didn't understand the first thing about politics or history, or their role in either of them.

In Estonia Ilves had made the idea of the Internet synonymous with post-Soviet progress. Now that he was among the social media companies he was disenchanted: they were empowering the very forces he had tried to free Estonia from, but didn't seem willing to recognise their responsibility. He wrote an essay for the Facebook Newsroom about how it could be exploited by undemocratic powers, but they took so long to publish it that by the time it came out, events had taken over: social media companies were being forced to investigate and reveal how the Kremlin used fake online accounts to covertly try and influence the US presidential election to help Donald Trump and fuel ethnic hatreds and social divides. Ilves rolled his eyes when he saw how the political and media classes in the US reacted as if nothing like it had ever been seen before: a 'digital 9/11', some called it, 'an online Pearl Harbor'. How narcissistic, thought Ilves; the attacks on the US were mild compared to what had happened to Estonia a decade earlier.

After the 2016 elections, academics and experts debated how to measure the effect of the Kremlin's information operations in the US. There were at least two separate ones to consider. One was the hack and subsequent leak of emails of senior staff in the

Democratic Party, which one could argue were influential as they became a major talking point in the election. The troll farm activities were much harder to make sense of. They were tiny compared to the overt and covert online political campaigning in the US. So should one ignore the effects of such a relatively small foreign campaign and focus on the impact of the larger, US-produced mass? Or should one focus on the foreign operation, as that could have tipped the scales in a tight race?

Or, I wondered, could one think about the impact of the Russian campaigns in another way: as eating away at a greater story and a set of associations between events and images that had defined 'democratisation'?

Estonia had been one of the places where the great non-violent protests that helped bring down the Soviet Union began. The Singing Revolution had started with ordinary people belting out patriotic songs in the main square of Tallinn in 1987, and culminated in 1991 with singing protesters facing down Soviet tanks. It was a constant reference point for advocates of non-violent revolutions, such as Srdja Popović. Now the Kremlin was working away at undermining the association between people demonstrating out in the streets in Eastern Europe and the greater story of waves of democratisation flowing in a single historical direction. When authoritarians create their own versions of protests, the effect is almost satirical, taunting and undermining the originals. Two could play at people protests, Moscow seemed to be saying.

In America one of the tricks of the St Petersburg troll farm was to take on the personas of American civil liberties campaigns – Black Lives Matter, for instance – and then use them to raise the vote for the more pro-Russian presidential candidate,

Donald Trump, or depress it for his rivals. The troll farm even organised protests in US cities, both for and against Trump, each chanting against the other. One protest in particular reminded me of a really crap copy of Srdja's political street theatre: when a troll posing as a Donald Trump supporter in a fake Facebook group called Being Patriotic convinced a woman in Florida to hire an actor to wear a rubber Hillary Clinton mask and then lock the actor in a makeshift jail cell and wheel them about as if in a carnival procession.[19]

And it's when the Kremlin's efforts are unveiled that they have perhaps their most significant effect. When one hears so many stories of fake accounts that seem to be supporting freedoms and civil rights, but which in fact turn out to be nothing of the sort, one starts doing a double take at everything one encounters online. Is that American civil rights poster over there actually being run out of St Petersburg? Is anything what it says? When the Kremlin crawls inside American protest movements online, the very notion of genuine protest starts to be eroded. Getting caught is half the point, making it easier for the Kremlin to argue that all protests everywhere are just covert foreign influence operations. After all, don't the Srdjas of this world get money from the democracy assistance complex? This reinforces the larger narrative the Russian (and Iranian and Chinese) media are trying to reinforce: that colour revolutions and the Arab Spring are not genuine but rather American-engineered 'regime changes'. Indeed, that there is actually no such thing as truly bottom-up, people-powered protest, a message that is only reinforced when the American government gets caught trying to use social media to covertly stir up anti-government sentiment abroad, as it has in Cuba.[20]

When exactly did the Kremlin start to think about how to crawl into digital pro-democracy movements to subvert them? After the troll farm's activities in the US were discovered, Dr Marcos Bastos, the London-based professor who had collected twenty million tweets from years of protests by 'rooted cosmopolitans', became curious: what had all those Internet personas been doing previously?

Bastos went back to his database. He returned to protests in Brazil, Venezuela, Spain, all the way back to 2012. And he found the Kremlin's masked accounts had been there all the time, right from the peak of the 'third wave of democratisation'. Even as the first protests had rolled through Brazil, Venezuela, Spain, the Kremlin was already experimenting with the possibility of penetrating and exploiting them from the inside. Back in 2012 the Kremlin sock-puppet accounts didn't do anything spectacular; they just embedded themselves, building capillarity, impersonating their way into the digital networks of the revolutionaries. When he dug deeper Bastos found that some accounts had even been created back in 2009, though whether those were created by the IRA or were organic accounts that were later compromised by the agency is another matter.

Bastos recalled a lecture he had given at the Higher Economics School in St Petersburg in 2013. It was about how influence in digital protest movements was achieved not by having a few powerful influencers with many followers, but by many small ones communicating incessantly. Usually his crowd consisted of fidgety academics or wealthy hipster students barely paying attention. This time there was someone else: two men, middle-aged, in suits, just staring at him, their heads not moving, taking in every word like recording automatons and writing careful notes.

———

Meanwhile, back in the western Balkans Srdja Popović has to watch his own tactics being used against his own ideals, like in some crooked hall of mirrors.

When (genuine) protests had begun against Macedonia's former prime minister, and Putin ally, Nikola Gruevski, in 2015, demonstrators poured red paint into the fountains near where Gruevski's bodyguard had murdered a student. They threw paintballs against the buildings of corrupt state institutions that had wire-tapped journalists and opposition parties, so that the city centre began to look like a huge Jackson Pollock painting. They held night-time rallies, bearing torches and wearing white masks to symbolise how the regime wore a fake face. So far, so Srdja.

But every time the opposition protested, the regime would bring in its own counter-protesters. They wore the same masks and bore the same torches, matching the original protests symbol for symbol. Gruevski would eventually be voted out, but the protests were a sign of how one could parody colour revolution tactics.

The parody would reach a different pitch the next year in Montenegro, where an oligarch who made his money in Russia, Russian oligarchs and the Kremlin's secret services tried to disrupt the Montenegrin government, which had brought the country into NATO.

'First, they united an utterly fractious opposition around a lowest common denominator – government corruption,' relates Srdja, talking about the creation of a Montenegrin opposition movement that brought together Serbian nationalists,

Orthodox Christians and Communists. 'They widened the battlefield by bringing in international players with Russian money; then they prepared to claim electoral victory, and when they lost the election they launched street protests.

'What happened in Macedonia and Montenegro is right out of my book, but reversed, and missing the most important parts,' argues Srdja, as he sits in front of the huge clenched fist that has become synonymous with all the protests he has inspired, scrawled on walls from Cairo to Caracas. 'They think that popular will does not matter, that you don't need to win elections, for example, while we make it the basis of our strategy. And they think you can use violence to make up for the lack of popularity, while we know that non-violent movements are the more successful.'

Throughout all this topsy-turviness, where the destination of the 'waves of democratisation' has come under question, Srdja has remained indefatigable. Anyone who is lucky enough to attend one of his workshops will experience the sense that change is just around the corner. Though with time some of the lessons have changed. Sometimes Srdja finds he is teaching his students not so much how to overturn authoritarian regimes as how to defend democracies. Increasingly he is asked to work in countries where democracy had been considered to be secure.

'What is the lowest common denominator among your institutions? Which are the ones you can gather a coalition to protect? Is it the courts? The media?' he asks.

When I talk to him, there is only one moment when he becomes frustrated: when I describe what he does as a 'technology', a 'model'.

'This is not a model. This is not a technology. We give people skills. We teach them how to play the guitar, not what to play . . . That's the great difference between us and them. They think you can use people like puppets. That you can import and export revolution. We train people to take power themselves.'

But what, I can't help wondering, if 'the people' who want to take power do so to abuse other people?

The Discord Channel

The Discord Channel is a closed Internet site usually used by computer-game fanatics, but it has become increasingly popular among far-right groups as a place to meet online and plan digital influence campaigns. Groups are private, and in order to gain access to the Infokrieg group you may first want to create an avatar who claims to be interested in the philosophy of Friedrich Nietzsche, and maybe spend some time developing an online alter ego which regularly reposts articles about migration and cultural cohesion. Once inside Infokrieg you will be able to download an 'Information War Manual', where you will be given a status depending on how many followers you have: twenty-five to a hundred makes you a 'Baron'; over 10,000 means you are 'an Übermensch Influencer'. You will then read up on different campaign tactics: how to coordinate online in order to taunt 'mainstream' journalists (known as 'sniper missions'); how to post nasty comments on the Facebook pages of politicians; and how to plan 'dislike' campaigns on YouTube, where you 'vote down' videos of your opponents. If you get into an online 'dogfight' with the enemy – a debate you can't win, for example – then you post to the hashtag #Air Support and other Infokrieg members will come to your aid, spamming the conversation with their taunts.[21]

Infokrieg also has its own meme factory, where activists are provided with existing pictures and then deface them with their own words in order to change their meaning. One meme created by Infokrieg, for example, showed a highly saturated drawing of a happy American family right out of a 1950s advert, with the words 'Right Wing Extremists' printed beneath it, indicating that traditional ways of life are being marginalised.

But what caught my eye on Infokrieg was the language used by some of the participants: 'Don't use any National Socialist memes. Focus on lowest-common-denominator themes: mass migration, Islamification, Identity, Freedom, Tradition.' 'Lowest common denominator' was a concept right out of Srdja's playbook.

Infokrieg was created by members of the 'Génération Identitaire' movement. Martin Sellner, leader of the Identitarian Movement of Austria, is perhaps the movement's most prominent figurehead and its intellectual leader. He advocates a culturally homogeneous Europe and the 'remigration' of Muslims: a sort of soft, peaceful path to achieve aims which sound not dissimilar to the ethnic cleansings Milošević supported.

Sellner is perhaps best known for a stunt he pulled called 'Defend Europe', when he chartered a ship to sail out into the Mediterranean and stop humanitarian organisations that help migrants making the dangerous crossing from North Africa to Europe. He has been banned from entering the UK on the grounds of 'not being conducive to the public good'.[22]

When we talked via video, Sellner, in black-rimmed glasses that made him look more like a philosophy student than a skinhead, told me that Popović had been a massive influence on him. He sounded genuinely impressed when I told him I knew Srdja and had even attended a workshop.

Sellner maintained that we are ruled over by a 'soft authoritarianism' that makes discussion of immigration taboo – an accusation that seemed absurd to me sitting in London, where the biggest-selling newspapers run on anti-immigration stories.

One could analyse Sellner's work through the prism of CANVAS's strategies. He has clearly articulated 'the change he wants to see' (a culturally homogeneous Europe). In migration he has found the 'lowest common denominator' that can unite disparate interests. When two researchers into the digital growth of right-nationalist movements, Julia Ebner and Jacob Davey, analysed the motivating ideas behind the different groups that supported Sellner's 'Defend Europe' ship escapade, they found that they included anti-Muslims and anti-leftists, those who were worried about terrorism and those who were worried about whites being displaced from Europe, general 'anti-Establishment' groups and conspiracy theorists.[23] Sellner has also what Srdja calls 'widened the battlefield', bringing in an international network of forces. He has built alliances with British anti-Muslim activists and makes regular appearances on Russian state broadcasters. His girlfriend is a leading US alt-right personality, like some sort of unification of royal families across borders. Almost half of the online support for 'Defend Europe' came from the US. And finally there is an electoral strategy: the Infokrieg campaign was to support the Alternativ für Deutschland party in Germany, which dominated social media to Twitter-storm its way into the German parliament for the first time in 2017.

After our video call Sellner sent me a message: 'Greetings to Popović ;),' it read.

Esfir pinned her most precious diamond earrings to Lina's lobes, and then someone – Lina could barely register who – took their cigarette, tapped the ash onto their fingers and smeared it on the earrings to hide the shine: 'If the customs officials ask, say they're just glass.'

We were at the airport. A crowd had come to tell us goodbye forever. As far as anyone knew, we would never see parents and sisters, brothers and best friends, or anything previously known as home ever again. All my parents could fit in their canvas bags were kilograms of reusable nappies (they were not aware of any disposable ones in the USSR). They had US $180 in cash, and that was it. Soviet citizenship was revoked. We were stateless. At the border we were strip-searched. My mother had held me so tight that when she took off her shirt there was an imprint of my face on her chest.

'In November 1977 Major MEL'GUNOV gave a formal warning to POMERANTSEV. The protocol listed circulating defamatory fabrications, regular listening to hostile broadcasts and contacts with foreigners. In the same month KGB Major A. L. IZORGIN advised POMERANTSEV to emigrate.'

In many ways Igor was lucky. He had the semblance of choice. The major had made it clear that if he stayed, he would have the full seven years in prison and five exiled in the Soviet provinces to face. If he had been a Ukrainian-language poet, he would have been locked up immediately. Repression in Ukraine focused on exterminating any signs of independent Ukrainian culture outside the cultural crèche of state-sanctioned Soviet 'Ukrainianness'. But Igor wrote in Russian, the language of the coloniser. He had been published in the Moscow-based cultural journal Smena, *which had over a million readers. If he were put away, there was a chance that someone in Moscow would kick up a fuss, and then it would be all over the Western 'voices', raised at international conferences. The charges against him no longer even led to arrest in Moscow, where conventions were more lax due, in part, to the presence of Western journalists able to make stars and saints out of dissidents (or at least write a column about them).*

The Soviet Union was still going through the motions of posing as a utopia. Minor poets elevated to prisoners of conscience for reading books were a bad look. In 1977 the most famous Soviet dissident, the physicist Andrei Sakharov, wrote a letter in support of other political prisoners to US President Jimmy Carter and had it published in the New York Times:

Dear Mr Carter, it's very important to defend those who suffer because of their nonviolent struggle, for openness, for justice, for destroyed rights . . . our and your duty is to fight for them. I think a great deal depends on this struggle – trust between the people, trust in high promises and the final result – international security.[24]

Sakharov provided a list of names he wanted Carter to raise with his Soviet counterparts. These weren't empty appeals. Ever since the Soviet Union had signed the Helsinki Accords promising to respect 'human rights' and 'fundamental freedoms' in 1975, American leaders would raise the issue of political prisoners at summits. Sometimes they even managed to get someone released. At the very least it embarrassed the Soviet Union and made the Americans look superior.

From the mid-1970s the Politburo decided that emigration was often an easier way of getting rid of troublesome dissidents than banging them up. It was also, according to some accounts, more profitable.

Igor and Lina saw themselves facing frightening choices about freedom, family, literature, but our fates were also decided by warheads and wheat. Technically we were being allowed to leave on a 'Jewish visa', the provision of which would, according to some sources, fluctuate depending on the amount of grain the USSR was allowed to export to the US. In 1976 14,000 'Jewish visas' had been issued. In 1978, as the US and USSR negotiated the SALT nuclear arms reduction treaty, which included easier grain exports, the number rose to 29,000. We were three of those 29,000.[25]

The visa allowed you to travel to Vienna, from where you had to choose between a final destination of either the US or Israel. My parents had no desire for either. They wanted to stay in Europe.

———

Dear Mark,

You were there to say goodbye to us at the airport and said goodbye at customs. I want to tell you what happened next. At customs we were strip-searched. I carried all our huge canvas bags as Lina had Petka in her arms. I was soon sweating and wanted a drink. On the second floor there was a sparkling mineral water dispenser, but I didn't have one Soviet kopek on me to put in the slot. Mark, if you ever emigrate, take some small Soviet change. It's illegal to take any Soviet money with you, but you will get away with this.

You then saw my hand waving to you from the window of the bus, but didn't see I was crying. We found seats in the tail of the plane. When the plane took off the stewardesses started to bring breakfast. We were treated like foreigners. They even served us wine. But in half an hour the plane began to shake like an autumn leaf: we had flown into a thunderstorm. Water sprayed on our cheeks. Snow fell through the cabin. There was an announcement in English that we would be making an emergency landing in Minsk, Soviet Belarus. Just to have something to say I told Lina to fasten her seatbelt. 'I'm nervous,' she told me. Petka was asleep on her knees. It was hailing from all sides, both, for some reason, from below and above. I put one hand over my head and the other round my son's face. The wheels collided with the Minsk landing strip and with a great crunch buckled, the airplane skidding on its belly another hundred metres, knocking down cabins and flags.

In the airport we were guided to the 'mother and baby' waiting room. Lina was crying and didn't want to go. I pushed her forward with my elbow and it came out rough so she cried even more. We were separated from the other passengers. 'Main thing is not to worry,' I told myself. 'We have foreign visas. We've been stripped of Soviet citizenship. We're foreigners now and that's it.' There was a man in a suit with his back to us when we walked into the room. For some reason I exclaimed, 'Good day!' to him in English. He paid no attention and began making calls. I could hear him say the names of our KGB interrogators from Kiev:

100

Villen Pavlovich; Valeriy Nikoaevich. Then he mentioned the Belarusian town of Babruysk. They took us away in the evening. We walked towards the van: I with my wet shirt; Lina with her face smeared and puffy with weeping, the sleeping boy in her arms. 'At least I don't have to carry the bags,' I thought. 'So they will take us to Babruysk. They will be there already. Villen will have taken off with some woman. Valeriy will be working on chess puzzles, checkmate in four moves, knocking the pen against his lower teeth, yellow with nicotine, squinting . . .'

Our van rattled on the rough roads. We were squashed in the back into one wet, salty mound.

We arrived in Babruysk at night. In Babruysk they executed us by firing squad.

Igor

———

Igor penned this nightmare scenario a few weeks after arriving in Vienna, a way of communicating the fear he felt during the flight. All through their first weeks, months in the West Igor would still instinctively listen for the click of the KGB eavesdropping on the phone line, for the knock on the door.

It was the colours that struck Lina when they first landed: she was almost blinded by the searing yellow of bananas, burning oranges. As Vienna came into focus around her she regained a sense of order: the architecture, with its art nouveau twirls, was comfortingly similar to Chernivtsi and Kiev. Then she found herself thrown again by the sight of so many handicapped people in the streets: old people in wheelchairs, groups of children with Down's syndrome. She struggled for an explanation. 'Is this some sort of punishment for what they did in the war?' she blurted out to Igor, even as she realised how nonsensical this idea was. Then she understood: in the utopia of the Soviet Union the disabled were locked away, hidden in horrible homes far from the city or trapped in apartments, censored.

We rented rooms in the dormitory of the Vienna Conservatory, so all these first impressions of oranges and children with Down's syndrome and art nouveau stucco swirls were bound together inside the sound of strings and trumpets and pianos tuning up and practising scales, in a din of dissonance that would some-times suddenly combine in harmony. Into this cacophony pulled up a large bright-blue Mercedes, out of which stepped a tall woman with a familiar face. It was Anneliese and she was here to guide us.

Anneliese was a German schoolteacher. She had visited Kiev and had got to know Igor and Lina. She had come to the USSR as a curious tourist, and left determined to help the dissident friends she made there. Now she had a plan to get us from Austria to Germany. She and one of her final-year pupils, Harold, had spent days researching the thick forest on the border and had mapped the quickest way to cross it by foot: they had it down to a brisk half-hour walk.

They drove the blue Mercedes to the border and Anneliese led us into the woods, while Harold drove on to meet us at the other side. Lina shushed me to be quiet. I stayed abnormally still. There was no path and soon everyone's feet were drenched, and what was meant to take half an hour was taking over sixty minutes. Every snapping twig made everyone start with fear. Anneliese had lost her way, but both Igor and Lina kept up the pretence that she knew what she was doing. She was the one taking the risk: if she were to be caught smuggling us across the border, she would, at the very least, lose her job. But she knew how badly Igor wanted to stay closer to Kiev, Odessa and Chernivtsi, which he in turn saw as part of a greater Europe.

Then, just as their strength was fading, they emerged at the other side, back by the autobahn, and the blue Mercedes drove us further into West Germany, past villages, across dark forests and along by the castles on the broad, curving Rhine to Anneliese's home village of Lahnstein, where she took Igor into the police station and he requested political asylum. If the policeman were to ask how we had made it into Germany, then Anneliese could have been in trouble. The policeman looked my father up and down, looked at Anneliese, and never asked the question. In 1978 West Germans were delighted to welcome political refugees from the Eastern bloc – proof their system was superior to East Germany's Communism. The application for asylum would take a year, but in the meantime we would be given an apartment in Adolfstrasse.

As part of the asylum application Igor was 'invited' to the regional capital to be screened by the German and French secret services. They were meant to check whether he was a spy. Two young, polite and smiling officials asked him what he did, where he had studied, what he wrote. He answered, and then waited for them to begin a more thorough vetting. When none was forthcoming he became worried: the Europeans were so naive, the KGB would waltz pass them. Why hadn't they tried to interrogate him properly?

Then the Americans asked him in for a chat as well. This time there was more intrigue: he had to go a bland office with no sign, where two men with crew cuts were waiting for him. *The Americans tried to catch Igor out: how many stairwells were there at your work? How many floors? What could you see out of the window? Igor was relieved. At least someone was investigating him properly. It even sounded like they had people in Kiev who could double-check what he had told them. Maybe there was hope for the West after all. The men with crew cuts asked him whether he could tell them about his army service, the size and location of the unit. He told them he had taken a military oath of honour not to divulge such secrets. The Americans were from the security services themselves and nodded respectfully at this sentiment.*

In Lahnstein, for the first time in his adult life Igor found he couldn't write poetry. He couldn't stop thinking about the friends he'd left behind. Some were now locked up in the USSR's last camps for political prisoners in Mordovia and Perm. He picketed outside the Soviet consulate with placards demanding their release. He wrote essays that tried to evoke the world he left behind, the dramas of Ukraine so often ignored by Western readers, who knew only about Moscow and St Petersburg. 'I have a motherland,' he wrote, 'and it remains within me forever. We are as inseparable as an eye and a tear.'

He described how they all felt revulsion at the Soviet invasion of Prague in 1968, how each of them could remember where they were that day. He wrote about the literary critic jailed for seven years who, during those years, had seen his wife exactly seven times, yet still wrote to her without a note of bitterness, merely asking her to send on new copies of Bakhtin. Igor wrote about the friends who woke up, read the morning newspaper and discovered that they were this morning's story and had committed some awful crime. The composer who discovered he had 'beaten up a construction worker in front of many witnesses right in the middle of Kiev'. Though the 'worker' didn't exist, the sentence was very real. The Jewish activist who was informed that he had viciously beaten up a female nursery teacher. He discovered that he went so far as to break her leg while she was walking home, carrying a cake. When his friends searched through every nursery in Kiev they never found any teacher with any broken leg.

Igor's angriest writing was saved for the cynicism he encountered in the West. The German journalist who told him 'the truth must be somewhere in between The Gulag Archipelago and official Soviet statements'. Or the newspaper editor whom Igor was trying to persuade to write about his friend Piotr Vince, who faced receiving another prison sentence while still serving his first one, in response to which the editor merely yawned and answered that 'This theme is old and boring. Does the Russian [i.e. Igor] want money?' Did the editor not realise that one article in his newspaper could change a prison sentence? Did the journalist not realise that there was no 'middle' in between truth and lies?

'No one needs you dissidents here,' an older Russian exile told Igor, meaning to say that no one in the West actually cares about all this business with 'rights', so why does he even bother? 'He who was a conformist at home is a conformist here,' wrote Igor. 'I'm sure the man who told me this lived in the USSR as if he didn't know or care about the thousands imprisoned inside political camps in Mordovia or Perm. His words were just an excuse, a lie. There are people here who care.'

Igor's essays were published in small literary magazines with tiny circulations, but which were, so the theory went, influential, as they targeted a cultural elite. There was Partisan Review, where Igor's essay on the 'Right to Read' appeared; decades later it would emerge the CIA helped the magazine survive by buying up copies when sales were low. There was Encounter, whose own CIA-funding scandal had already passed back in 1967.[26]

The Cold War had a cultural front, and Igor was rapidly finding himself drawn into it. In 1980 he was invited to London for an interview for a job at the BBC's Russian Service, which would have been vetted, as were all such interviews, by a member of MI5. MI5 never requested the vetting process themselves – no one at the BBC ever knew any classified information. It was the BBC itself that asked MI5 to do it. If the British government were ever to complain the BBC was being in any way disloyal to the country, the Corporation would be able to say that its employees had been vetted in advance. The vetting was not just for foreigners; many staff at the Corporation went through it.[27]

There was also a security consideration. In 1978 a member of the BBC's Bulgarian Service, Georgi Markov, had been walking to the office across Waterloo Bridge when he felt a twinge in his hamstring. He turned round to see a man passing by with an umbrella. A day later, as he lay dying, he would realise the ricin poison had been injected into him via the umbrella. Later, it would emerge the assassination had been carried out by the Bulgarian secret services, with ricin provided by the KGB poison factory near Moscow.[28]

Igor passed his writing test, and the vetting. We moved to London, part of a tiny quota of Soviet refugees allowed in – the British granted few entry visas to immigrants beyond their former empire. But we were being recruited for a Cold War effort.

Part 3: The Most Amazing Information Warfare Blitzkrieg in History

Today, talk of cold war has been replaced with discussion of information war. My office is stacked with thick reports and papers, such as 'The Kremlin's Firehose of Falsehood' and 'The Digital Maginot Line'. I have written about 'The Weaponisation of Information' and 'How to Win the Information War' myself, analysing the Kremlin's use of media in neighbouring countries.

During my research, I came across a Russian manual called *Information-Psychological War Operations: A Short Encyclopedia and Reference Guide* (the 2011 edition, credited to Veprintsev et al. and published in Moscow by Hotline-Telecom, can be purchased online for 348 roubles). The book is designed for 'students, political technologists, state security services and civil servants' – a kind of user's manual for junior information warriors. The deployment of information weapons, it suggests, 'acts like an invisible radiation' upon its targets. 'The population doesn't even feel it is being acted upon. So the state doesn't switch on its self-defence mechanisms.'

The encyclopedia seemed to take the idea of information war beyond just cyber- and media campaigns, as I had believed it to mean, and to hint at something more expansive. And the more I delved into the Russian literature on 'information war', the more it seemed to be not just a foreign policy tool, but also a quasi-ideology, a world view. How is it different to the Cold War, and how does one win, or lose, it?

Operation Perestroika

In the late 1990s and the first decade of the twenty-first century the idea of information war began to obsess a certain breed of security-agency-connected Russian geopolitical analyst attempting to understand history, and the failure of the Soviet Union in particular. Secret service agents turned academics assert the Soviet Empire collapsed not because of its poor economic policies, human rights abuses, lies, but because of 'information viruses' planted by Western security services through Trojan-horse ideas such as freedom of speech and economic reform (Operation Perestroika).[1] Alleged secret agents in the Soviet Establishment who posed as so-called modernisers, allied with a Washington DC-dictated fifth column of anti-Soviet dissidents, oversaw the dissemination of these 'viruses'.

For a long time such theories were not in the Russian mainstream. But as the Kremlin searched for ways to explain the colour revolutions and the growth of discontent at home, which erupted in hundreds of thousands protesting against Vladimir Putin's rule in 2011 and 2012, this all-pervasive information war philosophy became increasingly amplified by TV spokespeople and spin doctors. Today, runs the argument, the West wages information war against Russia with the cunning use of the BBC and human rights NGOs, fact-checking organisations and anti-corruption investigations.

One of the most outspoken public promoters of the information war is Igor Ashmanov,[2] a frequent guest on TV talk shows and radio. 'The fall of the Soviet Union, Yugoslavia, Iraq . . .

we've lived through many information wars,' said Ashmanov in one of his many interviews.[3] He's also told Russian law-makers that Google, Facebook and Twitter are ideological weapons aimed at Russia.[4]

But Ashmanov is no crusty spook. He is one of the fathers of the Russian Internet, the former head of the country's second-largest search engine. When I visited his high-tech office in Moscow, with piles of fresh fruit, dates and nuts on the table, I could just as easily have been in Palo Alto or Berlin. Ashmanov, in his sports clothes and wire-rimmed glasses, could fit in at any tech gathering.

Ashmanov's big idea is 'Internet sovereignty': government control over what information reaches the population, which China is well on the way to achieving with its Great Firewall and censorship, and which the West tries to undermine with talk about 'freedom of speech'. Information sovereignty can't be achieved, he argues, without an ideology to defend your rationale for letting some streams of information through and not others.[5]

'If your ideology is imported . . . as with liberalism, then you are always playing to foreign rules, which are always being changed by someone else. You can always be called guilty of breaking the rules of democracy . . . Ideology should be created inside a country, like operational systems, rockets, insulin and grain. Supported and defended by information sovereignty.'[6]

Information, in this world view, precedes essence. First you have an information warfare aim, then you create an ideology to fit it. Whether the ideology is right or wrong is irrelevant; it just needs to serve a tactical function. Instead of clashing ideas leading to a cold war, here information war necessitates the creation of ideologies.

Indeed, it's not hard to find many instances where the US acted, as Ashmanov argues, hypocritically when it came to freedom and human rights, supporting their promotion in adversaries and ignoring their violation in allies. In the sly words of diplomats, values and interests don't always align. On the other hand, as long as the US kept up the facade of believing in something when promoting its image abroad, it would have to at least sometimes do something about it.

As the Oxford University professor Rosemary Foot relates, you can trace the roots of the American foreign policy freedom narrative back to President Franklin Delano Roosevelt's 1941 'Four Freedoms' speech, which called for freedom of speech and religion and freedom from fear and want as the basis for a democratic world. Proclaiming the message so loudly meant that policy and practice needed to at least vaguely match promises.

As early as 1949 the 'Negro question' had been highlighted by the US embassy in Moscow as a 'principal Soviet propaganda theme', one which had to be battled at home for the sake of US foreign policy.[7] During the 1950s the US Justice Department could argue that desegregation inside the US was important as it would help promote the country's international image as a bastion of freedom. In the early 1970s, in the aftermath of the Vietnam War, American support for coups in Chile and US intervention in the Dominican Republic, Congress held hearings on human rights abuses in those countries. The resulting report established a human rights bureau within the State Department, meant to make rhetoric on freedom and human rights closer to policy.

Meanwhile, inside the Soviet Union dissidents could use the Helsinki Accords to insist that the regime 'obey their own laws', in an attempt to at least embarrass them internationally.

These were tiny victories in the grand scheme of the horrors of the Cold War, but the notion of information war as defining history demolishes even these achievements and replaces hypocrisy not with something better but with a world in which there are no values. In this vision all information becomes, as it is for military thinkers, merely a means to undermine an enemy, a tool to disrupt, delay, confuse, subvert. There is no room for arguments; ideals are in and of themselves irrelevant.

This leaves one with a tricky situation. In *Don't Think of an Elephant* the cognitive linguist George Lakoff defines winning and losing in politics as being about framing issues in a way conducive to your aims. Defining the argument means winning it. If you tell someone not to think of an elephant, they will end up thinking of an elephant. 'When we negate a frame, we evoke the frame . . . when you are arguing against the other side, do not use their language. Their language picks out a frame – and it won't be the frame you want.'[8]

I had already seen this in the Philippines, where the Rapplers had indulged Duterte's language of a 'war on drugs', thus making it easier for him to start his actual killing. The heads of Russia's international broadcasters, RT and Sputnik, indulge in the language of information war, even receiving military medals for their services to the government.[9] Western journalists and analysts, myself included, then call them out for being information war organs. But by describing them as such is one actually lending them a hand, framing them in the image that they need to secure more funding from a regime that wants to see everything through the frame of information war? By evoking the Kremlin's language of information war, does one end up strengthening it? Do the endless articles, senate hearings and think tank events with their sour coffee – I have written for and attended plenty – risk reinforcing the notion even as they try to expose it?

The long-term implications go deeper. If all information is seen as part of a war, out go any dreams of a global information space where ideas flow freely, bolstering deliberative democracy. Instead, the best future one can hope for is an 'information peace', in which each side respects the other's 'information sovereignty': a favoured concept of both Beijing and Moscow, and essentially a cover for enforcing censorship.

But to merely ignore the Kremlin's information operations would be foolish. The disabling of Estonia with a mix of media and hacking in 2007 had been a foretaste of how strong their effect could be. In Ukraine they had accompanied an actual invasion.

At endless panels held in think tanks in Washington DC, London and Brussels military theorists, journalists and officials have tried to make sense of the Russian approach to 'war' and international conflict. Some call it 'full-spectrum warfare', others 'non-linear war', yet others 'ambiguous' and 'grey-zone warfare'.[10] In Eastern Europe 'hybrid war' state research centres have sprung up, where 'hybrid' seems to be a diplomatic way of not saying 'Russian'.

There are some things that a few experts can at least occasionally agree on. First, that the Russian approach smudges the borders between war and peace, resulting in a state of permanent conflict that is neither fully on nor fully off. And in this conflict information campaigns play a remarkably important role. Summarising the aims of Russian 'next-generation warfare', Jānis Bērziņš of the Latvian Military Academy describes a shift from direct annihilation of the opponent to its inner decay; from a war with conventional forces to irregular groupings; from direct clash to contactless war; from the physical environment to the human consciousness; from war in a defined period of time to a state of permanent war as the natural condition in national life.[11]

This leaves us with a paradox. On the one hand, it is necessary to recognise and reveal the way the Kremlin, with a military mindset, uses information to confuse, dismay, divide and delay. On the other, one risks reinforcing the Kremlin's world view in the very act of responding to it.

It is in Ukraine where this paradox plays out at its most intense. This is where the Kremlin's next-generation warfare is being tried out, but also where it is trying to spread an all-encompassing world view of information war.

So how can one win an information war when the most dangerous part could be the idea of information war itself?

The Most Amazing Information Warfare Blitzkrieg in History

Of all the things one might think Tetyana could ever be, a soldier is not one of them. But back in early 2014, at the height of Ukraine's revolution against a pro-Moscow president, Tetyana suddenly found herself able to command life and death. Sitting in her father's apartment, in her pyjamas, she had her hand over a keyboard, knowing that if she pressed one key she might send many very real people to a very real death, and if she pressed another the revolution and all that she, her friends and thousands of others had fought for might be lost.

At the time Tetyana was running the Facebook page of Hromadske Sektor (the Civic Sector), one of the main opposition groups in the Ukrainian revolution against President

Viktor Yanukovich and his backers in the Kremlin. She posted photos and videos that were straight out of Srdja Popović's philosophy of non-violent action: a protester playing a piano out on the street while facing a row of riot police; photos of protesters holding mirrors up to the security forces; a drawing of a cop duelling with a protester, with the cop holding a gun and the protester 'shooting' with a Facebook sign, emblematic of how empowering social media was for the protesters. Online activists could organise everything from medical help to legal aid, coordinating million-strong protests and raising funds from Ukrainians abroad for food and shelter.

Tetyana had kept up the click-beat over many months of protests. Hromadske Sektor had 45,000 followers, and 150,000 visitors attended their protests – people who didn't trust politicians but believed in volunteers like Tetyana.

Tetyana had joined Hromadske because she wanted to be part of a historical moment, something to tell her future children about. The uprising was nicknamed the 'Revolution of Dignity'. It had begun when President Yanukovich had, very suddenly, dropped a long-standing pledge to sign an Association Agreement with the European Union in favour of a $16 billion loan from the Kremlin. After Yanukovich's police beat up protesting students, for many it had grown to symbolise the desire for a government that was less corrupt, for a more just society bound up in the word 'Europe' – 'Euro-Maidan' was the revolution's other nickname (Maidan being the name of the square where the protesters gathered).

Tetyana would post on the site as she filed stories for her real job as a financial journalist. She told herself she would somehow stay above the fray; she was for democracy and human rights, sure, but she wouldn't get dragged into disinformation, wouldn't get her hands dirty.

Tetyana's shift was in the morning. She was usually based in Kiev, but today she happened to be in her home town of Luhansk, one of the capitals in the far east of the country known as the Donbas, where most people watched state or Russian TV, which portrayed the revolution as a neo-fascist, US-orchestrated conspiracy. Out here Tetyana never mentioned her work for Hromadske Sektor.

She had woken at 9 a.m. and switched the computer to the live feed coming from the Maidan. At first she thought she had tuned into some action movie by mistake – snipers were mowing people down and there was blood on the streets. Then her phone rang: it was activists in the Maidan. She could hear guns going off behind them, and after a small time lapse heard them crackle on the live stream too.

'Get people to come to the Maidan. We need everyone here.'

But Tetyana could also see posts popping up on her Facebook feed from people in the square, warning everyone to flee and save themselves. Activists kept calling her, demanding that she tell her followers to come.

'But there are people being killed,' she said.

'The snipers will stop shooting if more people come.'

'And what if they don't?'

'It's your decision.'

It wasn't the first time she'd found her journalistic instinct to remain above the fray clashing with her revolutionary loyalties. A few weeks previously the pagan-nationalist, balaclava-clad Pravy Sektor (the Right Sector) had started hurling burning Molotov cocktails through the snowstorms at the riot police.

Few people had heard of Pravy Sektor until then. There were only a few hundred of them, but all the publicity around their violence had increased their profile wildly. Kids looking for a little ultra-violence were now signing up to join them.

Tetyana didn't approve of Pravy Sektor's violence or ideology. The Maidan was full of different 'sectors', everything from neo-Cossacks to neo-anarchists and neo-fascists, all able to organise with the help of the Internet. Their ideologies could be dissimilar. My parents' friends who had been put through the wringer of the KGB were there too. They could see in the Maidan a distant echo of their own struggles, though now raised to a level of mass protest one couldn't dream of in 1978. For them the Maidan was another stage in a much older struggle against the 'Chekists' in the Kremlin and their satraps in Kiev. Though now it wasn't just 'freedom-loving liberals' out on the streets; everyone had their own motivation. The different sectors had nothing much in common apart from being fed up with Yanukovich's corruption and casual brutality, and it didn't seem right to attack people who were beaten up by the same riot police who beat you up.

Hromadske Sektor decided to ignore Pravy Sektor's violence, but Tetyana couldn't ignore the massacre in Maidan Square that morning. What was her role? Was she, ultimately, a propagandist? A journalist? Was she reporting on the war, or was she a soldier in it? Every time you post or tweet, or just repost or retweet, you become a little propaganda machine. In this new information flux, everyone has to find their own boundaries. Tetyana had reached hers. She refused to encourage crowds to come to the Maidan. She simply reported on what was going on and let people make up their own minds.

Various Hromadske Sektor leaders logged on themselves and urged crowds to come to the Maidan. One hundred and three protesters died in those few days. But the crowds didn't stop coming. They kept pushing, storming the presidential palace, while in the regions local council after local council was stormed by protesters, many of them now armed themselves. President Yanukovich fled to Russia. Hromadske Sektor leaders joined political parties and stood for election. Tetyana didn't want to be involved in party politics and left the movement altogether.

Then the Kremlin began exacting its revenge. Russian TV filled up with invented stories about how Pravy Sektor was coming to slaughter ethnic Russians in Crimea, where most of the population are ethnic Russians. In Sevastopol, the Crimean capital, Cossack groups, separatist parties and Orthodox priests (all funded by the Kremlin) led crowds begging Putin to rescue them. He obliged and annexed the peninsula.

Russian TV broadcast scare stories about Pravy Sektor coming to murder Russians in East Ukraine too. The Internet, the medium through which the revolution had been empowered, was flooded with Kremlin content pumped out of the troll factory in the St Petersburg suburbs. Employees at Lyudmilla's old place of work were paid a few hundred dollars a day to post pictures, comments and videos, sowing confusion, enmity and panic in East Ukraine.[12]

The Kremlin's information campaign was the prelude to action. Irregular forces, local proxies of the Kremlin, seized cities in the east: Donetsk; Tetyana's home town of Luhansk. These parodied the same visual language as the Maidan uprising, with flag-waving crowds sometimes bussed in from across the border and piles of burning tyres, which had become the symbol of events in Kiev. It was labelled the 'Russian Spring' by Kremlin-controlled media, tapping into the language of the Czechoslovak rebellion against the Soviet Union in 1968. As with previous information campaigns around colour revolutions, the Kremlin was trying to satirise the Maidan into insignificance. At the same time it was desperately trying to reconfigure the Maidan uprising into a greater story of Ukrainians manipulated by covert American forces, all part of the American policy of 'regime change' which had brought catastrophe to Iraq and Libya. Igor Ashmanov and Russian state media honchos stated that the Ukrainian uprising was, of course, a product of information war.

If there was one aim to the Kremlin storytelling, it was this: to show that the desire for 'freedom', that hangover of Cold War logic, didn't lead to peace and prosperity but to war and devastation (a message meant, first and foremost, for its own people so they didn't become overenthusiastic about the idea). To make this narrative real meant ensuring Ukraine could never achieve peace. The country had to bleed.

When the Ukrainian military would attack the separatist strongholds, the Kremlin would send in tanks and crush them, then retreat and claim it had never been there in the first place. Over the following years – indeed, up to the time of writing – the conflict flowed hither and thither, not quite a full-blown war but never peace either. Towns in the Donbas are taken and then lost again. Shells go off on either side of the lines. The Russian army holds mass exercises on the border with Ukraine, and mass panics break out throughout the country. The violence has also had unintended consequences. In July 2014, when a Russian high-tech anti-aircraft gun shot down a Malaysia Airlines passenger plane full of Dutch tourists that was flying over territory controlled by Kremlin proxies, killing 298, the information operation went into absurd overdrive: the airliner had been shot down by Ukrainians who thought it was Putin's private jet; dead bodies had been put on the plane in advance and the whole thing was staged; Ukrainian fighter jets had taken the plane down . . .[13]

NATO's Supreme Allied Commander had called the Russian campaign to take Crimea 'the most amazing information warfare blitzkrieg' in history. But it was ordinary Ukrainians, often abandoned by a shoddy government, who had to find ways to make sure the information blitzkrieg wouldn't spread to the rest of the country too.[14]

———

'The worst thing about all of this', Babar Aliev told me, as we sat, on a burning hot summer's day in 2015, in a Severodonetsk cafe blaring out painfully loud techno overlaid with high-pitched Russian female vocals, 'is that I have to carry a weapon again. Ten years ago, I promised never to carry a gun. But I regretted that promise when the separatists came. Next time I will be ready.'

Severodonetsk is in East Ukraine, just a few kilometres from the Russian border, where in 2014 Russian troops were massing in what seemed to many the preparation for an invasion. A rumour had just swept through Severodonetsk's Internet portals about how Pravy Sektor were on their way to haul down the town's Lenin statue, a symbol of pro-Russian leanings. Local groups – Russian Cossacks and Russian wrestling, laser-tag and literary clubs – gathered to defend it. The rumour was false – someone was trying to get the pro-Russians fired up. This wouldn't be too hard. Severodonetsk is not a town that feels much historic loyalty to the Ukrainian state. It was built in the 1950s, a perfect grid of Soviet modernist white rectangles designed around sixteen science colleges and four chemical plants. Like much of the east, the inhabitants came from across the USSR. After the Second World War, it was one of the few places you could go with no papers – a bureaucratic trick to get criminals and vagabonds to come and work the heavy industry. After the end of the Soviet Union, the town went to pot: the plants are now stripped carcasses, the neat modernist rectangles cracked and peeling, the potholes in the roads so bad you drive in weird swerves. The writer Owen Matthews once compared parts of the former Soviet Union to an experiment abandoned by its scientists, the people lab rats left to rot and eat each other. In Severodonetsk, with its mix of symmetry and dilapidation, this seemed particularly apt. For many, Russia represents a better place.

Babar, a thirty-something web designer of mixed ethnicity from across the former USSR, had noticed that the pro-Russian clubs had started to proliferate here in greater numbers after 2012, just as Vladimir Putin was facing off mass protests against his rule in Moscow. Since the start of the Maidan uprising more had appeared. At the time Babar had thought nothing of it – Ukraine was a democracy after all. Now he suspected someone had been planning something for a while. During the day the pro-Russians would gather in the main square, where Orthodox priests (from the Moscow patriarchate) and Communist Party leaders were holding daily rallies calling for unification with Russia, claiming the Maidan had been led by fascists and fed by drugs.

'If we let them pass, then the country rolls backwards,' Babar thought to himself. He had been in Kiev during the Maidan and had felt that the revolution was some sort of historical leap into something new. He had been disgusted when he saw the riot police beating up students in Kiev. Over the last few years he had seen how Yanukovich's party was raiding businesses and pillaging the country: government run as a protection racket, propped up by Putin. Now, in a Severodonetsk abandoned by the government, he felt it was up to him to fight an information war against the enemy all by himself, hoping that he could galvanise others to join him.

Maybe he was motivated by the sense that there was also a part of his own past he didn't want to 'roll back' to. As a teen in the mid-1990s Babar had been a gang leader. His speciality was planning and executing complex burglaries (he always looked down on mere protection rackets: where was the art in that?). Then he moved on to stripping the local chemical plants of precious metals – gold and platinum (he had read up on the periodic table). He dropped the thug life after he was finally caught (he had studied law and knew how to bribe his way out). But even now, when he has long been a web designer and minor Internet PR guy, he has the swagger, shell suits and fast eyes of the smart hoodlum (as well as the sudden ecstatic grin of a toddler). In Severodonetsk many still find it hard to believe that Babar has, as he likes to put it, 'developed an aversion to slicing people up'.

During his time in the Maidan Babar had developed a Facebook following among pro-Ukrainians in Severodonetsk, and now he used it to fight back against the separatists online – to 'nightmare them', as the Russian phrase goes. Babar put out a story that separatists had beaten up some gay activists, and now a battalion of gay fascists was coming from Holland to take revenge. The story was ridiculous, but some of the separatists fell for it and started to get alarmed, which made them look like idiots. Babar also put out a story that two hundred undercover Pravy Sektor agents had holed up in flats in Severodonetsk; that they rode the trams listening to people's conversations; that when they heard pro-separatist talk the agents would take people off the tram and they were never seen again; that they recorded the names of taxi drivers who wanted Severodonetsk annexed. The separatists' portals were in a panic, and Babar felt he was winning the disinformation war. He wanted them to doubt everything and lose their bearings – to do to them what the Kremlin was doing to Ukraine.

Now he needed to build a coalition to take onto the streets. But how would he motivate them when there was no overall idea of Ukraine they related to, and when each tribe in the city lived in its own little information bubble?

Babar went to the organised crime bosses, known as *Vori v Zakone* (thieves-in-law), who lived according to a strict prison code. Some of them had been in Babar's first gang before he straightened out. 'How can you be on the same side as the cops?' Babar asked them, slipping into *Fenya*, the prison jargon which *Vori v Zakone* communicate in. 'You used to be an honest prisoner [i.e. someone who lives by the prison code]. Now you're a goat and you've got horns on your head [in prison jargon a "goat" is a turncoat, the lowest of the low].' The *Vori v Zakone* and Babar counted the cost to their business interests if the Kremlin invaded, so decided to back Ukraine. They offered Babar men and guns.

Babar also went to see the hoodlums who ran the protection rackets. Did they really want to have Russian gangsters come here? They would take away their territory. And while the local gangs had the Ukrainian police sown up, Russian police might have other ideas. The gangs told Babar they would back him.

Then Babar went to the businessmen. 'You guys have been to Europe,' he said. 'You know how much easier it is to do business there: no hassle from bureaucrats wanting bribes or gangs wanting protection money. Well, the Maidan is all about us having European rules. Don't you want that?' The businessmen came on side too.

Now he had his coalition, for backup Babar reached out to Kiev-based Maidan activists with connections to the new government. Just a few special forces would be enough. Throughout the spring of 2014 town after town in the east was being taken by separatists backed by Russian special forces, the flags of the independent Donetsk and Luhansk 'People's Republics' hoisted over local administration buildings. Babar kept on waiting for a sign from Kiev, but none came. He began to suspect the Donbas had been traded in for some deal with Moscow. He kept on calling his contacts, explaining to them that he'd done all the preparatory work – the disinformation campaign, building up the alliance of different groups . . .

In May the separatists took power in Severodonetsk. The local administration welcomed them, took down the Ukrainian flag and replaced it with the tricolour of the Luhansk People's Republic. The thing that hurt Babar the most was that when the separatists came for him, they only sent three men. When he had been arrested back in the 1990s the cops had sent three vans with SWAT teams wearing flak jackets. Now there were just three guys with guns who put him on a train to Kiev. His attempt to fight his own version of a one-man information war had failed. In a sense he'd tried to reverse-engineer the Russian approach: first spread disinformation to confuse the enemy, then use irregular forces, gangsters and mercenaries to hold a town. But the Ukrainians were still too slow to cotton on.

A few months later the Ukrainian military finally arrived, now reinforced by patriotic and ultra-nationalist volunteer battalions (including the Pravy Sektor). The army surrounded Severodonetsk and lobbed heavy artillery at it. The separatists hoped the Russian military would intervene, but no one seemed to care enough about holding 'Sever': they pulled back to the heartlands of their new republics, the areas around the cities of Donetsk and Luhansk. Babar returned home. But when we talked in 2015, he felt little sense of victory. The same politicians and cops who had backed the separatists were still running the town. Some of the Ukrainian soldiers and volunteer battalions had alienated the locals: there had been a shooting during a bar brawl; one of the volunteer battalions had decided to enforce their authority over the local mafia by forcing a gangster to swim across a river and then shooting him in the head when he was halfway across. This wasn't how you built coalitions.

I asked him what his plans for the future were. He told me that the financial crash that came with the war meant his old website development orders had disappeared. He wanted to set up media literacy classes for local people, but for the moment would do anything, even hauling crates, to get by. I asked him what his 'media literacy classes' would involve. He explained they would teach people how to check whether a piece of news online is real, to check it for the reliability of sources, to use a reverse image search to verify pictures were from where they claimed to be from.

Hadn't he used disinformation himself when he 'nightmared' the separatists with his fake rumours? How did he square that with promoting media literacy campaigns?

Babar smiled. 'I believe in disinformation for the other side and media literacy for my side.'

———

Information vigilante groups were sprouting in Ukraine, and I wanted to know what it was like to be on the receiving end of their campaigns.

'R u still alive you separatist? I wonder how long for?' said the SMS on Andrey Shtal's pre-smartphone-era mobile. 'As always, there's no number to trace it back to,' said Andrey. He seemed used to the messages and was more worried that activists from self-declared 'civic information war groups' had put him on a list of 'traitors' but given an old address. 'What if they go round and beat up the person living there now, someone totally un-related to any of this?'

Andrey was from Kramatorsk, just south of Severodonetsk. Like Sever, it had first been taken by Russian proxies and then retaken by Ukrainian forces. He worked at the Kramatorsk municipal gazette. When the proxies took Kramatorsk and announced it part of the Donetsk People's Republic, most of the staff fled, and Andrey stayed on as the editor. His paper pub-lished information about sewers and roadworks and schools – nothing political – and he never strayed into anything that was off-topic. This saved him when the Ukrainian army took the town back. He was arrested by a pro-Ukrainian volunteer battalion in Dnipropetrovsk. They beat him and held him for three days with a bag over his head, but eventually he was released.

It's Andrey's poetry, rather than his journalism, that gets him in trouble with the patriotic activists.

'In poetry I can be myself. The head of the Donetsk People's Republic likes my poetry and improvises verses back over Facebook.'

We walked across Kramatorsk's tidy city park and down a grand, neo-classical Soviet avenue to a local cafe with Wi-Fi so we could look up his poetry. In the distance we could see the sun shining off the hills of the Donbas.

There were dozens of pages of Andrey's lyrics on local poetry portals. We clicked through to his most recent work. It started with satires on the Maidan, done in the style of a Soviet children's poem:

> They will create hell here and horrid night,
> And turn you, my hero, into a sodomite.

'I was against the Maidan,' Andrey tells me. 'I sensed straight away it would lead to war. I get premonitions of the future sometimes.' He had grown up with the young men who joined the proxy Russian forces in Kramatorsk. In his poetry he conveys the careless, chaotic way they decided to take up arms. 'They were local druggies and gangsters, the kids of policemen and officials. How could I hate them? Nobody can hear the Donbas.'

'Nobody can hear the Donbas.' I heard that phrase often in the east, a catchphrase expressing the sense that politicians in Kiev didn't understand local needs.

As the conflict spread east Andrey's poems became more grim:

> I used to be a musician and artist,
> But now I woke up as a separatist . . .
> I live in Rus, Rus isn't dead yet!
> What I wish for is a bullet in the prime minister's head![15]

Much of Andrey's poetry evokes Soviet motifs and songs. He is haunted by a memory from his teens, when he was on a school trip to Lithuania in 1991 and witnessed the crowds trying to pull down the statue of Lenin. On the long train journey back to Donetsk he wrote his first poem, an allegory of the Soviet Union as a train that has become too old, and of a country falling into civil war.

'Lenins were falling then, and they are falling again now,' he sighs. 'Back then I already had a bad feeling about the future.'

When we met in Kramatorsk, the government in Kiev had just passed laws forbidding Soviet street names and symbols. The Lenin statue in the central square had been pulled down, leaving an empty plinth with a Ukrainian flag tacked on. Officials argued the street name changes and statue demolitions were a necessary part of the information war with the Kremlin, with its non-stop diet of Soviet movies and social media campaigns that reframe the present as an endless Second World War against eternally returning fascists. But the laws could also play into the Kremlin's hands, shifting the focus of the Maidan from the search for a better future to a battle over a past that could only ever be divisive.

'The Communists built everything here. Anyone who achieved anything was from the party – why should we forget them?' complained Andrey. 'There are a lot of people here who can't show what they think openly. They live online instead, and it's important for them not to be lonely. I can formulate what they feel.'

By embracing and parroting back the language of the Kremlin, Ukrainian information warriors risked playing Moscow's game. You were on either this or that side of an information conflict, either a traitor or a patriot. And this was just the sense of division that the Kremlin needed to foster its very real war. How could society hold together?

I started to get more of a sense in Odessa, the scene of my father's arrest, where the full-spectrum, non-linear, hybrid, ambiguous, next-generation war had one of its most deadly moments.

———

When Igor had been arrested in Odessa in 1976, the media that was accessible in the city was strictly censored. Today Odessa boasts fourteen local TV cable channels alone, not to mention the dozens of Ukrainian and the hundreds of international ones available in most free-to-air packages. Online there are dozens of local news sites and masses of social media groups.

Odessa has always been a port city, populated by Jews and Greeks, Russians, Romanians, Ukrainians and Bulgarians. Today the port is a major international thoroughfare for goods both legal and illicit coming into Europe. Many are traded at the Seventh Kilometre, which some locals claim is the world's largest outdoor market: acres of shipping containers stacked on top of each other in a multilayered maze, each one transformed into a shop where Nigerians sell fake Nikes, fake stereos and fake Gucci, Vietnamese trade money, Indians hang out silks and muslins. They say you can also buy weapons here, if you know who and how to ask. Not just guns, but anti-aircraft missiles too.

It was this delicate ethnic balance that the Kremlin tried to tip into civil war. In May 2014, just as Kremlin proxies were taking town after town in the Donbas, pro-Ukrainians fought with pro-Russians holed up in Odessa's Palace of All Trade Unions. A fire broke out, and even as the flames were still engulfing the building and the dead still being counted, the rumours and lies were already fanning through the media. The first YouTube videos were blurry and horrific. Hundreds of pro-Russian activists had been hiding out in the building. Pro-Ukrainians threw Molotovs and shot at them. A fire broke out. People began falling out of the windows – so quickly it looked like they were pushed to their deaths. Some of the Ukrainians cheered.[16]

The first photos from inside showed dozens of corpses in twisted poses. One was of a pregnant woman. Interviews appeared online with eyewitnesses who claimed Pravy Sektor death squads had been hiding in the building. The unnamed witnesses claimed the Pravy Sektor had been prepared, wearing gas masks and executing people on the spot. The initial death toll put the number of victims at around forty, but stories spread that actually there had been hundreds.

The story went international. Pro-Kremlin activists in Belgium and Italy campaigned to have a European square named after the 'Odessa Martyrs'.

In the days following the fire the people of Odessa, citizens of a city of ceaseless chatter, a city famous for its humour, stopped talking to each other. No one trusted anyone. The rumours began to turn the city against itself. Opinion polls showed an even split between those who wanted the city to be part of Russia and those who wanted it to be part of Ukraine. Pro-Russian bloggers began to ask Putin to save the city from chaos and invade. Later, recordings would emerge of Russian politicians talking on cell phones directly with gangs of thugs in Odessa, giving them orders on when to provoke more fights.

A group of Odessans, both pro-Russian and pro-Ukrainian, decided to take it upon themselves to launch a public investigation. They felt Odessans needed to know what happened in the fire if the city was to be whole again. It was clear that no official investigation would be forthcoming: too many bureaucrats would have to take too much blame for all the casualties.

The civic investigation pieced together the events of the day from video and multiple witness statements, autopsies and photographs. The trouble had started earlier in the day. It was found that both sides threw Molotovs and fired shots; that the barricades around the building had lit up accidentally; that the autopsies showed thirty-four deaths – all from asphyxiation, none by mysterious execution. The 'pregnant' woman had been over fifty and had died from the fumes, falling back into a position that made her stomach look swollen. The eight people who had fallen to their deaths had lost consciousness and tumbled out – none had been pushed.

The public investigation had managed to establish the essential truth about what happened during the fire, but when the results were presented, few were interested. 'There's no unity here,' Tatyana Gerasimova, one of the instigators of the public investigation, told me as we sat in a cafe by the opera house.

'Everyone lives in their own reality, everyone has their own truth, there is no reconciliation. We created the investigation to show that there is a difference between truth and lies. In that sense we failed.'

I would hear similar sentiments from students at the university, where I was giving a lecture about . . . information war. The students' friends and relatives just chose the story of the fire that better fitted their world view. As they sat and discussed it in their social media groups, pro-Ukrainians saw it one way, pro-Russians another. Faced with wildly conflicting versions of reality, people selected the one that suited them.

But despite this fracturing of shared reality, Odessa hadn't toppled into civil war. The week I visited summer was in full swing. The bars and discotheques were full. The opera was sold out. 'The city needs to feel alive again, after it looked death in the face,' said Gerasimova.

But this hadn't been achieved purely spontaneously. While the civic investigation had tried one way of unifying the city, other Odessans had taken a different approach. Zoya Kazanzhy was running government information campaigns when the threat of civil war was at its highest. She felt she knew something about her home town that Putin didn't. Yes, Odessa was as fractured as any globalised city, but its different communities had something deeper in common. Apart from a few fanatics, most saw Odessa as a wealthy, open trading port, a city of markets and merchants. They would go with the force that could guarantee their security, whether Russian or Ukrainian, the EU or NATO. So instead of playing on the ethnic tension, as the Kremlin might have wanted, instead of looking to divide the city further between patriots and traitors, Kazanzhy and her colleagues decided to target what all sides had in common. They put up posters across Odessa with pictures of the wrecked cities of the neighbouring Donbas, where the separatism had led to a destructive war. Despite their differences, no one in Odessa wanted that sort of future. No one wanted physical destruction. The most potent manoeuvre in the information war was to jettison the idea of 'information war' altogether and show what real war led to.

But as I headed into the zone of actual military conflict, I would soon find that even if the shooting and shelling was real enough, at the same time every action, including military action, was taken with its impact on the information conflict in mind . . .

How to Fight a War That May Not Exist

Dzerzhinsk is a mining town at the very edge of the territory held by Ukrainian forces. Separatist positions are a couple of kilometres away. There was a summer storm brewing when I arrived, thunder mixing with the sound of heavy artillery. A few days earlier a shell had hit the local lake. Fish had flown out onto the cracked paths or floated dead to the surface. The people of Dzerzhinsk ate the fish, but there were still a few drying on the paths and many more were floating belly-up in the lake. The smell was strong.

I travelled with a small crew from an Internet TV station in Kiev, one of the few Ukrainian media organisations not in the pocket of an oligarch. Driving through town we passed along roads with coffin-sized craters, saw empty factories with their walls ripped out; a young boy leading his drunk mother down

the lanes; local men with scabs on their faces. I stopped to pho-
tograph a concrete coal store with a gaping hole in its walls. I
assumed it had been shelled, but it turned out it had been taken
apart long before the war by locals looking for scrap metal.

Dzerzhinsk is named after Felix Dzerzhinsky, the man
responsible for the first Soviet secret police force, the notor-
ious Cheka. When I asked a local teenage girl whether she
knew who he was, she told me she'd 'heard of him at school but
couldn't remember'. This wasn't unusual: a few weeks earlier a
TV channel had done a joke report about how young people in
Dzerzhinsk had no idea whom the town was named after. Later
that year it was renamed Toretsk, in accordance with the laws
against Soviet names. There were no great protests.

The mineshafts were dark against the thundery skyline.
Some of the mines were now disused. Others were rusty, but
functional.

The local administration of Dzerzhinsk has weathered every
revolution. In April 2014 it welcomed the separatists with open
arms. The two newspapers under its control supported the
Donetsk People's Republic. When the Ukrainian army retook
the town a few months later, they shelled the town hall. The
administration quickly cut a deal with them. But though the
town is now officially in Ukrainian territory, you still can't get
Ukrainian TV unless you had a cable package. Russian and
DPR TV stations are still available everywhere. Dzerzhinsk
may be in Ukrainian territory, but it is still under the Kremlin's
informational sovereignty.

The pro-Ukrainian activists were jumpy. There was Oleg, an
older man with a grey moustache and a cap. He had been one of
the miners who helped bring down the Soviet Union in the great

strike of 1989, blocking the roads with broken glass to stop the Kremlin's tanks. Volodya was younger, with big arms and a boy-band fringe. He was a miner too but had worked in Sweden for several years. He knew things didn't have to be this way.

Volodya and Oleg were sure the administration wanted the activists, with their annoying anti-corruption rallies, out of town. They were worried Kiev was ready to abandon them.

'If there's no mention of us on TV, then it won't be a big deal if the town is lost,' said Volodya. 'We're being erased.'

In the front of his van was a stack of leaflets:

7 TO 12 YEARS PUNISHMENT FOR EVERYDAY SEPARATISM:
CALL THIS NUMBER IF YOU SPOT AN EVERYDAY
SEPARATIST!

HOW TO SPOT AN EVERYDAY SEPARATIST?

– CALLS FOR RUSSIA TO INVADE
– INSULTS UKRAINIAN VALUES
– SPREADS LIES
– PLANTS DEFEATIST FEELINGS

I asked Volodya where he had obtained the leaflets. He told me with no little pride he had made them himself. I asked whether that was such a good idea.

'The telephone numbers on them aren't even real,' he said. 'They're just to intimidate people. We're all alone here. We need to do something.'

We arrived at a Soviet block of flats, rising above an area of wooden shacks, several of which had been blown apart. The Ukrainian army base was five hundred metres away and this area was hit frequently. Oleg showed us the shrapnel holes in the metal door of the apartment block. Some women were on a bench outside the front door. They were angry that the Ukrainians had put their base near here. There had been no fighting when the town had been part of the DPR. The Ukrainian army had brought the war with them. One woman told me how a shell had exploded through her balcony.

Oleg got angry. 'Our mayor is a separatist. That's why the army is here. He should be in prison.'

'I worked all my life for pennies, and what's my reward?' said a woman going past in a sunflower-patterned dress. 'Bombs!'

'They came from over there – those are Ukrainian positions! That's not DPR,' shouted one of the women. Later, she showed me a crater in the ground. A tree had collapsed into it. 'Look,' she said. 'It's clear it came from the Ukrainian position.'

It didn't seem clear at all. I thought it unlikely the Ukrainians could shell themselves from five hundred metres away. But this wasn't about piecing together evidence. Journalists who had travelled the region had warned me about this phenomenon: people would rearrange the evidence to fit the world view they saw on television, however little sense it made.

'The Ukrainians are bombing each other!' said someone else. 'The Pravy Sektor wants to march on Kiev and they're fighting each other.'

'It's the Americans. They've come here to take our gas. I heard there are wounded American soldiers in the local hospitals.'

Oleg was becoming increasingly irate, shouting at the women that they were traitors. They started shooing him away. He took off his shirt and showed them a bullet wound: he said the Russians had shot at him when he was delivering food to the front lines. He said Putin was in Ukraine because he was afraid that Russia would fall apart. The women said Putin wasn't afraid of anything.

Oleg went to the car and came back with the leaflets and started handing them out.

'Ha – you think we're afraid of this?' The women laughed and threw the papers in the bin.

Then they turned to the cameraman and me and started shouting at us.

'You'll re-edit what we say anyway. Why should we trust you? Nobody wants to hear the Donbas!'

That phrase again, repeated here like a mantra: 'Nobody hears the Donbas.' It reminded me of a prayer, a religious lamentation for a lost God, the recurring theme of the Psalms crying out to a vanished God; the Yom Kippur prayers that beg God to hear the people.

'O God who answered Abraham, Jacob and Isaac, O God who answered us in Sinai, Hear, Hear, Hear the Donbas!'

———

I woke up in the billiards room. It was still dark and I nearly collided with some soldiers who were slumped, fully clothed, on sofas. One soldier was sleeping with his head on the floor, propping up his fat torso; he was so exhausted that he didn't notice he was sleeping in a half-headstand. Outside, the rose garden and tennis court were just becoming visible in the dawn light. The roses had wilted and the tennis net was missing. I could hear rhythmic splashing: a soldier was doing breaststroke in the outdoor pool. The light was coming on fast, revealing summer houses and garages, high-security fences, the hills beyond and the dark green, almost black pine forests of the Luhanschina. We were north-east of Dzerzhinsk, on the edge of the territory held by Ukraine, where it bordered the Luhansk People's Republic.

We were bivouacked on the country estate of a deposed local minigarch, formerly a senior judge in the territory now held by the 'separatists'. He was now lying low in Kiev, waiting to see which side would win. There was a hyperrealist portrait of his wife in the billiards room: a plump, grinning blonde lying in a summer field with a garland of red poppies over her head.

In a cottage near the pool an officer was making breakfast: chopped cabbage and corned-beef meatballs. The TV was bursting with war propaganda. The Ukrainian president was in military fatigues, inspecting well-equipped troops. There were slow-motion clips of proud wives waving soldiers off to war or meeting them by the train with tears of joy. It was the sort of war propaganda that was used to build national morale and spur mobilisation everywhere throughout the twentieth century.

But there was something strange: for all the war visuals it was never defined as a war rhetorically. On TV the president spoke of an 'Anti-Terrorist Operation', an ATO. 'What the hell is an ATO?' cursed the officer as he chopped more cabbage. One of the clever twists of the Kremlin's approach was that it waged war without ever openly declaring it, undermining the narrative of fighting a clear enemy.

Later, the soldiers took us to the front line. Every vehicle was a different make. I sat in the back of a small Nissan jeep and was told to look out of the window to watch for separatist snipers.

The window had been shattered in a previous gunfight and was held together with Scotch tape. You couldn't see a single thing through it.

We stopped on the edge of a bluff opposite the separatist positions on the other side of the river. You could just about see them with the naked eye. 'If they start shooting, jump away from the cars,' said the commander, known as the ComBrig. 'They will aim for that.'

The ComBrig ordered heavy artillery to spread out along the bluff in a show of strength. Then he timed how long it took the separatists to get their people into position: a ruse to get the other side to reveal where they had hidden their forces on the far side of the bluff. The story was that new Russian units had recently arrived.

From there we drove to the village of Lobachevo, a collection of single-storey wooden houses at skewed angles. A cow stood on the road, staring at an outhouse. Three elderly men in dusty string vests, flip-flops on dirty feet, sat drinking and smoking on some logs outside. One of them, known as Uncle Kolya, had no teeth. He claimed a separatist had knocked them out after he refused to sing the Luhansk People's Republic anthem. The soldiers suspected he had concocted the story just for them, and that the second their backs were turned he would curse Ukraine. 'We spent a long time winning their trust,' said the ComBrig. 'At first they thought we were all Pravy Sektor monsters from the Russian propaganda machine.'

Across the riverbank you could see the separatists with rifles slung over their shoulders, pacing up and down by the old ferry station. The ferry had been blown up during the fighting. Families who lived on different sides of the river had been split.

The school was on one side and the shops were on the other. Local women crossed in a tiny rowboat with a tiny motor. They complained that if they carried more than one bag of potatoes, they could be done for smuggling contraband. They didn't care about Ukraine, Russia or the Luhansk People's Republic. They cared about their village, and their potatoes.

We drove out from Lobachevo, past abandoned churches and blown-up bridges that had collapsed into the green river, past women walking with goats. There was no obvious profit to be made from any of this land. Kiev had done nothing to develop it in twenty years of independence, but the Kremlin had little need for it either. If you looked closely, both sides were prepared to lose Luhanschina: the Kremlin wanted to hand it back to Ukraine while maintaining covert political control; Kiev made noises about 'unity', but many people, from top brass to academics, argued that the best outcome was a frozen territory the Kremlin had to fund and feed.

War used to be about capturing territory and planting flags, but something different was at play out here. Moscow needed to create a narrative about how pro-democracy revolutions like the Maidan led to chaos and civil war. Kiev needed to show that separatism leads to misery. What actually happened on the ground was almost irrelevant; the two governments just needed enough footage to back their respective stories. Propaganda has always accompanied war, usually as a handmaiden to the actual fighting. But the information age means that this equation has been flipped: military operations are now handmaidens to the more important information effect. It would be like a heavily scripted reality-TV show if it weren't for the very real deaths. A few months after my visit, on 3 November 2015, the Kharkiv

92nd would be caught up in a firefight by Lobachevo. The ComBrig was wounded, but survived.

Our vehicles stopped by a bend in the river. The soldiers took off their donated uniforms, grabbed a Tarzan swing that drooped from a tree on the bank and leapt into the water, whooping. Some tried backflips and others bellyflopped: this was a daily ritual to help them wind down after the patrol.

The ComBrig was in the river when his phone went off. It was an emergency: shelling had started again over no-man's-land. The previous day the 92nd had agreed on a ceasefire with the separatists so that electricians could come into the firing zone and fix some cables. Now the separatists were shelling overhead. If the 92nd fired back, it would look like they were firing on civilians. 'Whatever you do, don't react,' said the ComBrig, fatigues hurriedly pulled over wet boxer shorts. 'It's a provocation for the cameras.'

In the evening we drank moonshine cognac from a plastic bottle and looked up at the stars, as thick as grapes, listening for the sound of shells and following traces of missiles in the sky. We were looking for signs of our military fate, like medieval men had looked at comets in search of meaning. Some of the stars moved around: drones, spying on us. I felt as though I were inside a modern icon: the information war had broken so much of my sense of scale. The activists behind their laptops seemed as big as ministries; mythological fiends from Twitter as real as tanks. The borders between Russia and Ukraine, between past and present, between soldier and civilian, rumour and evidence, actor and audience had buckled, and with that the whole rational, ordered sense of perspective suddenly gave way to a thinking that was magical and mystical, where reality was unknowable and seemed to be decided somewhere up on high by divine conspiracies. The layers of spheres and angels had been replaced with endlessly reflecting media stories, where information was no longer simply the recording of action but the point of it. We were all caught up in the recordings, revolving and refracting in the information heavens.

A drone paused up above us.

'Smile,' said the ComBrig. 'It's taking your photo.'

I had my first fact-check in my first year of primary school. I was three when I arrived in London. Playing football was my only way of communicating when I went to school; watching football on TV was my way into the language. Football commentary, which matches words to action, was a way to learn vocabulary. I learnt to read English from children's football magazines.

Between four and seven I spoke semi-English. I only half understood the people around me, and could only part communicate. I spent a lot of time in my head. I would compose football games in my mind, commentating on them in my handicapped English. I invented teams. I described the players' lives and moods in detail in the commentary. The players got older and had problems. They switched teams and were reinvigorated. I made up leagues. I kept pads with all my teams and the scores from games written down in them. I made up national squads. I spent my pocket money on cups from the local sports shop to present to the imaginary teams. I was a player too in this imagined world, and after many knock-backs I made it into the England side. But I used myself sparingly, often as a substitute; I preferred commentating on the others.

At school once I blurted out that I was off to Montevideo to play in a tournament (I had just discovered Uruguay on a map). My teacher, Mrs Stern, called my parents and asked if I needed time off school for my trip to Uruguay. They told her there was no trip. The next day she asked me to stay behind after class. I'd never been held after class before and I knew it was important.

'So it turns out everything you told us about going to Uruguay, about you playing football, was a fib,' Mrs Stern said. From her tone I could tell I had done something wrong, but the problem was I didn't know what the word 'fib' meant. Back home I looked it up. It didn't seem right. I hadn't thought of my imaginary world as a lie, just a parallel reality, and the one reality had spilled into the other.

By that time I was seven, it was 1984, and my English was improving. I had trained it up in the linguistic playing fields of my invented football universe. With the word 'fib' everything seemed to slot into place: I now had two words for the same thing ('lie' and 'fib') and it felt as if I had crossed a border into knowing English. The shock of people thinking I'd lied snapped me out of living so intensely in my imagination. Clearly this was not how to progress into acceptability.

In the early 1980s Lina had a job teaching Russian at London University. This too had its struggles. The other academics told her: 'Of course you were opposed to the Soviet regime. It was because you were dissidents! You can't be objective about it.'

'No,' she would try to explain, 'it's because of the objective nature of the regime we became dissidents . . .' They seemed bemused by this. They were nice but they weren't sure she was unbiased.

Igor now worked for the BBC, one of the foreign 'voices' he had listened to in secret in Soviet Ukraine. During school holidays he'd take me with him to that tall island in the middle of the Strand known as Bush House, home of the World Service. In 1929, when it was still only half completed, Bush House was already the most expensive building in the world, the Corinthian columns at its entrance crowned with six-foot statues framing a recessed portico and mighty iron doors worthy of a great cathedral.

It was a wondrous island for a child. As soon as my father was locked in the aquarium-like glass case of the broadcasting studio, I was free to roam every floor. Down the wide stairs I went, around me every colour and ethnicity the world knows, all speaking, shouting English, but with different accents. All typing, smoking, sprinting between slamming doors to break the latest news. Every section of the vast building was another country or even continent. From one floor to the next I travelled from Greece to the Middle East, then up in the lift to Poland. Sometimes I would find myself lost in Latin America, stranded in Africa, with only the gloomy London light in the windows a constant. Every other journalist seemed to be a great exiled poet or minister-in-waiting. When my father was too busy, I would play football in vast, purple-lit marble corridors with Egon from the Czech Service. He would later be a deputy prime minister, but when I was seven I beat him at penalties.

Igor's favourite shift was nightwatchman. After 9 p.m., with the office empty, he'd make his way down to the BBC members' bar, one of the few places in London where alcohol was served after eleven at night, acquire a bottle of Black Prince Bordeaux, uncork it, place it in a plastic bag, pick up some roast beef from the canteen, go back up to the office, pour a glass and consider his new place of work.

'There's a kind of gas in this building,' Barry Holland, Igor's boss when he first arrived in 1980, the editor-in-chief of the Russian Service and a former military translator, liked to say. 'Invisible, but very much present. It's an atmosphere, if you like, the ethos of a balanced view.' It was a 'gas' that would drive Igor's more partisan colleagues up the wall, frustrated at the amount of time the World Service would give to spokespeople of dictatorial regimes. 'If

145

you had the chance to interview Christ, you would give the Devil equal time as well,' one of Igor's colleagues lambasted Holland. 'Certainly,' Holland answered, 'but I would give Christ the chance to say the final word.'

The 'gas' was a means of gaining credibility. Trust. To project the image of Britain as the sort of place that you could rely on for the BBC trinity of 'accuracy, impartiality and fairness', which in turn was meant to promote what the founder of the BBC, Lord Reith, had called the 'British values' of 'reasonableness, democracy and debate', which in turn was meant to make Britain more admired globally. Unlike the rest of the BBC, the World Service was funded by a grant from Her Majesty's Foreign Office. It existed to 'serve the national interest' (which was not, every editor would insist, the same as 'the government's interest').

When he arrived, Igor's first assignments were to translate lectures on classic English writers, on how Christmas is celebrated in England. Maybe this was meant to be in the 'national interest', as it built bridges with Russian audiences. But why, thought Igor, when the Soviet Union censored so much, were they broadcasting something every Soviet schoolchild knew? He wasn't alone in his frustration. In the early 1980s a new generation of editors emerged who launched their own small cultural revolution at the Service.

Igor put on books and plays never broadcast in the Soviet Union: the love letters of James Joyce, full of sexual references unimaginable in late-Soviet-era broadcasting; Samuel Beckett's Krapp's Last Tape *(about a man who obsessively records himself and then repeatedly listens to and comments on his own recordings);* Audience *by Václav Havel (about a dissident who is persuaded to spy on himself. Havel listened to Igor's broadcast of the play on the Russian Service, while serving his prison sentence in*

146

Czechoslovakia. In 1978 he had called on people to stop repeating official language and rituals: it was the repetition of things you didn't believe which broke you. He had been jailed for 'subversion' soon after.)

At first Igor had looked down on radio from the heights of literature. Now he was finding himself drawn in by it.

'Most listeners use radio as a source of information,' he would write later, 'but what kind of information? And how does it differ from what you find in newspapers or on television?'

Igor made his programmes on the reel-to-reel machines, on which were magnetic tapes with recordings of voices. Editing tape was the work of an artisan: like a glass-blower blew glass, he was moulding sound.

'It is my belief that the meaning of radio is in the magic of the voice, the magic of sound. And in this sense poetry and radio share the same element – air. A free element.'

Russia and Ukraine were cut off physically from the rest of the world; books were censored. The rare phone calls he and Lina had with home took hours to arrange through a dispatcher, the secret services eavesdropping on every word. But barriers fell away when Igor entered the BBC radio studio; he felt himself piloting through censorship:

'The hermetically sealed and soundproofed booths, the control panels, the lack of outside windows make radio studios like spaceships. And your voice alone is capable of unlocking this closed space. I am convinced that, as they sit by the radio, many listeners are on a voyage round the world – no, into outer space, more like. I too am a travel maniac: I jump from wave to wave.'

There was a generation of recent Soviet émigrés who felt they knew what would matter to their audiences. Zinovy Zinik made

147

programmes about punks in east London for Soviet listeners whose idea of the city was stuck in Edwardian literature. Seva Novgorodtsev intermingled satire of official Soviet bulletins with heavy-metal bands banned in the USSR: 'Our metallurgists produce various metals for the people: from the graceful effervescent bronze to the stunning pig iron . . .'

Seva's show became a hit. The World Service received an unheard-of amount of letters from fans inside the USSR, one of the few ways the BBC could gauge its popularity beyond the Iron Curtain: listeners were ready to risk having their correspondence intercepted by the KGB just to express devotion. Soviet newspapers ran attack pieces on how Seva was corrupting Soviet youth. A panel of BBC managers was convened to judge whether he was being properly 'impartial'. All the playful humour was lost in the translation of his transcripts, and they came out as anti-Soviet diatribes. The World Service's big bosses were displeased. A new head of the Russian Service, a reformer himself, said he would do something about it – and then quietly let Seva get on with his heavy-metal Soviet satire.

The BBC's combination of 'balance' and absurdist theatre, heavy metal and 'accuracy' was competing with Soviet broadcasting, which was about to experience its first tremors.

In the corner of the BBC newsroom was a telefax, which every few hours would chug and squeal with fresh reports from a country house near Reading. This was where BBC Monitoring was based, where eighty monitors, all fluent linguists, would listen to the output of Soviet media in forty-two languages, which it broadcast no less intently than the BBC. Radio Moscow's usual style was so stiff it made the BBC feel informal. It would reel off statistics from Communist Party plenums about the supposed success of the Soviet Economy, the Onward March of Socialism across the world; state that the Objective, Scientific Progress of History was still inevitable . . . Even when it peddled what the KGB called 'active measures' – disinformation campaigns that claimed, for instance, that the US had invented AIDS as a weapon – it would do so with a Soviet seriousness, including interviews with fake scientists providing fake evidence, but all determined to keep up a facade of factuality.

In 1983 BBC Monitoring noticed something most unusual: a presenter on Radio Moscow's English Service began to call Soviet soldiers who had invaded Afghanistan 'occupiers' rather than the official 'limited contingent' of 'internationalist warriors' bringing help to the 'fraternal people of Afghanistan'.[17] What the presenter, a previously unassuming man called Vladimir Danchev, was doing was unheard of. He was quickly suspended from Radio Moscow and sent to a psychiatric ward in Uzbekistan. After the Soviet Union fell, he admitted he made the first reference to 'occupiers' by accident, but once he started he just couldn't stop himself from saying what he really thought.

Danchev's personal radio rebellion was a crack in the Soviet firmament of pseudo-facts. Soon Soviet listeners would be turning to the BBC in order to survive.

Like a transistor radio, a Geiger counter is also attuned to pick up invisible signals pulsating through the atmosphere. It measures radioactive emissions – gamma rays and particles – and when they increase the Geiger counter starts to make a clicking, ripping sound. On 26 April 1986 the Geiger counters of Scandinavian scientists, both professional and amateur, began to rattle hysterically: a radiation cloud of historic magnitude was moving towards Europe from Soviet Ukraine. The Soviet state media

149

gave one brief account of a minor accident at a nuclear reactor in Chernobyl, near Kiev. And then silence.

In Moscow and Kiev the May Day parades, with their vast columns of soldiers and warheads symbolising Soviet might, went on as normal. But while the Soviet media were silent, the BBC and other Western 'voices' began reporting on the radiation levels immediately. In Kiev rumours were quickly rife that the Communist Party elite were evacuating their children from the city. A pilot, so the story went, had been commissioned to fly out a whole plane-load of nomenklatura *brats, but had grounded the plane out of disgust at the injustice.*

In the absence of official health guidelines, folksy medical advice spread like a plague through the city. 'Drink lots of sweet red wine,' went one piece of advice. Everyone ran out to get drunk. Then came the counter-advice: 'Sweet red wine will make radiation poisoning worse!'

Throughout all this the BBC was giving regular bulletins on the greatest radiation catastrophe in history, with scientists commenting on the spread of the radiation cloud and medical experts giving advice on radiation poisoning. Tuning in became necessary for sanity and survival. It would take another two weeks before the Soviet media made any official announcement. By then any remaining faith in them was shot: you couldn't trust them to tell you what was in your milk, your meat, your bread, your water.

In 1987 the new general secretary of the Soviet Union, Mikhail Gorbachev, admitted that the lack of truth surrounding Chernobyl had been a disaster.[18] He promised to give new freedom to Soviet media. He removed restrictions on foreign books, films, video cassettes, on access to historical records and to Chernobyl itself. He called the politics 'glasnost' – literally 'giving voice'. It had been initiated in 1986, but it was only after Chernobyl that it began to be enacted in earnest. 'Glasnost' had been a term used by dissidents to demand more information about political trials; now it was the language of Soviet policy.

In 1988 the Soviet Union ceased jamming the BBC. At the World Service this was met with jubilation. Could the regime that seemed immortal, permanent, immovable actually be changing? Could Russia, Ukraine become something else?

For Igor it felt like the artist, activist and journalist in him were flowing into one: freedom to access information and creative freedom; individual rights and the right to be utterly individualistic. In much of his writing from the 1980s current affairs were conspicuous by their absence, but were latent in everything he wrote in its celebration of liberation from constraint. He wrote in stream-of-consciousness swirls of pure impressionism, breaking the borders between realism and fantasy, poetry and prose. He recreated Bush House as populated by hedgehogs and foxes gripped by panic as a sticky blue fog bursts the windows on every floor and each animal wonders, 'Who will be next?' – though the exact consequence of being next is never quite defined. He reinvented himself as a boy who wakes up with a fever, takes a thermometer and places it in his armpit, only to discover his armpit is now an abyss as he falls into it. He travelled to Ticino to cross the Italian border with Switzerland, hither and thither, over and over, revelling in the freedom to cross all barriers. In one of his poems he had written, 'If I were a red Indian, my nickname would be Barrier-Crosser.' Now all the barriers were coming down.

That year Prime Minister Margaret Thatcher, wearing a checked jacket and pearl necklace, strode into Bush House and conducted a live phone-in with Soviet listeners on the Russian

Service. Nothing of the kind had been attempted previously.[19] Soviet citizens rarely got to talk to their own leaders, let alone engage one – and a woman too! – in live conversation. To a question from Kaunas, Lithuania, about whether the changes in the Soviet Union (glasnost, as well as the political and economic reforms known as perestroika) were reversible if someone other than Gorbachev took charge, Thatcher answered:

'I think that once you have tasted the increasing freedom of speech and discussion, the liveliness of debate that you are having now, then I think that it would be very difficult to reverse that.

'But I do not think that they would go forward with anything like the same momentum if Mr Gorbachev were not there. I recognise someone who has a vision for the future.

'In a way, I felt like that myself when I became prime minister of my country.'[20]

At the end of the programme Thatcher was apparently heard to say, 'Oh, was that all? We could have done with more time on air.' There was a small drinks party with the Service staff. Thatcher had her usual whisky.

Part 4: Soft Facts

During glasnost, it seemed like the truth would set everybody free. Dictators appeared so afraid of the truth they had it suppressed. But something drastic has gone wrong. We have access to more information and evidence than ever, but facts seem to have lost their power. There is nothing new in politicians lying, but what seems novel is that they seem to be making a thing out of showing that they don't care about whether they tell the truth or not.

When Vladimir Putin went on international television during his army's annexation of Crimea and asserted, with a smirk, that there were no Russian soldiers in Crimea, when everyone knew there were, and later, just as casually, admitted that they had been there, he wasn't so much lying in the sense of trying to replace one reality with another as saying that facts don't matter. Similarly the president of the United States, Donald Trump, is famous for having no discernible notion of what truth or facts are, yet this has in no way been a barrier to his success. According to the fact-checking agency PolitiFact, 76 per cent of his statements in the 2016 presidential election were 'mostly false' or downright untrue, compared to 27 per cent for his rival.[1] He still won.

Why has this happened? Is technology to blame? The media? And what are the consequences in a world where the powerful are no longer afraid of facts? Does that mean one can commit crimes in full view of all? And then just shrug them off?

Objectivity Is a Myth Imposed Upon Us

Forty years later, my office is opposite the old Bush House. The BBC World Service has long since abandoned it. First it was mooted that Bush House would be sold to Japanese property developers and converted into luxury apartments. This plan failed when the UK property market started sagging in the wake of the 2008 financial crash. It now houses a university.

All of the BBC – World Service and domestic, news and entertainment, TV, radio and 'multimedia' – is squeezed into a building at the top end of Regent Street that is curved like a compressed accordion, with people sitting far too closely together, so that it feels like the architects forgot to factor in the right amount of desk space in their design.

When I talk to BBC editors and managers, the architectural misproportion seems to mirror a media one: the world has changed and the old values of the BBC – of accuracy, impartiality and fairness leading to democracy, reasonableness and debate – have been upended.

During the Cold War the BBC defined 'impartial' as a balance between left-wing and right-wing opinions. In the 1990s and 2000s things got more complicated. There was no clear left or right any more. In the late 2010s audiences have fractured even more, seeing the world through the distinct values and causes that define them.

'Even as affiliation to political parties has weakened, the importance of values people identify with, such as religion, the monarchy or minority rights, have become stronger,' James

Harding, the former director of BBC News, told me. 'And so, with it, perceptions of bias and how people understand impartiality have changed, well beyond traditional ideas of left and right.'

The BBC used to determine what to be impartial about by following the agendas set by the political parties and, to a much lesser extent, newspapers. These were meant to be representatives of greater interests. But what happens when newspapers are no longer read and parties are so fractured that they no longer represent anything coherent? When I was in Britain as a child, we lived in a series of sublimations, our sense of self squeezed into the vessels of media and sucked through the cathode-ray tube of the TV to join a greater whole. For better or worse, those vessels have burst. And as a consequence the concepts which the BBC used to negotiate reality have been scattered. Even at the best of times the BBC struggled to get 'balance' right,[2] but what does it mean to be impartial in such a fractured world?

To be fair, impartiality always was a slippery term. Back in the 1980s Margaret Thatcher's government was fighting a war against the domestic BBC, accusing it of being biased for attacking Conservative politicians, of being disloyal for broadcasting Irish terrorists. There were even threats to close the BBC down: why should one have a publicly funded broadcaster if Thatcher believed in market freedom? But now the attacks are not just on the BBC's impartiality, but on the very idea that impartiality and objectivity can exist at all.

In Russia, Kremlin-controlled media heads and stars insist that broadcasters such as the BBC can't be trusted as they all have hidden agendas,[3] that 'objectivity is a myth that is proposed and imposed on us'.[4] It's a far cry from Radio Moscow, with its commitment to upholding scientific, Marxist truth. And you can see the difference in the content. When, in the 1980s, Radio Moscow broadcast 'active measures' claiming that the CIA had invented AIDS as a weapon against Africa, the lies were carefully curated over many years. They involved scientists in East Germany who had supposedly found the evidence. An effort was made to make the elaborate lie look real. Today the Russian media and officials push similar stories, claiming that American factories were pumping out the Zika virus in East Ukraine to poison ethnic Russians, that the US is harvesting Russian DNA to create gene weapons,[5] that the US is encircling Russia with secret biological warfare labs. But these claims are just thrown online or spewed out on TV shows, more to confuse than to convince, or to buttress the phobias of audiences predisposed to seeing US plots all around them.

In the US, impartiality is also under attack. Ted Koppel was one of the country's most famous news broadcasters during the Cold War, objectivity personified. In 2017, on his CBS morning show, Koppel accused partisan cable news channels on the left and the right of undermining reasonableness and debate. Koppel was placing himself above the fray, implicitly making the case that balance and objectivity were still possible. After all, there has to be a position from which you can judge partisanship. One of his main targets was the Fox News prime-time TV host Sean Hannity, as virulent a defender of Donald Trump as Russian state TV presenters are of Vladimir Putin. Hannity responded that by attacking opinion shows, Koppel was actually just 'giving his opinion'. Hannity described himself as honest because he admitted to being an advocacy journalist, whereas Koppel's facade of being impartial was actually fraudulent. All pretence at objectivity was just subjectivity.

With the possibility of balance, objectivity, impartiality undermined, all that remains is to be more 'genuine' than the other side: more emotional, more subjective, more heroic. Hannity's studio features a superhero-style shield, reminiscent of Captain America's, with the Stars and Stripes and his name emblazoned upon it. In the Hannity mythos, the Fox hero has to fight off the monsters of the 'alt-left-destroy-Trump media', who have declared 'war on the American people'.

When Hannity lands on a failing of other media – the way some channels spent so much airtime trying to detect direct, covert, criminal 'collusion' between Trump and the Kremlin, for instance – his response is not to try and restore impartiality, but to say it is impossible per se.

The irony is that the rejection of objectivity pushed by the Kremlin and Fox News plays on ideas that originally championed 'liberal' causes which the Hannitys and Putins of this world oppose. 'Objectivity is just male subjectivity,' was a slogan of the feminist movement; the student protests of 1968 celebrated feelings as an antidote to corporate and bureaucratic rationality.

But now Fox and the Kremlin exploit the same ideas: if reality is malleable, why can't they introduce their own versions too? And if feelings are emancipatory, why can't they invoke their own? With the idea of objectivity discredited, the grounds on which one could argue against them rationally disappears.[6]

––––

With the objectivity and impartiality of a network like the BBC or CBS undermined, online fact-checking agencies have stepped into the fray. However, they too face a problem: the very technology they work in, social media, where falsehoods spread faster than facts.[7] It's become something of a ritual: hauling up representatives of tech companies and lambasting them for normalising lying.

Take the summer of 2018 in Rome, where I attended the annual gathering of the world's fact-checkers.

'If this group can't help make the information disorder problem a little less terrible, if this group can't clean up this mess that we're in, who will? We are the wrinkly arbiters of a take-no-prisoners war for the future of the Internet,' announced Alexios Mantzarlis, developer of the 'Fact-Checkers Code', which defines the 'Five Principles of Transparency and Methodology'. The principles establish who is a real fact-checker and who isn't. Mantzarlis's code was often invoked in Rome. Prospective fact-checkers are monitored over a year to ensure they live up to the five principles. Among the greatest dangers to the movement are the wrong kind of fact-checkers, who claim the status for themselves without following the principles. Perhaps it was the fact that we were in Rome, but I began to feel that there was something a touch religious about the fact-checkers. In a world where facts have become sullied, they wanted to make them sacred again.

In the cloister-like courtyard of St Stephen's School in Rome I met everyone from a guy in Los Angeles who monitors the accuracy of celebrity gossip through to those for whom facts are matters of life and death. Fact-checkers from India, for example, told me about efforts to stop murder sprees by squads of vigilantes. Hindu nationalists were spreading surreptitious rumours on closed social media groups about Muslim butchers, falsely accusing them of slaughtering cows, the Hindus' sacred animal. Fanatics would then descend on the innocent butchers and slaughter them instead. In Burma and Sri Lanka, where Facebook has been used to incite ethnic cleansing, the situation was even worse.

Looking around the arches of the courtyard I could see editors from Rappler, fact-checkers from Ukraine, the western Balkans, Mexico . . . When the representative from Facebook took the floor, she was pilloried for allowing blatantly untrue news stories to spread on the platform and for allowing it to be a conduit for threats against fact-checkers.

The insurmountable problem is that for all the social media companies' statements of concern about this problem, it's the way many of their platforms are designed and how they make money that create an environment in which accuracy, impartiality and fairness are, at best, secondary.

Back in 2011 Guillaume Chaslot, an engineer at Google with a PhD in artificial intelligence, discovered that the way YouTube was designed meant that it served people ever more of the same content, creating and reinforcing one point of view – and not one necessarily based on its factuality. So if you were to watch one video full of inaccurate, often downright disinformative content, the algorithm would keep feeding you similar material. YouTube didn't want to be the judge of what is true, but it wanted its algorithms to be the judge of what gets promoted. As a consequence, untrue content could get massively augmented. Chaslot offered his bosses potential ways of fixing the problem. Couldn't one offer people more diverse content? He was told this was not 'the focus'. YouTube was primarily interested in increasing the time people spent watching it. It struck him as a terrible way to define desire: purely by how much time someone spent staring at a screen – a far cry from the patrician 'public service' ethos of the BBC.[8] It's also, Chaslot told me, easy to manipulate: if you have the resources to hire huge numbers of people to watch certain videos and create tons of content on a specific subject, that helps to promote those videos. Having many YouTube channels working together was also a good way to get your content 'recommended'. There was a reason, he argued, why the Russian state broadcaster RT had such an impressive array of YouTube channels.

In a study on 'Emotional Dynamics in the Age of Misinformation',[9] Dr Walter Quattrociocchi of the University of Venice analysed fifty-four million comments in various Facebook groups over four years and found that the longer a discussion continued, the more extreme people's comments became. 'Cognitive patterns in echo chambers tend towards polarisation,' he concluded. This, argued Quattrociocchi, showed up the emotional structure of social media. We go online looking for the emotional boost delivered by likes and retweets. Social media is a sort of mini-narcissism engine that can never quite be satisfied, leading us to take up more radical positions to get more attention. It really doesn't matter if stories are accurate or not, let alone impartial: you're not looking to win an argument in a public space with a neutral audience; you just want to get the most attention possible from like-minded people. 'Online dynamics induce distortion,' concluded Quattrociocchi. It's a lamentable loop: social media drives more polarised behaviour, which leads to demands for more sensationalised content, or plain lies. 'Fake news' is a symptom of the way social media is designed.

There's something even more insidious going on here. In his early Cold War essays, Igor celebrated being as individualistic as possible as a way to resist oppression. Another exiled Soviet poet, the Nobel Prize-winner Joseph Brodsky, who had emigrated in 1972, put it best in his commencement speech at Williams College in 1984: 'The surest defence against Evil is extreme individualism, originality of thinking, whimsicality, even – if you will – eccentricity. That is, something that can't be feigned, faked, imitated.'[10]

In the Cold War 'extreme individualism' was interlinked with the struggle to receive and transmit accurate information, while freedom of speech was associated with freedom of artistic self-expression, both opposed by regimes that censored facts and 'whimsicality'. Now social media offers limitless fields for a form of extreme individualism. Express yourself to your heart's content! But its very construction pushes away from factuality.

And there's another twist. This self-expression is then transmuted into data: the frequency of certain words, times of postings and what that says about us, our movements and language – all passed to forces that influence us with campaigns and adverts we might not even be aware of. But if you were to look for your own data imprint among the data brokers in the hope of finding a reflection of your true self, you will be disappointed. Instead, there are broken bits of information (something about health, something about shopping), jagged edges that can be added and stacked in different patterns according to various short-term purposes, little writhing squiggles of impulses and habits that can be impelled to vibrate for a few seconds to get you to buy something or vote for someone. Social media, that little narcissism machine, the easiest way we have ever had to place ourselves on a pedestal of vanity, is also the mechanism that most efficiently breaks us up.

That extreme individualism comes with its own dangers is already there in Igor's early stories. Reading them again I notice how often the impressionistic, self-obsessed narrator ends up subtly undermined. At the end you realise they have been so caught up in themselves that they don't notice what is going on around them, are losing touch with reality altogether.

Why We're 'Post-Fact'

Social media technology, combined with a world view in which all information is part of war and impartiality is impossible, has helped to undermine the sacrosanctity of facts. But the more I thought about the issue, the more it seemed to me I was asking the question the wrong way. Instead of questioning why facts had become irrelevant, I should ascertain why they had ever been relevant in political speech at all. And why were we seeing such similar tactics from both of the former Cold War superpowers?

Facts, after all, are not always the most pleasant things; they can be reminders, as I had discovered with my teacher Mrs Stern, of our place and our limitations, our failures and, ultimately, our mortality. There is a sort of adolescent joy in throwing off their weight, of giving a great big 'fuck you' to glum reality. The very pleasure of a Putin or a Trump is the release from constraint they offer.

163

But though facts can be unpleasant, they are useful. You especially need them if you are constructing something in the real world. There are no post-truth moments if you are building a bridge, for example. Facts are necessary to show what you are building, how it will work, why it won't collapse. In politics facts are necessary to show that you are pursuing some rational idea of progress: here are our aims, here is how we prove we are achieving them, this is how they improve your lives. The need for facts is predicated on the notion of an evidence-based future.

In the Cold War both sides were engaged in what had begun as a debate about which system – democratic capitalism or Communism – would deliver a rosier future for the world. The only way to prove you were achieving this future was to provide evidence. Communism, for all its many perversities and cruelties, was meant to be the ultimate scientific Enlightenment project. Those who lived under it knew it was a sham, but it was connected to a paradigm of Soviet economic growth based on Marxist–Leninist theory, whose objective laws of historical development were supposedly playing out as the theory maintained. Thus, it was also possible to catch the USSR out by exposing how it lied, by broadcasting accurate information or by confronting its leaders with facts.

After the Cold War there was only one political idea and one vision of the future left: globalisation fostered by the victory of 'freedom' – free markets, freedom of movement, freedom of speech, political freedoms. In democracies, political parties still had to prove that they could manage this process better than their rivals, though this was more a technocratic process than a battle of new ideas.

We can find many moments when that vision of the future crumpled. The invasion of Iraq, which was called 'Operation Iraqi Freedom', undermined the idea that political freedom was a historical inevitability. When Saddam Hussein's statue was torn down in Baghdad, in scenes reminiscent of the destruction of Lenin's statues in Eastern Europe, the visual imagery seemed to suggest a historical equivalence, a montage of shots signifying one great story. Great Cold War dissidents, including Václav Havel, backed the war, in terms that echoed their own battles against dictatorship.[11] Those who led the overthrow of Saddam invoked the struggle against Soviet rule and posited it as part of one continuous history.

'President Reagan said that the day of Soviet tyranny was passing, that freedom had a momentum that would not be halted,' President George W. Bush announced in 2003, before connecting the battles of the Cold War with his vision for the Middle East post the US invasion. 'Iraqi democracy will succeed, and that success will send forth news, from Damascus to Tehran, that freedom can be the future of every nation.'[12]

Instead the invasion brought civil war and hundreds of thousands of deaths. Words and images that were imbued with powerful meaning in East Berlin and Prague lost that significance in Baghdad.

But we still lived in a world in which there was an idea of the future, at least an economic one of ever greater globalisation. Then came the financial crash of 2008. The idea that free markets could deliver freedom from want became risible; the dream that Europe's carefully tended market was sheltered from vast economic shocks was shattered. With that the last of the old, Cold War-framed notions of a universal future fell away for many. Elsewhere, from Mexico City to Manila, they had already been dissolving gradually, like an old bar of soap coming apart in mushy flakes.

But if the need for facts is predicated on a vision of a concrete future that you are trying to achieve, then when that future disappears, what is the point of facts? Why would you want them if they tell you that your children will be poorer than you? That all versions of the future are unpromising? And why should you trust the purveyors of facts – the media and academics, think tanks, statesmen?

And so the politician who makes a big show of rejecting facts, who validates the pleasure of spouting nonsense, who indulges in a full, anarchic liberation from coherence, from glum reality, becomes attractive. That enough Americans could vote for someone like Donald Trump, a man with so little regard for making sense, whose many contradictory messages never add up to any very stable meaning, was partly possible because voters felt they weren't invested in any larger evidence-based future. Indeed, in his very incoherence lies the pleasure. All the madness you feel, you can now let it out and it's OK. The joy of Trump is to validate the pleasure of spouting shit, the joy of pure emotion, often anger, without any sense.

And it's no coincidence that so many of the new breed of political actors are also nostalgists. Putin's Internet troll armies sell dreams of a restored Russian Empire and Soviet Union; Trump tweets he will 'Make America Great Again'; Turkish and Hungarian media dream of restoring phantoms of ancient greatness.

'The twentieth century began with utopia and ended with nostalgia. The twenty-first century is not characterized by the search for newness, but by the proliferation of nostalgias,' wrote the Russian-American philologist Svetlana Boym, who saw nostalgia as a way of escaping the strictures of rationally ordered time. She contrasted two types. One, which is healthy, she called 'reflective' nostalgia: it looks at individual, often ironic stories from the past, tries to tease out the difference between the past and present to formulate the future. The other, harmful type she called 'restorative' nostalgia. This strives to rebuild lost homelands with 'paranoiac determination', thinks of itself as 'truth and tradition', obsesses over grand symbols and 'relinquish[es] critical thinking for emotional bonding . . . Unreflective nostalgia can breed monsters.'[13]

'Restorative' nostalgia has taken hold from Moscow to Budapest to Washington DC. The last things desired by those who purvey these phantom, fabricated pasts are facts.

But if in Western Europe and America this manifests itself in eccentric elections, the consequences of a politics where facts have lost their potency are far deadlier elsewhere.

In Aleppo

When the Syrian regime's rockets, shells and bombs were lobbed into eastern Aleppo, Khaled Khatib would grab a camera and record the destruction of his city. People would turn on him, screaming, 'Aren't you ashamed to film us? Do you like to see our tears? We've lost everything.'

He would try to explain that he was here to help, that if the whole world knew how innocent people were being targeted, then it would have to do something. There were rules after all. Things from the UN. Laws . . . You can't just bomb civilians, children, old people like this.

Scores of young men and women were constantly scurrying around the city, filming and uploading video of the damage at what they called the 'Aleppo media centre'. Some had travelled to Beirut for video training from humanitarian organisations. 'Capture the crimes and this will help stop the atrocities,' they had been told. They were now 'citizen journalists', 'media activists'. President Assad's helicopters were circling over their town, hovering overhead, then pushing off barrel bombs – oil drums, fuel tanks and gas cylinders filled with explosives and metal fragments – onto the city. Aleppo's citizens were helpless beneath them. But they could film, and that, they felt, hoped, connected them to something greater and more powerful than the helicopters.

In 2011 several Syrian cities had risen up against the forty-year dictatorship of the Assad family, in the Syrian iteration of the Arab Spring. The protests had been sparked when the regime tortured teenagers who dared to graffiti anti-Assad slogans on a high-school wall,[14] a subversive act under a system whose power was predicated on making people repeat its ridiculous slogans publicly as a sign of fealty, whether they believed in them or not. 'This obedience makes people complicit, it entangles them in self-enforcing relations of domination,' wrote the anthropologist Lisa Wedeen in her study of the Syrian regime,[15] and it reminds me of Havel's interpretation of late Soviet Communism. When I have talked to Syrians involved in those first demonstrations in 2011, they often come back to the intoxication they felt at finally saying, screaming, shouting, singing publicly what they thought about Assad.

Assad responded with bombs, rockets, snipers, chemical weapons, more executions and more torture. In 2012 rebels took eastern Aleppo, and its bombardment by the regime began. A million people fled.[16] Khaled was sixteen. He wanted to do something that had meaning, show the world what was happening in Aleppo.

The first people on the scene after an attack were the rescue services, who pulled victims out of the rubble. When they arrived they would ask everyone to be quiet, listen for the sound of sobbing under the stones and then begin digging. Many of them had no background in rescue operations; they were taxi drivers, bakers and primary-school teachers. After 2013 they started to get money, training and bulldozers from the UK, Dutch and US governments. They became known as the 'White Helmets' for their distinctive headwear. Khaled began to record their missions. He spent days filming his first rescue operation after a barrel-bomb attack had flattened several houses at once. When you film you have to focus on every detail. You focus so long it stays with you and you remember the world as a sequence of close-ups: torn-off hands, screams, limbs, tears, everywhere dust, more dust, more hands, rubble. During that first rescue operation Khaled's dreams became full of body parts. After he uploaded the footage at the media centre he swore never to film again. Then he checked social media and saw his material going viral. He realised his efforts were worth it.

At first he hadn't told his parents about his filming; they would have thought it dangerous. But when he came home one time caked in dust, after nearly being caught in a bomb attack, he couldn't hide it any more. His father was furious initially. Then, when Khaled explained to him how they were pulling people out of the rubble, how his footage was appearing on international TV channels, relating Aleppo to the whole world, his father relented. Shots of children being pulled miraculously out of the wreckage were particularly popular (there were many more they couldn't save, but that footage didn't always go so viral).

Life in the city became guided by sound: a hiss, pause and then rumbling and an expanding explosion meant barrel bombs; a spluttering sound signified rockets. Khaled would listen for them in the background as he watched the 2014 World Cup finals. He wanted Germany to win. He would watch his favourite player, Mesut Özil, ghost into the penalty area, then hear the hiss or splutter and run out to film the damage. He always had to be careful about a 'double tap': when a helicopter drops one bomb, waits for a crowd to gather, then drops another.

When the rescue services, led by former school teacher Ammar Al-Selmo, arrived after an attack, people would react differently. Some of the survivors would rush towards Khaled's camera lens, right up close, and start crying, 'Why are they bombing us? There are no soldiers here'; or demanding justice; or saying it was their neighbour's fault, the one who'd joined the revolution – 'The bombs had been meant for him, not me!'

Khaled got used to the sight of slaughter. At first much of what he shot was out of focus; he waved the camera around too much, chasing the action around him, when what was needed was to make a mental map of the surroundings first, then choose what to capture. He had to start breaking reality down into separate shots that together told a story: corpses in the rubble; craters; the remains of toys and clothes; photographs on the collapsed walls – any details proving civilians had been bombed. The dust from the destroyed buildings was a permanent problem, misting over the lens, clogging up the mechanics.[17]

In 2015 Russia entered the war on Assad's side. The Soviet

Union had propped up his father, Hafez. Now Russia was rescuing his son. For the first time since the end of the Cold War the country was back on the biggest stage of global politics. Putin's domestic image is founded on the idea that there is no alternative to his rule, that he is immense. Now he was showing he was supreme not just at home, but in the Middle East. When Russia joined, Assad controlled only 20 per cent of his own country. The stated aim of the Russian campaign was to help defeat Islamist terrorists. Instead, the Russian air force turned its attention to crushing any resistance to Assad's rule, and Aleppo in particular.

The siege intensified in April 2016.[18] Supplies to eastern Aleppo were cut off. Barrel and cluster bombs crashed down on bakeries, markets, schools. Over 4,000 barrel bombs would fall in 2016.[19] The work of the White Helmets became ever more relentless. One morning they pulled a man out of the rubble of his home and took him to Al-Bayan hospital; when a bomb landed in the vicinity of the hospital it was evacuated, and the man was taken to a suburb that was subsequently bombed in the evening. The same rescuers who had pulled him out in the morning now came to rescue him again. He began screaming at them to go away – they brought him nothing but ill. He had lost his wife and child in the morning's bombing.

When the European Football Championship came round in the summer of 2016, Khaled was too busy to pay attention to how Özil was doing. Hospitals were being targeted repeatedly to break the will of the resistance; doctors had to operate underground, in semi-darkness. Tens of thousands fled.[20]

Increasingly people just sighed when they saw Khaled's camera: what was the point of all this filming?

———

Mary Ana McGlasson was in Starbucks. She was an American nurse and ran humanitarian medical aid for Syria, based in the Turkish border town of Gaziantep, a city of one million, where an extra 500,000 Syrians had arrived as refugees. Working first for Relief International, then for Doctors Without Borders, she had spent the last five years coordinating the construction of hospitals that would then be destroyed again. She had just managed to get six months' worth of medical supplies into Aleppo, but as the siege intensified over the summer of 2016 it became clear that was not going to be enough. As she sat in Starbucks she was getting live text and WhatsApp messages from doctors inside Aleppo: 'The bombings have started again . . . we are operating in the basement . . . the generator has gone. We are operating by the lights from our mobile phones.'

Her job as a humanitarian worker was to be neutral. To build hospitals, deliver supplies, report on fatalities and war crimes. She relied on there being, beyond her, a system of international norms, ideals, institutions to which she provided the necessary evidence.

After 2015, as Russia began its bombing, Mary Ana and dozens of other humanitarian organisations compiled report after report showing that the attacks were aimed not, as the Russians claimed, at areas held by ISIS, but at Aleppo itself. She still assumed the weight of evidence would mean something. She wrote letters to US congressmen and UN representatives. She had long given up thinking there would be military intervention, even a safe zone – that moment had passed when the

Russians began bombing – but at least more sanctions, an outcry, last-ditch negotiations . . . Or, more importantly, millions in the streets, protests . . . Where were they? She knew the politicians would react only if they saw people were upset. Did it not matter any more if a regime gassed its own people? Did that elicit just a shrug?

The WhatsApp messages from Aleppo kept on coming through: 'We have run out of gauze and bandages. The bombs are getting closer.'

She struggled to look Syrians in the eye. They kept coming to her, thinking she had some sort of influence, planting hard drives of evidence in her hands. 'We have been killed by barrel bombs,' they told her. 'We have been killed by sarin gas and by Sukhoi rockets. But what is killing us now is the silence.'

At one moment in May 2016, there was hope: the Security Council of the UN, which included a representative from the Russian Federation, passed a resolution calling for a halt to the bombing of medical centres in Syria. It seemed, suddenly, that all their frenetic report writing had not been entirely in vain.

The resolution was passed on 3 May[21] – but in the following months attacks on medical facilities in Syria increased by 89 per cent. There were 172 attacks between June and December – one every twenty-nine hours.[22]

The medics' messages from Aleppo flashed on her phone: 'Paediatric hospital was targeted today by aircraft. Many fatalities and injuries.'

As the fall of Aleppo became ever more inevitable, Mary Ana's Syrian employees started asking for a month's pay in advance. She knew what that meant: they had given up any hope of ever going home, were prepared to risk everything on a boat taking them across the Mediterranean to Greece, and from there on the long march through the Balkans to Europe. There were different prices: if you had $10,000 or so, smugglers could take you in a luxury yacht that dropped you on a pleasant beach in the Peloponnese; sometimes as little as a few hundred could get you on a very overcrowded dinghy.

The Syrians she knew in Gaziantep had always thought they would go home. There was the doctor who walked around Gaziantep with the keys to his Aleppo apartment in his pocket, as if expecting to return there at any moment, though he had been away for years. Other refugees in Gaziantep lived in squalor, middle-class families squatting in empty shipping containers, eking out a living cutting shoe leather for local factories, but even they had not moved on from the border town, in the expectation that their time away from home was temporary. Now, with the final bombardment, they were abandoning all hope.

Since 2015 the TV news had been full of stories of boats with refugees capsizing, the bloated corpses of toddlers washing up near sunbathing tourists on the beaches of Greek islands. So refugee families sent their strongest sons, used their last money to get them on the best boats possible, arming them with mobile phones, the most important navigational aid for the journey. But this in turn provoked negative reactions from those watching television in Europe and the US. One could feel sorry for drowning babies, but instead columns of young Syrian men were marching into Europe.

When Mary Ana spoke to her parents in Arizona, they would ask her why weren't these men fighting? Why did they have mobile phones? Weren't they all terrorists? Her parents were deeply Christian, watched Fox News. She could tell how they were torn between their concern for her and sympathy for her work, and what they were being told on television. Nationalist politicians used shots of the exodus of refugees walking across Europe to fuel the fear of being overrun by foreigners, with one such photo being used on a poster advocating Britain's departure from the EU. 'Breaking Point', it read.

On 23 September the Russian and Syrian air forces launched forty air strikes a day on eastern Aleppo to prepare the way for a ground assault.[23] Over the next month there was an average of one attack every hour, every day and night.[24] Whole parts of the city went up in flames. The UN Special Envoy to Syria described the use of incendiary bombs that 'create fireballs of such intensity that they light up the pitch darkness in Aleppo as if it were daylight'.[25]

'We have twenty-seven more casualties,' went the messages on Mary Ana's phone. 'About half of them children. Here are the photos . . . please tell people.'

As the rebels tried to break the siege, they shelled government-held western Aleppo indiscriminately too: the Syrian Observatory for Human Rights recorded seventy-four civilian deaths there in October.[26]

Mary Ana went on writing the reports, reciting the facts of crimes against humanity, facts that no longer seemed to have any power. On television Donald Trump was debating Hillary Clinton for the US presidency. He wanted to build a wall; he wanted to stop Muslims coming to America, he said Muslims were terrorists. He made numbers up as he went along: there were thirty million illegal immigrants in America; Clinton would let in 650 million more.[27] No one took his chances seriously. Mary Ana knew different, that many would vote for him back in Arizona. And if facts didn't matter in Aleppo, why would they in the US?

The sitting US president, Barack Obama, had often talked about history having a 'right side' and a 'wrong side' (which he accused Russia of being on). Like Cold War leaders, he invoked the idea that history had an 'arc', a direction, a future, 'the hope of a better day'.[28] But in Aleppo such lofty words appeared utterly meaningless. History's direction was being barrel-bombed to nowhere. By November the siege was reaching its crescendo: the Russians seemed keen to finish it before a new US president came in. Schools, orphanages, hospitals were relocated into cellars. Even there bunker-busting bombs, the kind usually used to destroy military installations, were used to reach the inhabitants.[29]

Mary Ana was in Washington DC on the night of the election, 8 November. She watched the results in a bar by the Capitol. There were balloons: everyone was preparing for a Clinton victory. When the first states went to Trump, she sensed immediately he'd win. Two Republican campaign managers, already jolly, came up to her and told her she looked like the most distraught person in the bar. She walked out and grabbed a taxi back to the hotel. She sat in the back seat and wept. The taxi driver tried to console her: 'Don't worry, it will be OK.' He sounded Middle Eastern. She asked where he was from. He said, 'Afghanistan.' She asked whether he had a green card. 'No.'

She told him she was crying for him, not her. For the turning of immigrants into undesirables, of immigration into an evil.

Aleppo, the US election – they felt like different expressions of one phenomenon, where all the 'evidence-based rules' and 'humanitarian norms' Mary Ana had worked towards had become hollowed out. And in this new world the taxi driver would be the first victim.

In December 2016 Aleppo fell. Mary Ana helped organise the final evacuations of the acutely injured from the city. The Violations Documentations Centre in Syria estimates that 30,000 died in Aleppo between 2012 and 2016, the vast majority in opposition areas.[30] Over 70 per cent of those killed were civilians. The Syrian Network for Human Rights (which discounts reports provided by the Syrian regime) puts the civilian death toll in the war at 207,000, 94 per cent of which was at the hands of the Syrian government and Russian forces.[31] No numbers in this conflict are 100 per cent reliable. The UN gave up counting casualties in 2014, when it put the overall death count in the war at 400,000, give or take.[32]

Khaled had got out of Aleppo in August, when the rebels managed to open a road out of the town, his bag packed with video archive (a lot had been taken to Turkey previously). Some of the footage he shot in the city was included in a short documentary film about the White Helmets, which won an Oscar in 2017.[33] He travelled to LA but sounded a touch awkward about it when we talked: Khaled was glad his footage had been seen by so many, but he hadn't filmed death and the destruction of his city in order to go to parties in Hollywood.

We met in Istanbul and then Amsterdam to conduct the interviews I have used in this book. Khaled wants to make films about the slivers of Syria still free from Assad and radical Islamists. Facts didn't save Aleppo; perhaps telling stories is more powerful? He's only in his early twenties but is trying to preserve his home on camera before what's left disappears, whether from continuous bombardment or under the deluge of disinformation. 'They say we are all terrorists. I need to show the world what we are really like.'

At first Mary Ana hadn't taken the disinformation about Syria very seriously. Then she began to look further and saw that it was everywhere. When she punched 'White Helmets' into YouTube and found wall-to-wall coverage claiming that they were actually terrorists, or that they were actors and everything they did was staged, or that they were a British secret service psy-op, or that they didn't actually exist at all . . . Mary Ana feared these stories were part of a larger effort to wipe out the facts regarding what happened in the country.[34]

But here she encountered the great paradox of the Syrian slaughter. In all the other historical examples of crimes against humanity that Mary Ana has looked into, there was always the excuse that the world wasn't aware of what was going on. The Holocaust? We didn't know (or pretended not to). The slaughter of Bosnian Muslims by Serbs in Srebrenica? Happened too quickly to react to. Genocide in Rwanda? Politicians claimed they hadn't known the extent of what was happening. And now? Now everyone knows everything all the time. There's an abundance of video, photo and eyewitness testimony, scientific analysis, SMSs, JPEGs, terabytes of data showing war crimes, communicated virtually in real time, all streamed on social media for everyone to see. And yet the reaction has been inversely proportional to the sheer mass of evidence.

But if everyone knows everything and still does nothing, feels nothing, and the truth about what happened isn't locked into what Mary Ana has taken to calling 'the psyche of history', what does that lead to? That anyone can carry out mass murders and it's now seen as just OK? A globe lacerated with black holes where no known norms apply?

Look around and black holes are opening up everywhere. 'Maybe the world should be held responsible, because the world is a dangerous place,' retorted the US president in late 2018, when confronted with mounting evidence that his ally, the crown prince of Saudi Arabia, had ordered the killing of a journalist inside a Saudi consulate in Turkey, the president's phrase encapsulating an attitude whereby no amount of proof leads to accountability.[35] And when one looks at the slaughter of civilians by all sorts of forces in the Middle East (Saudi- and US-led, Iraqi, Israeli, Iranian),[36,37] the social media-powered ethnic cleansings and mob violence in Burma and Sri Lanka,[38] which one can see instigated live, online, in full view, it's hard not to feel Mary Ana's worst fears are coming true. And is disinformation then just the excuse we use to let ourselves off the hook – 'We didn't do anything because we were confused by a bot farm'?

Meanwhile, 22 TB of video recorded by the White Helmets sits in safe houses across Europe. To that one can add 60 TB of videos, tweets and Facebook posts held by the Syrian Archive: 800,000 documents and over 3,000 witness statements collected by the Commission for International Justice and Accountability that link crimes to senior Syrian officials.[39]

It is as much archive as we have ever had relating to torture, mass murder and war crimes. And it sits there, waiting for facts to be given meaning.

'Excuse me, are you English?'

'What do you feel: English or Russian?'

The incessant questions of my childhood, pursuing me from the mouth of every curious parent of my school friends as they drove me beyond London at weekends to visit country houses full of second cousins, infinite uncles and great-aunts, a rooted- ness so different to our wandering family. On those long rides in the back of other people's cars I would stare, transfixed, at the borders between the fields. The hedgerows parcelled up the land so irregularly yet somehow coherently; even the fields seemed to be involved in a conversation so intricate and entrenched that it could feel rude to interrupt. The English were defined so precisely by class, accent, schools, postcodes, counties, parties and sports teams that for an immigrant like myself, it could be hard to know where to fit in.

One of the first things I worked out as an immigrant child is that you're not meant to rush into Englishness. You can do that in the US maybe, but it would be utterly un-English to try to be English fast.

'Your English is so perfect, one would never suspect you are a Russian,' I would be told, making me feel that my English was some sort of deception (should I fake a Russian accent to be more genuine?).

To make matters more complicated, I couldn't simply answer, 'I'm Russian.' I had been born in Ukraine after all, but into a Russian-speaking family. What did that make me – Soviet?

181

Russia, Ukraine, the entire USSR were just vast splodges on the map that hung in our kitchen, splattered with coffee and wine; places I'd never visited, a territory I could only populate through the books that I had read. Is that where I came from – books?

The only way my identity fused with England was through the mass media, the television and radio synchronising my attention and emotions with the nation. This could be surprisingly intimate: in the 1980s Igor's stories were being translated and broadcast on BBC radio, including Reading Faulkner, *which, narrated by an English actor, made Chernivtsi sound like somewhere near Suffolk:*

Better to try again, to describe Chernivtsi once more.

My childhood smelt of grapes, greenery and caraway.

It passed under the watchful eyes of grandfathers (later I figured out only one was my grandfather, all the rest were his brothers). Can't remember any winters in my childhood; perpetual July, the air flowing from the swelling apples and tickling so your head swam . . .

In 1987 Igor moved from the BBC World Service to the London bureau of an American 'voice' that broadcast into the Communist bloc. Radio Free Europe (RFE) had been set up in 1949 by American strategists in what they called a 'citizens' adventure in the field of psychological warfare'[40] in order to help exiles from states newly controlled by the USSR express a different political vision of their home countries. In 1953 Radio Liberty was added to broadcast into the USSR itself. Unlike the BBC, where British editors controlled all output, here the exiles had more control. The first iteration of the 'experiment' ended in disaster in 1956, when, during the Hungarian uprising against Soviet occupation, broadcasters on Radio Free Hungary made incendiary speeches and gave protesters tactical advice, implying American military assistance was on its way. However, the US government didn't provide any, and Hungarian dissidents felt lethally betrayed.

When Igor joined RFE, such escapades had long been reigned in and the broadcaster was legally bound to create news that was 'accurate, objective, comprehensive'. It had changed in other ways too. At its inception RFE had been sponsored by the CIA, under the cover of private donations for a campaign called 'Crusade for Freedom'. Since 1971 it had been funded via Congress and a 'Broadcasting Board of Governors', full of grandees from the media and academia appointed to safeguard its independence. But its mission remained different to that of a broadcaster like the BBC, which existed to represent Britain in the world. RFE/Radio Liberty was known as a surrogate station, whose aim was not to express the US or Britain abroad, but to articulate a different political identity for Russia, Ukraine and other countries under Soviet domination. To better understand its audience, RFE had an ingenious method of polling (which it shared with the BBC). Starting in the 1950s sociologists would visit the bars in busy ports or international fairs in the West that Soviet sailors and delegations would be allowed to visit, strike up conversations and ask them casually but systematically what sort of radio programmes they liked to listen to and why. When the Cold War ended they felt confident enough to ask Soviet tourists to fill in more formal questionnaires. Despite the best efforts of Soviet signal jamming, some 5–10 per cent of Soviet adults wiggled and waved their antennas to tune in to Radio Liberty between 1972 and 1988, a figure that was much higher among the well-educated and those in the big cities, rising to 15 per cent after jamming was removed in 1988, when Igor joined.[41]

Igor was now empowered to create his own worlds. 'I have no interest in describing culture. But to create and blow culture like glass is thrilling,' he would write later.

His aim was to intermingle Russia and Ukraine with a greater Europe: 'I am not a cosmopolitan, I am a patriot. But I have a different patria. I feel a sense of home in Istanbul cemeteries, Rome, Chernivtsi, London, Sergiev Posad.'

He made programmes about glass, windows, billiards, colours – things that brought together different nationalities, junctures where they could meet and mix. He made programmes in which every one of the contributors spoke Russian with an accent, widening the boundaries of the language.

Igor's weekly slot was called Across the Barriers, *and from 1989 the real barriers were crashing down. It was a time of miracles on our Grundig television, with its four channels (two of which were BBC). Press the remote and there was Václav Havel, now free from prison and the president of Czechoslovakia, waving from a balcony to a great swell of cheering crowds in Prague; press it again and statues of Lenin were being pulled down throughout Central Europe, swaying in mid-air on chains hanging from cranes, like burnished bronze trapeze artists; press once more and people were clambering over the Berlin Wall, bashing away at the concrete with hammers, something they would have been shot for a few weeks ago.*

Igor's own writing moved away from first-person impressionism: the unmitigated 'I' had begun to feel self-indulgent without the heavy breath of authoritarianism bearing down on him. Instead, he drew on anthropology, zoology, ways of reimagining and redefining groups, identities, interconnections. Viticulture, winemaking, became an incessant theme, a tradition that travelled across and transformed continents. A glass of wine had magical properties, could transport you in time and space. In a story from July 1991 the first person is almost entirely absent. The tale is based on a meteorological dictionary of winds. He's talking about freedom, but there's little mention of himself, just detailed descriptions of gales, breezes, gusts, breaths.

On 21 August 1991 Igor woke to find that a putsch had broken out in Moscow. The head of the KGB, the army, the prime minister and the deputy president had announced a state of emergency. Gorbachev, they claimed, was unwell in his country house in the Crimea and too ill to serve the country any longer. They were taking power and planned to save the Soviet Union.

Soviet television was showing Swan Lake on a loop, so people turned to the Western 'voices' in even greater numbers. On Radio Liberty Boris Yeltsin, the president of the largest Soviet republic, Russia, called the state of emergency a coup, asking for crowds to come to the centre of Moscow, with hundreds of thousands forming a human shield to defend the Russian parliament from the tanks and KGB battalions that had been pulled into the middle of the city.

In Crimea, Gorbachev, who wasn't sick at all, had been placed under house arrest by the coup plotters and had all his communications cut. The only thing he had left was a battery-powered radio. He and his staff gathered around it, wiggling the antenna to get good reception, tuning desperately into the foreign 'voices'. On Radio Liberty British prime minister Margaret Thatcher exhorted her friend Mikhail to hold on. This was Igor's work. He had spent the night trying to persuade Downing Street to let him interview the prime minister. They told him repeatedly she didn't give interviews like this. 'This isn't about just politics,' Igor told them. 'Her personal friend Mikhail is in danger. Has she nothing to say to him?' That worked.

The coup failed. Within a year the Soviet Union itself was gone. The map on our kitchen wall began to change. Fifteen new countries were created in one go. The colours on the map I had grown up with, a globe shaded into two blocks, started to mix like a messy palette. The geography of identity that I had grown up with – 'there', 'here', 'them', 'us' – no longer made sense.

Our personal geography was shifting too. In 1992 Igor was transferred to the central bureau of RFE in Munich, Germany, to sit with the language sections of dozens of other now former Communist bloc countries, housed in a building that looked like a medieval fortress, with high, thick walls covered in spikes and with even higher security – the legacy of an attempt to blow it up by the Stasi-sponsored Venezuelan terrorist Carlos the Jackal in 1981. In the corridors and cellars of that fortress Igor was delighted to discover vast, forgotten cabinets containing reels of the great émigré writers who had worked at Radio Liberty over the last forty years. He was becoming ever more enamoured of the power of radio to create new worlds, to blend past and present, here and there into something strange and new:

'Drama, dramatic effect is born on radio when sounds collide, rub noses, give each other a slap. Radio language is wider, richer, more full-bodied than any spoken tongue. With it you can convey ageing, the approach of madness, dying.'

He and his producers travelled everywhere with their audio recorders, picking up noises to be used in programmes: the crunching of an apple made one think of snow in winter; a dingo howling in a zoo was yearning love.

One is perhaps not very aware in childhood that one is part of vast experiments in the culture, the mindset, the language that make politics possible. While Igor worked for a station that symbolised American support for a Europe that was, as the US president said in 1989, 'whole and free', I was sent to a special school created to change the political psychology of the continent.

Munich was home to one of nine European Schools, which were created by the founders of the European Union (then the EEC) to forge a new, 'European' model of identity. Under the foundation stone of each school lay the mission statement, allegedly written by Jean Monnet, the creator of the EEC, himself:

Without ceasing to look to their own lands with love and pride, they will become in mind Europeans, schooled and ready to complete and consolidate the work of their fathers before them, to bring into being a united and thriving Europe.

Primarily intended for the children of the EU's multinational civil servants, the schools were also open to anyone who could get in via a lottery and an exam. Indeed, the dream of their founders had been that they would become a model for all education in the Union.

Every morning our headmaster, Herr Hoyem, a former Danish minister for Greenland, would greet us at the entrance of the school, which was built in the shape of a star, in honour of the stars on the European flag. The architects had forgotten to include EU-regulation fire escapes, and the building was later encased in a metal exoskeleton of stairs and walkways; at first glance it looked like scaffolding, as if the school was under permanent construction. The school was split into different language sections – English, French, German, Italian and so on – with history and geography taught in a foreign language and from that country's point of view. When the first school had opened in 1953, less than a decade after the end of the Second World War, it must have been a stunning idea for French children to be taught history in German from a German perspective – and vice versa.

The kids in the English section had been in Germany so long their connection to the UK was tenuous. Fresh from London, I was in some ways the most English person there. This was novel. Back in London I had been known as 'the Russian'. Now I was suddenly a representative of England.

The children of the European School played up to the caricatures of their homelands. The French were moody; the boys read graphic novels and the girls dressed beautifully. The Italians were appalled by the food and seemed to take to multilingualism badly. The Germans were the jocks. We in the English section, the boys anyway, posed as eccentrics: we quoted Monty Python and made a point of eating Marmite. At playtime we would teach our Italian counterparts cricket, not because we had any passion for it, but simply because as the 'English' that's what we felt we ought to do to identify ourselves.

I was taught history and geography in French. For me this was less a case of sink or swim, more simply sinking and having to survive by breathing underwater. Overwhelmed in my first months I gradually began to grow linguistic gills, could make out the dim outlines of glowing underwater kingdoms: the St Bartholomew's Day massacre, Versailles, Napoleon. But this Napoleon was different to the one I knew. In England I had learnt that he was a villain. For the French he was a star of democracy promotion, not a despot. I ended up with two Napoleons: one English and one underwater.

I became amphibian. I joined the other pupils in the aula, where conversations would start in German and flow into French and then English; or everyone would speak their own language but understand everyone else's. I remember looking across the aula at an English classmate once and momentarily not recognising him because, when speaking German, he shed his camp grimaces and laughed like a Bavarian, slow and macho. So, on the one hand, national traits were more pronounced as we defined ourselves against one another in the playground rituals; but they were also less fixed, something you could put on and take off again, not 'you'. It was an existence I found quietly ecstatic. After an immigrant, bilingual, awkward childhood – knowing I wasn't English like the majority around me, but not quite sure what I was – here was a system that celebrated stepping outside of and outstripping one's identity, the one thing I was actually quite good at. This was what 'European' meant: not some superimposed identity, but the ability to wear identity lightly, to be able to wriggle outside of one and inside another.

As Igor and I were working out what Europe meant, Lina was immersing herself in Russia. She had been the first of our family to return: since 1989 she had been joining documentary crews filming in the USSR and the newly independent states. On her first landing she had the curious sensation that everything she saw was out of synch with what she heard, as if her hearing were straggling behind her sight. She saw the long queues of people all standing far too close to one another, the movements of the taxi driver's mouth, but would only hear them moments later.

189

When sound and vision synched, she found herself in a country the stomach of whose society had been ripped out, the intestines of its tragedies and traumas everywhere. Some of her earliest films were about the street children of St Petersburg. There were whole colonies of them, sleeping underground alongside warm gas pipes, living in networks of dark, wet, bare-walled cellars, where they mimicked normal apartments by bringing in settees and watercolour paintings they found in dumps. Many of the children spoke educated Russian but had run away from homes where their parents had become drunk, deranged, as all sense of normality, family, sanity collapsed. All social roles were being overturned. Prostitution, previously taboo, suddenly seemed acceptable. Students would support their parents, answering ads for work as secretaries with 'no complexes' – a euphemism for being prepared to sleep with the boss.

The political language was in utter chaos too. In 1994 Lina worked on a documentary about a popular new politician, Vladimir Zhirinovsky, sailing with him on a cruiser down the River Volga as he, dressed in a flamboyant all-white suit, gave speeches to excited crowds gathered along the banks. Zhirinovsky was the head of the Liberal Democrat Party, but he was neither a 'liberal' nor a 'democrat' in the way the words had previously been used in Russia, when they signified someone tolerant, well spoken, pro-Western. Indeed, it was hard to pin down what he was. His speeches seemed stream-of-consciousness, yet somehow unerringly picked up on the audience's desires. It was impossible to tell when he was joking and when serious. He promised he would end poverty and homelessness within a few months of coming into power, and that Germany would pay for it as they owed Russia Second World War reparations. He railed against the US with its 'Mickey Mouse dollars', which, under his rule, would no longer be able to undercut the glorious Russian 'golden rouble'; claimed Russia would control the entire territory from the Pacific to the Mediterranean, that Russian soldiers would wash their boots in the Indian Ocean, annex Alaska. But he also told crowds that the reason they lived in penury was Lenin and his Communist economics; that he, Zhirinovsky, would make them like successful Westerners, owning their own homes, new cars and widescreen televisions. He also promised the bands of Cossacks, who stood on the shore with whips, that he would empower them to go and fight against the 'enemy to the south . . . We will give you weapons. Take your whips and ramrods, go to the regions where there is anarchy, disruption and anti-state activity and restore order.'

Zhirinovsky meant the breakaway republic of Chechnya, where a year later Russia would be fighting a hapless war with little regard for civilian casualties, and where a new strain of Islamist extremism was beginning to breed. Lina filmed with the Chechen separatists up in the mountains of the Caucasus. They described their struggle as one of national liberation, but Lina also noted something new for Russia: Islamist preachers from the Gulf; women veiling their faces with niqabs.

It was easy in those days for Lina to film everyone from politicians to warlords: just saying you were from the BBC or British television made you a symbol of something better from 'over there', an envoy from another world which still had a sense of norms, justice, clear identities, where words stood for something.

Away from her filming Lina went to smoke-filled-to-suffocation performances where the artists and poets of the 1990s tried to make sense of the all-pervasive uncertainty. It was an inspired time. Lev Rubinstein delivered spoken-word performances where he stood with a stack of Soviet library catalogue cards, those little emblems of cultural order, on which he wrote cryptic stanzas, throwing them away as he read through them, a symbol of old meanings falling apart. Dmitry Prigov would howl and chant sound bites of Soviet agitprop until they bent into shamanic dirges. Oleg Kulik discarded language altogether, transforming himself into a growling dog for days, down on all fours and snapping at visitors to his gallery. If words were meaningless, all that was left was action.

'Soviet time has stopped,' Zinovy Zinik wrote, 'while the universe it rules disintegrates.'[42] The art critic Boris Groys described the moment as the 'Big Tsimtsum', a term borrowed from the Jewish mystical tradition of the Kabbalah, an alternative version of Creation where God first brings the world into being and then retreats from it. 'The withdrawal of Soviet power, or the Tsimtsum of Communism, created the infinite space of signs emptied of sense: the world became devoid of meaning.'[43]

In 2001, after university, I followed Lina's trail, moving to Russia to eventually work in television. 'Moscow', I would write later, 'seemed a city living in fast-forward, changing so fast it breaks all sense of reality. Russia had seen so many worlds flick through in such rapid progression – from Communism to perestroika to shock therapy to penury to oligarchy to mafia state to mega-rich – that its new heroes were left with the sense that life is just one glittering masquerade, where every role and any position or belief is mutable.'

Part 5: Pop-Up People

Thirty years later, it is not just Russia where signs are 'emptied of sense' and the world is 'devoid of meaning'. The 'Big Tsimtsum' feels relevant among the victors of the Cold War too, in countries where professional pollsters struggle to define models for our identities, where what was previously assumed as 'normal' has dissolved. Who will be first to form new identities out of the flux?

Othering

As I was experiencing experiments in multilayered identity at the European School, Rashad Ali, also a child of first-generation immigrants, was going through a very different process in Sheffield, Yorkshire.

Back in 1996 Rashad had been immediately impressed by the men from Hizb ut-Tahrir the first time they came to his school to give a talk on Islam. These were the days before 11 September 2001, before ISIS, when no one in the school's management thought anything bad could come of the well-dressed, erudite young college lecturers in engineering and science speaking so engagingly about big ideas: about whether you could prove God exists, evolution, identity.

'What kind of Muslim are you?' they asked the pupils. 'A Friday Muslim? A part-time Muslim? Can you be a complete Muslim?'

'Complete' sounded interesting to Rashad. What could that mean? He went along to the Hizb study groups, held in an ordinary terraced house, among streets of russet-bricked terraced houses built for workers in the city's once-mighty steel factories that stretched towards the green-sprouting hills of South Yorkshire.

The recruiters explained that in Bosnia, Muslims had spent hundreds of years integrating with the locals: they drank, they smoked, they fornicated like secular Europeans. And what had happened? They were now being slaughtered by their secular and Christian neighbours, who were armed and supported by Slobodan Milošević's government in Belgrade. And what about Chechnya, where Russian forces were bombing Muslims mercilessly? What was the West doing to help these Muslims? Nothing. 'Muslims in Bosnia are your brothers,' said the recruiters. 'They are your family, not the secular people around you, not the English.'

Growing up Rashad had always known that he was different. His father, who died when Rashad was eight, had come to England in the 1960s to work in the steel mills. He had done well, bought a house, opened a restaurant, wore a suit he had custom-made from the tailor on the corner, watched the BBC news religiously twice every evening. But for all this veneer of Englishness, both of Rashad's parents spoke with strong Bangla accents. His home smelt different to English ones. He was a different colour.

And then there was the God thing. Rashad was religious in the way everyone in his community was: it was just something that was indelibly part of you, like a limb, and something most English people just couldn't understand. But Rashad had never defined himself as 'Muslim'. In the early 1990s all the talk was of an Asian identity, 'Asian British', which encompassed Sikhs, Hindus, Indian Muslims, Pakistani Shia. But what did these Asians really have in common, when back in their homelands they were at war with one another? Rashad had visited Bangladesh and knew he didn't belong in the home of his parents' past. He was aware he wasn't quite English either. Now he was about to be offered a new home, a place where he would belong perfectly because it didn't exist yet: an Islamic state.

Each week Rashad and the other members of his study group would immerse themselves in Hizb's founding texts, which laid out in stunning detail every aspect of how the ideal Islamic state should look. There were books on law, government, ethics, epistemology; everything from the powers to be granted to judges through to how reality was shaped by a priori thoughts. Hizb had been founded in the 1950s by a Palestinian Islamic scholar, Taqiuddin al-Nabhani, who had previously been a senior member of the Arab Socialist Ba'ath Party. For al-Nabhani the creation of Israel was a sign that Muslims were weak, unable to stand up for each other, corrupted by Western notions such as 'the nation', which had splintered them into different countries. It was the very language and concepts through which people saw the world that had to change.

At the foundation of Hizb's ideology was the idea of the 'Islamic personality'.[1] It argued that a person has natural instincts that have to be fulfilled, but training yourself to think in the correct way would channel those instincts into the 'right' behaviour. So, for example, man has a natural instinct for security, which is articulated in the quest to acquire things and property. Marxism suppressed that instinct and was therefore destined to fail. Capitalism, however, overindulged it, while undermining another instinct, defined by Hizb as 'procreation', which expressed itself as the need to feel part of a community. Political Islam fulfilled both needs: it allowed you to both fulfil the need for security by allowing a certain amount of private property, and for procreation by defining your obligations to the *ummah*, the greater community of Muslims.

Rashad asked his study group leader what methodology would bring about an Islamic state. The man invited him for a drive in his gold Honda Shuttle.

As they drove through Sheffield, the group leader explained to Rashad that their plan was to convince the military in Jordan,

Egypt, Iraq and Syria to launch military coups, take power and then unite into one supra-Islamic state. For a moment Rashad paused: this sounded, even to his sixteen-year-old self, reckless. The group leader saw his reaction and continued: 'Remember what the Prophet did at Mecca and Medina. He had no forces of his own, but he managed to persuade the tribal leaders to back him and be his army. It's the same with us.'

That coming together of past and present, of holy books and current history, helped Rashad hurdle his initial doubt. And soon enough the notion seemed less fantastical. The movement was growing stronger by the day. Between 1996, when Rashad joined, and 2003 the number of activists in the UK grew from thirty to 3,000, with hundreds of thousands globally. The party leadership issued statements claiming that generals throughout the Middle East were turning in their favour. The leadership consisted of al-Nabhani's successors and a handful of close allies, who lived in such secrecy in Lebanon and Jordan that when they 'spoke' at Hizbi gatherings across the world, it was only via audio link, their voices beamed in to thousands of followers in a hall, but their faces not revealed.

By the turn of the century Rashad was one of the leaders of Hizb in the UK. He would organise university debates about, for example, whether it was possible to be both Muslim and British simultaneously, arguing that the two were incompatible. In 2000, at the age of twenty, he authored a core text of Hizb literature, a copy of which would later be found in the library of Osama bin Laden in his safe house at Abbottabad.[2] *The Method to Re-Establish the Khilafah* spends over three hundred dense pages outlining Koranic arguments for how to correctly establish the Islamic state. The process starts with 'Culturing'

– uniting drives, instincts and ideas to form the Islamic personality. Then comes the 'Interactions' stage, the public outreach campaigns that are meant to convince populations in the Middle East that their interests are best served by military coups to overturn their corrupt governments, who are nothing but lackeys of Western colonialism.

'After this the military would be capable of establishing the authority of Islam . . . and Jihad to the rest of the world.'

One of Rashad's many roles was to answer email questions from party members about the finer points of Hizb doctrine, liaising with the heard-but-not-seen leadership on what was the canonical response. He had now read enough religious commentary to know that some of the answers the leadership were giving were simply wrong. When a member asked why the Prophet hadn't enforced all his decrees onto his followers, the leadership answered that no scholar allowed any Muslim to follow the Prophet's example in this regard. Rashad was aware that the leadership themselves knew this was false. Many scholars argued that it was acceptable not to enforce all decrees. The leadership were simply misusing people's ignorance to create a system whereby they had more control. And now that he was better versed in Islamic ideas and history himself, Rashad was discovering that many of the Hizb teachings were factually incorrect. There had never been a golden moment of a Caliphate under a single ruler. There had been many small and fractured treaties throughout Islam's history, a patchwork of jurisdictions, but there was no original Caliphate to restore.

There had been no one moment when the scales had fallen from his eyes. After eight years Rashad had noticed how far Hizb was from fulfilling any of its promises. The leadership sent circulars stating that their *coup d'états* were just around the corner, but it was becoming obvious nothing of the sort was happening. Then there was the question of violence. Hizb claimed it opposed violent acts. However, it did not disapprove of others committing them under the right conditions. Officially Hizb had condemned the attacks of 9/11, but only on a technicality: the planes were privately owned; if they had been Israeli ones, it would have been different as Israel was an occupying state. The contradictions seemed, to Rashad, absurd.

He began duelling with the leadership, questioning the movement's underlying assumptions. Slowly the idea that being Muslim and being English are mutually exclusive fell away, and the notion that the only place where he could be truly fulfilled was in an Islamic state unwound. He found he could be simultaneously Muslim and from Yorkshire, British and Asian, all held together with a core belief in human rights, which he threw himself into vehemently defending, from Palestinians in Gaza to anti-Semitism in Europe.

In the summer of 2018 I took the train with Rashad to towns in England in which he had grown up and preached. On the way, as we passed fields parcelled as intricately together as I remembered from my childhood, Rashad told me how he would practise recruitment techniques on strangers during train journeys as lessons for younger Hizb disciples, who would observe him. One time, on a train to Durham, he saw a woman reading a newspaper in which there was a distressing report about how a ten-year-old boy had killed his baby brother when, for a laugh, he put him in a washing machine and switched it on.

Rashad approached the woman and asked her what she thought about the article. The woman told him the story angered her. She blamed the parents. They had gone to the pub that evening, left the children all alone. She was a nurse, and every day she saw how narcissism, irresponsibility, negligence caused harm to others.

Rashad had his in. He asked the woman whether she thought this sort of behaviour was inevitable in a liberal, secular society, where people were encouraged to think about nothing but their personal gain and pleasure. What we needed, argued Rashad, was a society where all the economic and social laws would encourage care for one another, where people would know good deeds brought high rewards.

The woman nodded.

It may sound novel, Rashad concluded, but had she considered that an Islamic state could be a way of establishing just such a society . . .?

Rashad and his pupils got off soon after, and we will never know what the nurse made of his proposal. But the essence of the recruitment arguments was clear: whatever issue a target cares about, your job is to connect it with the need for an Islamic state.

In Birmingham, Rashad and I walked through the streets, among red housing and low sky, but which had been brought to life with street vendors selling fruit and sandals, McHalals, Sudanese supermarkets with brightly coloured shawls, graffitied murals calling to 'Free Palestine', Somali passageways selling niqabs. But what struck me were the bookshops. I counted at least three large ones on a single short stretch of street, with long rows of hardcover books of holy texts and commentary, and garish paperbacks on everything from *Polygamy* to *God's Gentle Artistry*, *Jihad*, *Islam and Karma* and *The Prohibition of*

Homosexuality. All were sponsored by different Islamic movements and by different states, all tussling over the minds of English Muslims. At one point Rashad drove out to a warehouse by a flyover, where we were met by a man with a beard and a key who took us up in an industrial lift to a floor where books were piled high, whole valleys and alleyways of spines with gold Arabic lettering, which Rashad clambered through excitedly. 'I've found it! Al-Ghazali, *The Ninety-Nine Beautiful Names of God!*'

It's his knowledge of Islamic law and recruitment techniques that make Rashad so good at what he does today: extracting people from the sort of movements he was once a part of. He works at an organisation blandly entitled the Institute for Strategic Dialogue (ISD), which tracks online extremist campaigns, advises governments and technology companies on what regulation they should (and shouldn't) introduce to tackle them, and experiments with what it calls 'counter-speech', reaching out to audiences coming under the sway of extremist movements. The ISD defines extremism as 'a system of belief that posits the superiority and dominance of one "in-group" over all "out-groups", propagating a dehumanising "othering" mind-set that is antithetical to the universal application of Human Rights.' Sometimes they simply refer to it as 'othering'.

Across the ISD office there are dozens of people. There are teams looking at how hatreds are inflamed online in Kenya, with Islamist movements trying to define the country according to religion, while political parties try to redraw the lines of loyalty along tribal ones. Next to them researchers track computer-gaming sites where neo-Nazis recruit new converts. The neo-Nazis stalk online forums where awkward teens spend their days playing Second World War games. Those who seem the most angry, lonely, the neo-Nazis direct towards other chat rooms, where they instruct the new recruits on digital marketing campaigns to promote far-right causes: which videos on YouTube to like or dislike; how to create swarms of automated accounts to boost far-right campaigns on social media. The recruits move from computer games to digital political campaigns that feel like another sort of game, all the while never leaving their bedrooms, slipping from one virtual reality to another.

On Reddit and 4chan sites anonymous administrators provide an online 'crash course in mass persuasion', which in the Cold War would have been the province of the secret services and 'civilian psy-ops'. There is advice on how to use the values of your enemy against them. So if you are attacking a leftist politician, you should create a fake liberal persona for yourself online and point out how politicians are part of the financial elite, or how their 'white privilege' has allowed them to rise to the top and avoid arrest. There are instructions on how to 'control an Internet forum', including tips on 'consensus cracking': using a fake persona to introduce the ideas you oppose in such a weak and unsubstantiated way that you can then use another fake persona to knock them down. Campaigns can come from anywhere. The ISD once found a Russian freelance bot herder in Nizhny Novgorod promoting German far-right memes, next to their other campaigns for escorts in Dubai, medical clinics in provincial Russia, attacks on Russian opposition figures.

The ISD also has teams creating educational videos for schools, so teenagers learn how to recognise far-right and Islamist campaigns, which are becoming ever more intermingled with a young person's everyday social media life. Jihadi recruiters, for instance, will first scan a potential target's social media profile, see what a person's favourite interests and hobbies are, and then try to engage with them accordingly. If they feel a young woman is interested in religion, romance, a family, they might strike up a conversation about the virtues of a Salafi husband. If a person doesn't respect God, they argue, how could they be expected to respect their wives?

The Internet has made recruitment quicker and more dexterous than when Rashad was first in Hizb, but the underlying techniques of envelopment are similar. Today it is ISIS that is best known for propagating the need for an Islamic state, and though Hizb has officially condemned the movement, Rashad can see how it echoes Hizb's original interlacing of feelings, concepts, language and behaviour.

———

'Tell them how much you miss them, and that tearing yourself away from family is haram.'

Rashad is direct-messaging the parents of two teenage girls who have joined an Islamist movement in the Middle East. The parents are in an English market town and are simultaneously talking to the girls, who are somewhere in Iraq. They are asking their parents' permission to marry Jihadi fighters. The girls write that they miss their parents, they're sorry, they don't want to cause them pain, but this marriage is their duty to the soldiers of the Caliphate. This is their contribution to a great cause.

Rashad knows the parents brought the girls up as conservative Muslims and sent them to study medicine in Khartoum, and then found, to their horror, that the girls had been turned towards a form of Islam so radical and political that they could barely recognise it. At their wits' end, they have asked Rashad for help.

For Rashad, the fact the girls are even writing to their parents for permission is a good sign: it means they still feel a bond to Mum and Dad. This is where the extremists' hold on them could be weakest, where he can unpick a strap that binds them to their new identity.

The girls keep on asking for their parents' blessing. They explain that it's only in the Caliphate they can practise the pure version of the religion they believe in.

Rashad and the parents try to argue that the girls can practise Islam fully in England, that they don't give their blessing to this marriage, that their 'Caliphate' violates all genuine Islamic ethics, justice.

'ISIS are to Islam what adultery is to marriage,' writes Rashad.

The girls don't respond immediately. Could they be thinking? After a while they come back with cut-and-paste quotations in medieval Arabic, misquoting arcane scholars. Clearly these aren't their words. Rashad can tell that their ISIS handler has stepped in and is dictating to them. The conversation, for now, has become pointless.

Rashad opens up another window on his computer to reveal the Facebook wall of a young man in the Midlands. Photos of the bungalows he rents out during his day job as an estate agent sit next to conspiracy videos 'proving' terrorist attacks in Europe are 'actually' CIA; comments about how he prefers his new Samsung to his old iPhone intermingle with clips of preachers advocating the killing of gays. He writes about how he feels sickened by the sight of drunks on a Friday night while British drones hit innocent Muslim children in the Middle East. 'It's a duty to support the Khilafah. The land of the Kuffar will never be a home for the believer!'

Rashad direct-messages him, explains he was once part of a radical Islamist group himself, but left. Does the young man in the Midlands want to talk?

At any one moment he might be involved in dozens of such conversations online. For reasons of privacy, data protection and security the extracts above minimise, mix and blur the personal details of his conversations. Though I've tried to make them as faithful as possible within such rules, Rashad rolls his eyes every time I try to squeeze his 'interactions' into neat little scenes with clear plot lines like in a TV drama. In reality it doesn't work that way. There are no clear beginnings and endings. Everything is bitty, smudged. A lot of the time success is measured just by getting an 'at risk' individual to respond to Rashad. If 5 per cent answer when he contacts them, that's already success. Conversations can take years, and even if you can 'engage' someone, it can be hard to help them. Rashad eventually helped persuade the young women that they should go back to their parents. But there was no way for them to physically escape from ISIS territory. There has been no news of them since then, even after ISIS was pushed out of Iraq and Syria.

When Rashad initially engages with an 'at risk' individual online, his first job is to work out that person's motivations. Are they driven by political passions, a radical who just happens to be Muslim? A tell-tale sign would be if they accused Rashad of being an agent of Western imperialism. Or are they actually interested in religion? A personal grievance? Mental health issues? Or a combination of the above?

Then Rashad tries to parse the logic he knows recruits have been subjected to, find the contradictions. When they argue it's a religious duty to unite in one state and impose Sharia, Rashad points out that since the time of the Prophet there have always been different Islamic empires and rulers; there's no one model. Or when they suggest cartoons of Muhammad should be banned in the West, Rashad asks them whether that means one should ban the Koran too? Surely if one side has freedom of speech, the other should too? Or if they were to claim the West makes up Islamist terrorist attacks, but that terrorism is a natural response to Western foreign policy, Rashad focuses on the contradiction of claiming that terrorist acts are both invented and justified.

And then he will zero in on one of their core false beliefs – let's say Holocaust denial – and overpower them with so much evidence it becomes irrefutable. After all, Rashad argues, how do we know about the existence of the Prophet? Because authorities confirm it. We have historical evidence. Tradition. Conspiracy theories undermine the entire premise of Islam . . .

Rashad tries to help those he talks to understand how they have been manipulated, to break down the idea that one's Islamic identity is inherently mutually exclusive to a British (or American or Danish) one.

But there's a problem. The types of thinking he looks to unwind, the belief in conspiracies, the 'othering', is now becoming ever more pervasive. 'Extremist' should not be confused with 'marginal' or 'fringe'. An extremist movement can be the main one in a country. Indeed, it is increasingly hard to tell where the centre and the fringe are these days. One of the barometers the ISD uses for its work is the 'Positive Peace' index, which has an indicator called 'the acceptance of the rights of others'.[3] And that particular indicator has plummeted in Europe and North America particularly, even as movements that push a mindset which 'posits the superiority and dominance of one "in-group" over all "out-groups"' surge.

Looking around, Rashad even sees politicians from long-established parties adopting a version of the approach popularised by organisations such as Hizb. One chooses a theme – religion, immigration, an economic principle – then builds it up so that it becomes the marker of who you are, not just a policy to be debated but a line on the other side of which everyone is deemed untouchable, lassoing the whole with conspiracies that divide 'us' from 'them'.

'In religious terms we would call it sectarianism,' says Rashad, 'identity masquerading as ideology.'

In a recent report the ISD described the environment it works in as a 'liquid' society, invoking a world where old, more solid social roles have slipped the leash, where information moves so easily it fractures old notions of belonging, where a sense of uncertainty pervades everything and where all sorts of forces can more easily reshape you.[4]

Pop-Up Populism

'All politics is now about creating identity' – that was the argument a spin doctor made as we sat in a bar in Mexico City, the terrace so shaded by dense foliage it seemed like night down below, while the sky was curaçao-blue above. He explained to me that the old notions of class and ideology were dead. When he ran a campaign now, he had to take disparate, discrete interests and unite them under a new notion of 'the people'.

The spin doctor wore a pinstripe shirt, his hair was slicked back – he looked quite the yuppie. 'Populism is not an ideology, it is a strategy', he asserted, invoking two theoreticians from the University of Essex, Ernesto Laclau and Chantal Mouffe, who first coined the notion of 'populism as strategy', though they had meant it to advance a new sort of socialism. I was surprised at his choice of favourite theorists – he didn't look like much of a socialist himself. He told me his personal preference was for the left, but he would work with anyone who paid the rent.

The nature of social media encourages populism as a strategy. Take a look at things from the point of view of the spin doctor. People on social media are organised across vastly different interests: animal rights and hospitals, guns and gardening, immigration and parenting and modern art. Some of these might be overtly political, while others are private. Your aim is reach out to these different groups in completely different ways, tying the voting behaviour you want to what they care about the most.

This sort of micro-targeting, where one set of voters shouldn't necessarily know about the others, requires some big, empty identity to unite all these different groups, something so broad these voters can project themselves onto it – a category like 'the people' or 'the many'. The 'populism' that is thus created is not a sign of 'the people' coming together in a great groundswell of unity, but a consequence of 'the people' being more fractured than ever, of their barely existing as one nation. When people have less in common than before, you have to reimagine a new version of 'the people'.

Facts become secondary in this logic. After all, you are not trying to win an evidence-driven debate about ideological concepts in a public sphere; your aim is to seal in your audience behind a verbal wall. It's the opposite of 'centrism', where you have to bring everyone together in one big tent, smooth out differences. Here the different groups don't even need to meet each other. Actually, it might be better if they don't: what if one perceives the other as their enemy?

To seal this improvised identity one needs an enemy: 'the non-people'. Best to keep it too as abstract as possible so anyone can invent their own version of what it means: 'the Establishment' will do, or 'elites', 'the swamp'. The spin doctor in Mexico admitted that, sadly, this could get nasty. Consider the US. The Trump presidential campaign targeted free-marketeers, American preservationists, 'anti-elites',[5] the working class – and that doesn't even touch on the multitude of micro-groups targeted on social media. Some social media ads didn't even mention Donald Trump himself, avoiding showing the reality-show star and focusing instead on touchy-feely messages that were quite out of synch with his vitriol. But, unlike their rivals in the Clinton camp, the campaign team then managed to unite all these different groups in a general anger at 'the swamp' and foreigners.

Or one could look at Italy, where the Five Star Movement started as a series of Facebook blogs representing completely different grievances for different audiences, from ecology to immigration, potholes in roads to foreign policy. The fault for all of these was laid at the door of 'the Establishment' and channelled through the manic energy of their anarchic, curly-haired, sweary leader, the comedian-turned-politico Beppe Grillo.

And then there's England. I used to think the English were different: that if anyone in the world knew who they were, it was them, a people defined so precisely by class, accent, schools, postcodes, counties, parties and sports teams it could be hard to know, for an immigrant like myself, how to fit in. But something has shifted. An air of uncertainty underlies everything.

I'd first noticed something was changing in Britain while talking to one of the architects of the Brexit campaign soon after his referendum victory, in a pub in London. He started a sentence by saying, 'The problem for people like you is . . .' I can't remember the rest (it may have been something like 'metropolitan liberals are so out of touch') because his opening words made me feel so unexpectedly at home. I'd always been the 'Russian' foreigner. Now, finally, I was no longer being asked to play the part of the outsider; I was in. This made me feel warm. That happiness, however, was quickly followed by dismay. The only reason I was being included was to play the puppet 'globalist', the enemy. 'People like you' was only being invoked as a contrast to the 'real people'. In the following months I heard other variants of this theme. 'It must be hard for people like you,' a Brexit activist consoled me. 'Can't you tell Brexit happened because of people like you?' a philosopher scolded me. It was confusing. What 'people' did they mean? I had always considered myself at most a lucky guest in England, and had been treated courteously as such, yet now I had woken up to find myself an enemy.

I got a more detailed picture of the logic of the Vote Leave campaign when I met with its lead digital officer, Thomas Borwick, who explained to me how the vote was won, revelling in the nerdy detail of his craft. Borwick comes from a family of

Conservative Party politicians (his mother is the former MP for Chelsea), and he approaches his work like a precocious schoolboy solving a puzzle or playing Risk.

Borwick's job as a digital campaign manager is first to gather as much data as he can about voters and then to try and calculate which ones are most likely to vote for his side. Over the decades the way one perceives the electorate has changed. Back in the Cold War one used to define the electorate along simple lines of economic class; ideological left versus ideological right; *Guardian* readers and *Telegraph* readers. Then, during the 1990s and early 2000s, when politics was reduced to just another consumer product, pollsters would draw on the categories provided by marketing companies. Tony Blair's New Labour would target categories like 'Ford Mondeo man' (a person who was very attracted to a certain kind of car), trying to satisfy their economic desires. Now that too seems outdated: people don't vote according to simple categories of consumer choice. Nor do newspapers or political parties necessarily represent clear social categories any more. In the early 2010s it became fashionable to define the nation along psychological lines, substituting economic class with types of psychology. Other pollsters looked for maps that measured status and self-reliance, secure versus insecure, closed versus open.

Now social media groups can give one the most accurate reflection of the thing that might motivate different groups to vote. Animal rights or potholes? Gay marriage or the environment? A country of twenty million, Borwick estimates, needs seventy to eighty types of targeted messages. His job is then to connect individual causes to his campaign, even if that connection might feel somewhat tenuous at first.

In the case of the vote to leave the EU, Borwick confessed that the most successful message in getting people out to vote had been about animal rights. Vote Leave argued that the EU was cruel to animals because, for example, it supported farmers in Spain who raise bulls for bullfighting. And within the 'animal rights' segment Borwick could focus even tighter, sending graphic ads featuring mutilated animals to one type of voter and more gentle ads with pictures of cuddly sheep to others.

Animal rights supporters may actually have a very different stance on immigration – they may well be for it – but that doesn't matter, as you are sending different targeted ads to various groups. And, of course, Borwick had the great catchphrase 'Take Back Control', so utterly spongy it could mean anything to anyone, with the EU framed as the enemy conspiring to undermine whichever cause it was you cared for.

'I believe that a well-identified enemy is probably a 20 per cent kicker to your vote,' he told me, always keen to add a data point to any statement.

And the EU has made for an easy enemy, distant and aloof. I was struck by this when I went back to visit my old school in Munich. There was a new glass and steel cube next to the original star-shaped building. The school's population had increased from 900 to 2,000 after EU enlargement to include many of the countries formerly under Soviet domination. The aula was now packed, and I could barely pick my way through the encampments of teenagers sitting cross-legged on the floor. There were so many people I couldn't make out any distinct languages, so great was the din. The way they dressed also seemed more uniform: Gap-style jeans and hoodies everywhere.

There were now so many EU bureaucrats with so many children that there was no room for pupils from outside, such as I had been. The dream for the European Schools had been to be a model for others, even to seep into the communities where they were located and transform them. Instead, the school in Munich, the new headmaster admitted, was disliked by locals, who couldn't send their children to it. When I looked up the headmaster from my time there, Herr Hoyem, he was even more strident: 'The schools were meant to be a pedagogical laboratory for Europe. Instead, they are becoming isolated company schools.'

The European Schools had become closed off from the Europe they'd once hoped to transform. It felt like a metaphor for so much of the EU project, as it struggled to articulate why it was a vision for all its citizens.

———

The Brexit vote had been one way of reconfiguring identity around a notion of 'the people'. But it would be a mistake to think it was the only way of reorganising political identity. For the next general election the Labour Party quickly came up with its own formula. Its slogan became 'For the many, not the few'. 'The many' combined utterly different groups, from those in the north of the country who voted for Brexit and resented well-heeled west Londoners, to well-heeled west Londoners who had voted to stay in the EU and thought Labour would reverse the Brexit vote. Labour managed to gather enough votes in the election to destroy the Conservative Party's majority. 'The people' had been reconfigured into 'the many', the 'enemies of the people' into 'the few'.

We are living through a period of pop-up populism, where each social and political movement redefines 'the many' and 'the people', where we are always reconsidering who counts as an 'insider' or an 'outsider', where what it means to belong is never certain, where bubbles of identity burst, crack and are then reformed as something else. And in this game the one who wins will be the one who can be most supple, rearranging the iron filings of disparate interests around new magnets of meaning.

One person excited by Labour's rise was Chantal Mouffe, the theorist who first formulated the idea of populism as a strategy, and who wanted to reinvent the left for an age when categories of economic class were no longer fixed.

Her husband Ernesto Laclau has passed away, but Mouffe is as active as ever. When we met in Vienna and then at her apartment full of plants and books in London, she told me that despite living in the UK since 1972, she had never felt British (it was the humour she couldn't understand), but she now saw a great change taking place in the country where she had lived for so long, and throughout much of the rest of the world as well.

In the decades since the 1980s – and the victory of capitalism over Communism in the Cold War – we have lived, argues Mouffe, within a sense of 'normal' to which there has seemed to be no alternative. Terms that had been so important for those struggling under authoritarian rule Mouffe saw as having been co-opted by economic interests. 'Choice' had become a way to justify relinquishing public control of schools and hospitals; 'liberty' had transmuted to selling off state assets.

'Thatcher managed to convince people that the state could only deliver benefits in a collectivist, oppressive way, while

215

privatisation would bring you liberty,' Mouffe told me in her highly accented English. 'Liberal democracy', she argued, had been skewed too far in favour of the word 'liberal', which had been used to privilege giving more freedom to financial powers, while what we needed was more 'democracy', or what she termed 'equality'. It was as if she wanted to prise apart words which, she felt, had been soldered together incorrectly.

Since the financial crash in 2008 everything was up for grabs again. It is in the space where words, desires, meanings and behaviours are put together and dissolved that the most important battles for power are played out, similar to Hizb's process of 'culturing'. This is what defines 'normal'. Mouffe used the term 'meta-politics', coined by the Italian philosopher Antonio Gramsci, to denote this process.

Mouffe is much more than a theorist, having worked with the Podemos movement in Spain and La France Insoumise in France. She told me an anecdote from France, where left-wing politicians had travelled to parts of the country that had always voted for the right-nationalist, anti-immigrant party of Marine Le Pen and tried to convince them that their actual enemy wasn't foreigners but the financial elites who kept them poor. 'Identities are the result of political construction,' she asserted.

But for all of Mouffe's enthusiasm, I was also worried. Hadn't some of the old freedoms, if one could still use that term, been there for good reason? Mouffe spoke about the need for a charismatic leader as an 'articulating agent' who could bring together the very different causes and grievances of the newly created 'people'; about the need for strong passions, the expressions of our deepest, unconscious drives, to bind them; about how important it was to define the enemy.[6] She argued this could be done within democratic rules, but it wasn't hard to imagine how it could turn into something frightening.

Mouffe agreed it is a dangerous time. 'It can go into a more authoritarian direction, or it can go also towards a more democratic thing. The whole question is how you construct the "us" and "them".'

There was perhaps no one who understood the game better than Martin Sellner, the Identitarian leader whom we met in Part 2 using Srdja Popović's protest tactics to pursue his vision of a 'culturally homogeneous' Europe.

'We don't want Mehmed and Mustafa to become Europeans,' the manifesto for Génération Identitaire runs. 'Europe belongs to the Europeans alone. Because we are Generation Identity.'

Sellner, like Mouffe, talked about meta-politics (and Gramsci). When I reached out to him again, this time for a BBC radio documentary, he explained that 'Our job as the avant-garde from the right is to show the people that the normality of tomorrow doesn't have to be what is considered normal today. Political normality is something very volatile, dynamic and relative.'

He taps into the language of rights and freedoms – women's rights especially – and connects them to his aims. In one stunt female Identitarians attended a meeting in support of women's rights in Germany, and then let off rape alarms to advertise cases of rape by Muslim migrants (of which there have been several, though the vast majority of sexual assaults are committed not by wandering migrants, but by people who know the victim well). In another stunt Sellner put a burqa over the statue of the Austro-Hungarian Empress Maria Theresa in Vienna. But instead of violence his language invokes freedom of speech, democracy, openness to new ideas . . .

'The powerlessness of our enemies is they are still trying to describe and fight us as if we were the old right-wing fringe-group parties that they faced decades before,' he told the programme I presented, as we all worried whether by interviewing him we were only helping to make him all the more mainstream, if such a concept even existed still.

The Future Arrived First in Russia

As I wondered about these endless transformations of 'the many' and 'the people', these desperate, fluctuating attempts to reinvent identity on the fly, I was struck by how I'd seen all of this before – in Russia, where I lived between 2001 and 2010.

'I first invented the idea of the Putin majority,' one of President Putin's early spin doctors, Gleb Pavlovsky, had told me when I still lived in Moscow, 'and then it appeared!'

I had left Russia in 2010 because I was exhausted with living in a system where, as I'd put it in a previous book, unconsciously invoking Hannah Arendt, 'nothing is true and everything is possible'. Those were still relatively vegetarian days in Moscow, before the invasion of Ukraine (though the invasion of Georgia and carpet-bombing of Chechnya should have been premonitions), but it was already a world where spectacle had pushed out sense, which left gut feeling as the only means of finding one's way through the fog of disinformation. I returned to London because, in the words of my naive self, I wanted to live in a world where 'words have meaning', where every fact was not dismissed with triumphant cynicism as 'just PR' or 'information war'.

Russia seemed to be a country unable to come to terms with itself since the loss of the Cold War, or with any of the traumas of the twentieth century. It was ultimately, I thought, a side-show, a curio pickled in its own agonies.

Then came the revolutionary year of 2016, and things became a touch more topsy-turvy. Suddenly the Russia I had known seemed to be all around me: a radical relativism which implies truth is unknowable, the future dissolving into nasty nostalgias, conspiracy replacing ideology, facts equating to fibs, conversation collapsing into mutual accusations that every argument is information warfare . . . and just this sense that everything under one's feet is constantly moving, inherently unstable, liquid.

And not only were attitudes I had witnessed in Russia uncannily prevalent, the country was also headlining the news all the time, invading Ukraine, bombing Syria, hacking the US, buying Europe. Putin smirked at me from newsstands and from the top of the ten o'clock news. 'You thought you could get away?' he seemed to be saying.

Despite all my efforts to escape Russia, it had followed me. What if I had been wrong during my years there? What if Russia was not an agonised curio in a historical blind alley? What if it had been a pre-echo of what was to come in the thing once known as the West?

With these questions in mind, I found myself turning back towards Russia, to the roots of the system I saw during my own years in Moscow, and to the 1990s, when Lina was making her films there. I got back in touch with Gleb Pavlovsky. He agreed to let me interview him over the phone, and as I sat in a BBC recording studio while he explained his tactics for creating the idea of 'the majority', 'the people' in 1990s Russia, it all began to sound remarkably familiar.

'The Communist ideocracy was sluggish, but it was an ideo-logical entity nonetheless,' he told me, gently advising me to ask more precise questions. 'Even up to the end people could at least argue over the positives and negatives of Communism. Now a vacuum arose, requiring a new language. We were an absolutely blank canvas. We had, in a sense, to reinvent the principles of the political system as best as possible.'

The vision of a pretty future of 'freedom' had fallen apart in the devastations of the early 1990s. Instead the landscape was dotted with new micro-movements making up their own terminology as they went along: National Bolsheviks; Liberal Democrats who were actually conspiratorial nationalists; Communists who were Orthodox monarchists with social programmes. When he polled the country, Pavlovsky found Russians believed in contradictions that didn't fit into any old conceptions of left and right. Most people believed in a strong state, if it didn't involve itself in their personal lives. Soviet categories such as 'workers' and 'intelligentsia' were useless in elections.

Pavlovsky experimented with a different approach to assem-bling a winning electorate. Instead of focusing on ideological arguments, he took quite different, often conflicting social groups and began to put them together like a Russian doll. It didn't matter what their opinions were, he just needed to gather enough of them.

'You collect them for a short period, literally for a moment, but so that they all vote together for one person. To do this you need to build a fairy tale that will be common to all of them.'

That 'fairy tale' couldn't be a political ideology: the great ideas that had powered collective notions of progress were dead. The disparate groups needed to be unified around a central emotion, a feeling powerful enough to unite all of them yet vague enough to mean anything to anyone. In 1996 the 'fairy tale' that Pavlovsky wrote for the campaign of the ailing, unpopular president Boris Yeltsin played on the fear that the country might collapse into civil war if he didn't win. He cultivated the image of Yeltsin as someone so reckless and dangerous he would be prepared to plunge the country into war if he were to lose. Survival was the story, fear of losing everything the feeling.

Pavlovsky's agency, the Fund for Effective Politics, went about smearing the opposition Communist Party in an early echo of today's 'fake news' and 'sock puppets'. Pavlovsky created posters that purported to be from the Communist Party and which claimed they would nationalise people's homes. He filmed actors posing as Communist Party members angrily burning anti-Communist pamphlets. He hired astrologers who would go on TV and predict that electing the Communists would lead to nightmare scenarios – even war with Ukraine.

Yelstin won an unlikely victory.

Pavlovsky had conjured up a new notion of 'the majority', but as this was no more than an emotional trick with little political content it fell apart soon afterwards, and work immediately began on a new one. He polled incessantly, an emerging science in Russia. When it became clear that the candidate people most respected would be an 'intelligent spy', a Russian James Bond, the Kremlin and its oligarchs began to search for potential successors from the former KGB. They landed on Vladimir Vladimorovich Putin.

This might seem a strange place for someone like Pavlovsky to end up. He had, after all, started as a dissident. In a book of conversations with the Bulgarian political scientist Ivan Krastev,[7] Pavlovsky recounts how as a schoolkid in 1960s Odessa he was already pulling pranks by sticking sheets of paper to teachers' backs which read, 'I vote for John F. Kennedy' – quite an act of anti-Soviet rebellion. As a young man he proliferated samizdat copies of Solzhenitsyn's *Gulag Archipelago*. When the KGB hauled him in in 1974, Pavlovsky, to his own amazement, panicked under pressure and ended up shopping one of his acquaintances. He would later recant his testimony, which meant his friend had to serve only a small stint in a psychiatric ward rather than in prison. In the early 1980s Pavlovsky went up to Moscow, edited one of the main dissident journals, *Searches*, and was arrested again. This time he confessed that he was guilty of 'slandering the Soviet Union'. Such a confession was seen as shameful in a dissident culture that prized the sovereignty of the individual in the face of state pressure above all else. After his arrest in 1982 Pavlovsky spent the years in prison and internal exile writing letters to the KGB, saying it should work with dissidents for the good of the Soviet Union. He was released in 1986. During perestroika he continued to believe that a reformed, cosmopolitan USSR was a better vehicle for progress than a potentially racist Russian nationalism. The need for a strong, centralised state became his great concern. By 1999 he was working to bring a KGB man to power.

For the 2000 presidential election the guiding 'fairy tale' was to pull together everyone who felt they had lost out during the Yeltsin years, the 'left behind', and imbue them with the sense that this was their last chance to be winners. These were completely disparate segments of society who in Soviet times would have been on different sides of the barricades – teachers and secret-service types, academics and soldiers – whom Pavlovsky would bundle together under the idea of the 'Putin majority'. As the likes of Borwick and others would discover decades later, in an age where all the old guiding ideologies have gone, where there is no coherent competition about political ideas for the future, the aim becomes to lasso disparate groups together around a new notion of 'the people', bound around an amorphous but powerful emotion which everyone can interpret in their own way, and then sealed with enemies who will threaten to undermine that feeling.

Putin won the election, the candidature of someone with a security-service background made all the more prescient as the news became filled with horrifying, panic-inducing footage of Islamist terrorists from Chechnya setting off one devastating bomb after another in Russian suburban apartment blocks, with hundreds killed under the rubble.

During Putin's almost two decades in power since Pavlovsky helped him become president, the idea of 'the majority' has been reorganised over and over, shuffled around, but always managing to unite utterly disparate groups around a rotating enemy: oligarchs at first, then metropolitan liberals, and more recently the whole outside world. Like some actionist performance artist, Putin poses bare-chested in photo ops of derring-do; instead of ideological coherence he offers the emotional highs of the local equivalent to 'Make Russia Great Again', bringing 'Russia off its knees'.

In that time Pavlovsky has been busy. He helped found Nashi, the patriotic youth movement that launched the 'denial of service' attacks at Estonia and harasses dissidents and journalists, and whose name, which literally means 'Ours', reduces politics to a series of pronouns: 'them', 'us', 'ours', 'theirs'. According to Dr Ilya Yablokov of Leeds University, an analyst of conspiracy theories in Russia, Pavlovsky's frequent media appearances in the first decade of the twenty-first century invoked an image of Russia besieged by enemies, with the West planning to turn Ukraine into a 'huge testing area for anti-Russian technologies'. The 'Putin majority' that he helped create became a 'truncheon to delegitimise its opponents. The division of society into Putin's majority and its enemies became a dominant political tactic.'[8]

At one point Pavlovsky got on the wrong side of the divides he helped instil, arguing that Putin should not return to the presidency in 2012 after a stint as prime minister. He was thrown out of the Kremlin. Having worked across such different shades of the Russian political spectrum, he remains an object of fascination and the subject of much comment, a sort of Everyman popping up in Russia's many tales.

———

When Pavlovsky looks at the West today, he sees it going through the same changes that Russia underwent in the 1990s, a delayed reaction to a similar crisis.

'The Cold War split global civilisation into two alternative forms, both of which promised people a better future,' he told me when I interviewed him from the BBC's studios. 'The Soviet Union undoubtedly lost. But then there appeared a strange Western utopia with no alternative. This utopia was ruled over by economic technocrats who could do no wrong. Then that collapsed.'

In this flux of identity and ideology political campaigners in the West have ended up adopting strategies strikingly similar to Pavlovsky's, though enhanced by social media and big data.

'I think that Russia was the first to go this way, and the West is now catching up in this regard. In general, the West can be considered to follow a proto-Putinism of sorts,' remarked Pavlovsky, wryly.

This is the great paradox of the end of the Cold War: the future, or rather the future-less present, arrived first in Russia. We are just catching up. Though maybe there's a simple cultural logic at work here: if our own ideological coherence was based partly on opposition to the Soviet Union's, when it collapsed we would inevitably follow.

In his book of conversations with Krastev, Pavlovsky invokes his mentor, a Russian historian of the Holocaust called Mikhail Gefter, who in the late Soviet era had already argued that mankind was running out of unifying, universal visions of historical development. In the 1990s Gefter predicted that the end of the Cold War would usher in an era of 'sovereign murderers'. In the absence of norms we have vacuums in which chaos agents behave according to rules they make up for themselves as they go along, who murder people and indeed whole peoples according to their own 'sovereign' logic. Pavlovsky sees this as prophetic, a vision from the early 1990s that anticipates 2019. 'The image of a common mankind is impossible, and no alternative has emerged. Everyone invents their own "normal" humanity, their own "right" history.'

The current Russian regime finds itself at ease in this environment because it has been finding ways to adapt to it for longer. There's nothing mystical at work in its all-pervasiveness;

it simply has a slight head start. And as our world becomes more uncertain and liquid, in ways which echo the new Russia, the more one can be tempted to yearn for the seeming certainties of the Cold War: if the Kremlin is the great enemy again, then maybe we will rediscover our own, once victorious meanings, a desire which in turn augments the current Kremlin's status, which risks playing into what it wants.

If there was one overarching aim to all of Pavlovsky's 'political technology', it was to resurrect the idea of the strong state when it had all but come apart. Back in the 1990s he'd figured out that though the Kremlin might be weak, he could make it seem strong domestically by spreading it everywhere in the information flows and media landscapes of people's lives. Now Putin, Pavlovsky told Krastev, can simulate global influence by purposefully leaving the fingerprints of his hackers and information operations all over the world. 'It's all just theatre for a world audience. *Theatrum mundi!*'

Part 6: The Future Starts Here

Conclusions and Recommendations

Before he came to meet me at South Kensington Tube station, Nigel Oakes had visited an exhibition at the Victoria and Albert Museum entitled 'The Future Starts Here'. While strolling through the exhibit he suddenly found himself riveted by a display. His heart rate shot up, he started trembling, he had to rush outside for air.

The display, which was called 'Can Democracy Survive the Internet?', was dedicated to a 'global election management' company called Cambridge Analytica. Cambridge Analytica claimed to have gathered 5,000 'data points' on every American voter online: what you liked and what you shared on social media; how and where you shopped; who your friends were . . . They claimed to be able to take this imprint of your online self, use it to understand your deepest drives and desires, and then draw on that analysis to change your voting behaviour. The boast seemed to be backed up by success: Cambridge Analytica had worked on the victorious American presidential campaign of Donald Trump; it had also run successful campaigns for US Senator Ted Cruz (twice); and others all across Africa, Asia, the Caribbean, Latin America.

The reason Oakes was so overwrought was that here, finally, was proof that he had been right all along. Cambridge Analytica was a spin-off from a company he created, Strategic Communication Laboratories (SCL), and it drew on his philosophy. All his adult life he had tried to prove that he had discovered the secret of mass persuasion. At first he had been laughed at, then criticised, but now his ideas were being paraded as an exhibit of the future in a world-renowned museum.

When we meet a little later the same day, Oakes is wearing a grey suit and a cap with the SCL logo on it, pulled low over cornflower-blue eyes.

'The thing about most advertising and influence campaigns – they're absolute bollocks,' he tells me at the start of our conversation. His dream, he repeats several times, was to create the ultimate influence weapon. Like any weapon, argues Oakes, it could be used for good or ill. He readily calls himself amoral.

He hadn't started off thinking about 'strategic communication'. He had originally wanted to be a composer, but there were no courses for composers at the Royal College of Music and he wasn't good enough at playing any one instrument to get in. After leaving school, he wrote theatre scores, but there was no money in that. He still composes organ pieces for weddings in the style of late baroque. Oakes smiles beatifically and hums when he recounts the joy of holding a whole crowd transfixed by music. But as a young man he needed a real career, and in 1988 he joined the advertising company Saatchi and Saatchi.

Oakes never went to university and at his exclusive, aristocratic public school, Eton College, had always felt himself both less academic and poorer than the other boys. Perhaps it was the need to overcome that feeling of academic inferiority which drove him to adopt such a scientific approach at Saatchi. Could the agency actually prove, he asked his colleagues, that its ads changed people's behaviour?

To his surprise he found there was little empirical evidence. Advertisers were good at shiny campaigns that got attention (agenda-setting). They could make a food or a politician or a country look more, or less, positive by associating them with things people liked, or disliked (framing). But changing attitudes, argues Oakes, is not the same as behaviour. Consider smoking. A campaign can show that smoking kills you. Smokers will agree it is bad but still continue with their habit. You need to work out why somebody smokes, argues Oakes, if you want to stop them from doing it. Young women, he found during his research, smoked because they thought it made them look attractive. So to change their behaviour you focus on how smoking makes their hair and breath stink, how it makes them unattractive.

In 1989 Oakes created the Behavioural Dynamics Institute, whose mission was to collect all the historical research on persuasion. Over the next four years, backed by investors from the advertising industry, he commissioned studies from dozens of academics. They wrote, to give but one example, about how Goebbels, Hitler's propaganda minister, promoted the use of the raised-arm *Sieg Heil* salute because he had worked out that the forceful exhalation of breath combined with strenuous arm movements caused hyperventilation and exhaustion in the audience, which made them more susceptible to messaging, almost putting them in a trance-like state.

The Institute developed new ways to define social groups. Descriptive categories (age, gender, social class) were of limited use as predictors of behaviour. Oakes pioneered surveys by teams of anthropology students, who, usually without revealing their mission, spent long periods penetrating a community, enquiring about who people hated and trusted, what they most desired, which friends would influence them, what dictated how they behaved within a group.

One research visit in particular stunned Oakes. It was to Moscow in 1990. After he gave a three-day talk on advertising at the state energy company Gazprom, he was offered a tour of the research centre of the KGB's Service A, as a sign of mutual respect and exchange of knowledge. The chief scientist was keen to tell Oakes all about his work. He had the freedom to conduct tests on whole villages, to test how communication and persuasion work. Oakes thought for a moment about the ethics of this (could you kill someone to test a hypothesis?) but was too excited to dwell on it. Such research was impossible in the UK. It was November, and Oakes was wrapped in a thick overcoat and mountain walking shoes, with suit shoes in his bag in case the KGB expected him to look more formal. The building wasn't heated, and he soon found that all the academics, sitting in one large open-plan office with few computers, were wrapped in thick coats themselves. Later, they sat down to lunch and the soup was served. It was watery, and Oakes realised the chef had given him the portion with the bone and a little meat on it as a sign of hospitality. The research that Service A was conducting was epic in its sweep, but the whole system was coming apart.

In 1993 the Behavioural Dynamics Institute collated its findings and Oakes created SCL, expecting to be swamped with offers. But instead of clients beating down his door at Lots Road, Chelsea, no one could understand what he was talking about. Why would you spend months penetrating a community with teams of anthropologists to sell a chocolate bar?

Then Oakes got a call. From South Africa. Apartheid was ending, black people were being given the vote for the first time – but would enough actually go to the polling stations?

Oakes was asked to identify who locals would listen to in each region to encourage them to vote. It worked. He realised elections, rather than chocolate bars, could be his game. In 1995, in Indonesia, he persuaded President Suharto, who was holding elections for the first time, to create completely separate political campaigns for the country's thousands of islands and across its 200 million population. It worked.

More elections followed, but Oakes was never in the big league of PR companies. His methodology was slow and expensive. His clients could be the sort of rulers who might hire him, take his research and then refuse to pay; and as they were in countries where the courts were not exactly independent, there was little Oakes could do to get his money.

In 2008 another Etonian, Alexander Nix, joined SCL. He was a different type of Etonian to Oakes: he came from a fabulously wealthy background, had studied art history at university and his friends called him 'Bertie', a nickname out of Edwardian England. Oakes says Nix wanted to drag the research into the digital age, wanted to make money. He was better with clients. In 2012 Nix took the elections part of the company and made it his own, renaming it Cambridge Analytica (a whistle-blower would later claim that mentioning the prestigious university, which the company had no official affiliation to, impressed American clients).

Cambridge Analytica furiously tested ways of replicating 'behavioural change' methodology by looking at people's social media use. They explored the potential of 'psychographics': the idea that your social media preferences and language predict your personality. Imagine you were running a campaign to support the right to bear arms. If the campaign manager knew someone was an anxious person, then they could target them with messages that argued they needed guns to keep them safe. The promotional literature the company put out boasted that their approach boosted voter turnout for their candidates in the 2014 US midterms by 30 per cent and over.

This is the potential nightmare of the new media: the idea that our data might know more about us than we do, and that this is then being used to influence us without our knowledge. What's unsettling isn't so much that 'they' know something about me that I considered private, hidden – though that's unpleasant, it's also somehow comforting, reinforcing the idea that there's a stable 'me' I am fully aware of, to protect me from 'them'; more disconcerting is the idea that 'they' know something about me which I hadn't realised myself, that I'm not who I think I am – one's complete dissipation into data that is now being manipulated by someone else.

Oakes, however, told me he was sceptical that Facebook likes and online product purchases could replicate months of in-depth, in-field research. He had refocused his own work onto Western militaries. The invasions of Iraq and Afghanistan had been disasters partly because no one had paused to understand the local populations. 'At least by the time we got out of Afghanistan we understood the locals. We left in a much more thought-through way than when we came in,' says Oakes. He called his part of the business SCL Defence.

In 2018 Nix was recorded by journalists telling a prospective client from Kenya he could use prostitutes as a honeytrap for the man's political rivals. It later transpired that Cambridge Analytica had access to the data of eighty-seven million Facebook users, without their consent. The sordid details seemed a far cry from the high-tech claims of psychographics.

The scandal destroyed Cambridge Analytica. At SCL Defence Oakes's military clients disappeared: no government would touch anyone even remotely associated with Analytica. But Oakes doesn't sound bitter about Nix. They had been partners. Nix had shared some of his profits with Oakes. And though he's lost his business, Oakes feels he's won the intellectual war. Everyone now agrees that influence means understanding your audience more fully than the next person, fitting your message to them rather than pushing an ideology top-down.

'Isn't that democracy,' asks Oakes rhetorically, 'when you give people what they want?'

His former colleague Nix made a similar argument when testifying to the UK Parliamentary Committee on Disinformation and 'Fake News', which I had been brought into as one of many 'specialist advisers'.

'We are trying to make sure that voters receive messages on the issues and policies they care most about . . . that can only be good for democracy,' Nix told the Committee, utterly unrepentant about any of his actions.

By the time I joined, the Committee had already been going for two years, and it had become obsessed with the question of what exactly was 'good for democracy' in an age of 'information abundance'. It had started by looking into 'fake news', but after astounded Members of Parliament heard testimony about how ethnic cleansing in Burma had been fuelled via Facebook, about Kremlin interference in Europe and the US, about how people's online information was used to target them in political campaigns, the members of the Committee decided that 'our existing legal framework is no longer fit for purpose'.

In this environment, people are able to accept and give credence to information that reinforces their views, no matter how distorted or inaccurate. This has a polarising effect and reduces the common ground on which reasoned debate, based on objective facts, can take place . . . the very fabric of our democracy is threatened.

In February 2019 I sat at the back of a room in the House of Commons as the Committee, made up of MPs from all parties, and their advisers went through detailed edits of their Conclusions and Recommendations. This was just the start of a long process. Their report would then be submitted to the government, which in turn was producing a White Paper with its plans on the subject, which would then be debated in Parliament. The editing process of the Committee was pernickety: MPs would question the meaning of each small phrase, the validity of each point of reference. It was slow going, but I found it oddly reassuring. Many novels of the nineteenth and twentieth century satirised the fussy language of bureaucracy, policy, the law. But in an age of utterly unstable meaning the slow, legalistic, evidence-scraping work of the Committee seemed a touch heroic.

Behind the MPs was a wide painting that showed a scene from the House of Commons in the eighteenth century, depicting men in wigs making some sort of elegant argument, while the other side listened politely and attentively. It was unlikely to have been a realistic scene – the House of Commons has always been a rowdy place full of cads and liars – but it did, at least, envision an ideal, what I imagined the Committee meant by 'reasoned debate' and 'fabric of democracy'. The room we sat in featured oak panelling and thick, emerald-green wallpaper emblazoned with paisley prints; there were oil paintings of nineteenth-century prime ministers on the walls, their eyes all arrogance and wit; the fireplace was engraved with wood carvings of heraldic signs. Sitting there one felt part of a tradition. Could it adapt to the present?

The Committee began their report by emphasising the need to have a common set of definitions. They had originally described themselves as being concerned with 'fake news', but then found the meaning of those words was morphing to denote any content that someone didn't like. They tried instead to differentiate between 'disinformation' (content designed to mislead) and 'misinformation' (content that misleads by accident). But many of the most pernicious campaigns I'd seen didn't necessarily use 'disinformation'. And even if 'disinformation' is identified, would, or indeed should, that make it illegal necessarily?

What if one were to refocus 'disinformation' from content to behaviour: bots, cyborgs and trolls that purposefully disguise their identity to confuse audiences; cyber-militias whose activity seems organic but who are actually part of coordinated campaigns full of fake accounts; the plethora of 'news' websites which look independent but are covertly run from one source, all pushing the same agenda? Shouldn't one have the right to know if what looks organic is actually orchestrated? How the reality one is interacting with is engineered?

Ultimately, what does it mean to be an empowered, 'democratic' citizen, the kind that Srdja Popović envisions, online? How can the digital world become the space where 'freedom', 'rights' – all those big words that have become bled of their vitality – are regenerated and given meaning?

One part of this is, as cybersecurity specialist Camille François argued, protection from coordinated campaigns of harassment and intimidation by the powerful. Another part is protecting privacy, so you decide which bits of your online activity end up in whose hands and for what purpose.

Sitting in the committee room I began to imagine an online life where any person would be able to understand how the information meteorology around them is being shaped; why computer programs show you one piece of content and not another; why any ad, article, message or image is being targeted specifically at you; which of your own data has been used to try and influence you and why; whether a piece of content is genuinely popular or just amplified. Maybe then we would become less like creatures influenced by mysterious powers we cannot see, made to fear and tremble for reasons we cannot fathom, and instead would be able to engage with the information forces around us as equals. Could we even be empowered to have a stake in the decision-making process through which the information around us is shaped, with public input into the Internet companies who currently preside over how we perceive the world in darkness?

If one could instil these principles, then much of the framework of information war would fall away. The way to judge information would not be whether it came from 'over there' or 'over here', but whether the way it is offered allows you to engage with it on equal terms, rather than being belittled by some force that takes away your understanding of how you are being acted on.[1]

Sitting in that emerald-green room, under the oil painting of idealised parliamentary democracy, I considered other ideas

I'd come across which could help find the 'common ground on which reasoned debate, based on objective facts, can take place'. In Denmark I had first been told about 'constructive news', a journalism which goes beyond merely 'balancing' one set of opinions against another, but is always trying to find practical solutions to the challenges which face its audience, forcing politicians to make evidence-based proposals, which one could then evaluate over time, pegging their words back to reality, generating a conversation where facts become necessary again. This approach could help reinspire trust in journalism, because we trust those who work together with us for some greater goal. And by putting change back into our own hands, it can overcome the sense of helplessness which conspiracy-peddling politicians so like to push to make you feel that only they can guide you through a murky world of insurmountable and hidden powers . . .

The bell rang to signal a new vote in the House of Commons, and I snapped back to the present. It was the middle of February 2019, and Parliament was still struggling over how the UK should leave the European Union, as ordained by the Brexit vote Tom Borwick and his team had won just over two years earlier. Maybe, hopefully, by the time you read this the question will have been happily resolved. Political language will be clear again, political parties will represent clear interests, the future will be clear. But in that moment Parliament was somewhat different. Round the curved, mock-Gothic stone stairwells, through narrow green and beige corridors, in crowded bars and on the terraces that seem to almost tumble into the Thames, you heard the same words repeated and echoed and reverberating: 'Brexit', 'the people's will', 'sovereignty'. What any of them meant was moot. Borwick had won the vote by talking to so many audiences in so many different ways that one couldn't say what the will of the people really was. Had the country voted to stop immigration? To protect animal rights? 'Brexit means Brexit', the prime minister had said, but what did 'Brexit' actually mean? And were the people whose will it claimed to represent the same as 'the many', whom the Labour Party now claimed to champion vis-à-vis 'the few'? But 'the few' Labour wanted to oppose were often the very ones who claimed to represent 'the people's will'. And who did these parties represent anyway, as in the middle of February 2019 they were all in a state of civil war, not only over leadership ambitions, but over their very meaning?

Leaping the Wall

Britain, Russia, the thing once known as the West, so many of the countries that had experienced 'democratisation' after the end of the Cold War were in a swirling state where notions of progress and identity were in flux. It would take more than a few regulations to fix that.

But what about China? Was it on another trajectory, one that perhaps I wouldn't like, but which at least could have coherence, a concept of the future one could engage with, even if in opposition to it? Could I find the future in Beijing?

It was my first-ever visit, and at Chinese passport control I had my fingerprints recorded and my photo taken, to be fed into a system of web cameras across the country which would instantly identify me wherever I might be – a reminder that China represents a sort of Dismaland of mass persuasion and surveillance, with every method of manipulation and control I have touched on in this book, and some more besides. Out in the west of the country there are labour camps right out of early-twentieth-century totalitarian dictatorships; in other places things resemble the 1970s. China has a human rights movement called Charter 08 (signed in 2008), which echoes Charter 77 (signed by Václav Havel and Czechoslovak dissidents in 1977). As with Cold War dissidents, Chinese signatories are imprisoned, marched onto television to confess their 'crimes', exiled.

For more contemporary techniques there are the legions of the Fifty Cent Army, so-called for the fifty cents they are paid to leave pro-government comments on Chinese social media. Researchers at Harvard University have established that these troll farms allow some criticism, but immediately censor any hints at protest. 'The Chinese people are individually free but collectively in chains,' concludes one study.[2]

Many Western websites are blocked in China behind the Great Firewall, so one has to use Internet services controlled by companies loyal to the regime. If any country would be first to perfect the use of data imprints to target people according to cognitive, psychographic and behavioural patterns, it would be China.

And then there's the 'social credit score', still under development, which promises to gather all the information about every individual Chinese person's behaviour, from how much money they spend on alcohol to their financial health to whether they visit their parents regularly, and then crunch it into a number that defines whether one can get a bank loan, a job, permission to travel.

China also has a full suite of foreign policy informational approaches. There's the vast international broadcaster, CGTN; the social media trolls who taunt politicians in neighbouring Taiwan; the pressure exerted on foreign academics who investigate the country.[3] A 2013 Pentagon paper reviewing China's doctrine of 'Three Warfares' (economic, media and legal) concluded that it showed 'twenty-first-century warfare guided by a new and vital dimension: namely the belief that whose story wins may be more important than whose army wins'.[4] This had been exhibited in the South China Sea, where China had annexed vast maritime spaces by first building artificial islands and then claiming the surrounding waters as its own, all without firing a shot.

But what, I thought as I moved through the immaculate, ambitious airport, created as a symbol of China's emerging strength for the 2008 Beijing Olympics, were all these techniques there to buttress?

———

2049. The date is repeated like a mantra in Beijing – in Communist Party speeches, on posters, in newscasts, pop videos, social media posts – so that it seems the whole vast country is being concentrated into a single year. The politburo of the Communist Party has declared that 2049 is the year the Chinese People's Republic will finally achieve 'full modernisation'. 2049 also coincides with the centenary of the founding of the People's Republic of China, still run by the Communist Party created by Soviet agents in the 1920s to spread the revolution to the East, but which has long since outgrown its original progenitor and transformed into something far more rich and strange.

When I first landed in Beijing, 2049 intrigued me. Could it be that here, after futureless, flattened Moscow, London and Washington, after all the nebulous nostalgias, I would find a hint of historical perspective?

The cityscape of Beijing reinforced the impression of progress, rising from the narrow alleys of the old town, where workmen in white vests slept in dark doorways with steaming barrels of soup behind them, up through the smog-shrouded, endless cubist hills of Communist apartment blocks, which often make Beijing indistinguishable from Moscow, and then up to the boastful, bullying ambition of the Central Business Area, with skyscrapers that manage to be both gargantuan and somehow squat, as if they are titans taking dumps in a line. These lead to the mind-bending building that houses the headquarters of CGTN, promoting China across the world as something big, inevitable, immovable, intimidating. From a distance the building looks like a giant pair of empty trousers striding across the skyline, but as you draw closer you realise it's one continuous tube, with the two towers at the side joined at the top and bottom into what the designers call a 'three-dimensional cranked loop structure', a vast, jagged, glass and steel uroboros.

In the staff cafeteria of Tsinghua University, an establishment with immaculate lawns that features its own opera house, I asked two academics what the future designated by 2049 was meant to bring. They immediately started disagreeing. One argued the official line: China was still on the path to Communism, but as the Communist idea of objective history presupposed that Communism had to proceed from capitalism, the party had fostered its own capitalism in order to be able to then surpass it with a return to true Communism. The other academic thought China was using capitalism as a way to return to a previous model of Chinese greatness, to a Confucian empire which, she argued, had little notion of linear historical development. 2049 was meant to see China's return to a futureless past.

China was sounding more familiar.

The next day I met with Angela Wu, a media and communications scholar from Beijing who now taught at New York University, and who had researched the formation of political identities on the Chinese Internet. I wanted her to explain to me what being pro- or anti-regime here really meant.

As we walked along the side of a traffic-congealed motorway, we passed posters bearing the latest government slogans:

'Community of Shared Future of Mankind!'

'Democracy! Liberty! Justice! Friendliness!'

The terms were in such contradiction with reality that their effect was to strip these pretty words of any intrinsic meaning, so they became signals that had to be loyally repeated to show fealty.

We were on our way to the school Wu had attended as a child, where her own journey into investigating 'self-formation' on the Chinese Internet had begun.

On the outer walls of her old school were head shots of the latest, most successful leavers, along with the names of their destination universities, printed on laminated posters to protect them from the rain. The vast majority were heading to the US. Opposite were huge sports fields, where Wu's exploration of political identity first began, quite by accident. As a pupil she had never understood why she wasn't being allowed to join the Communist Youth League. She had been marked down for 'political performance', but she had never even had any thoughts about politics at the time. Finally a teacher told her the reason. Every morning all the school had to gather in the playing fields for 'radio calisthenics': mass warm-up exercises performed to music and instructions blared out from a radio loudspeaker. Officially it was exercise, but the teachers used it as a way of measuring 'political appropriateness': was one prepared to fully participate in collective activities? Wu thought herself too cool and clever to dance with too much determination. She hadn't meant it as a form of political rebellion, but her teachers had marked her down for it.

Later, when she was studying at the Chinese University of Hong Kong, she began to ask more questions about the system she was brought up in. In the library she discovered books with photos of the Chinese murdered after the anti-regime demonstrations of 1989 in Tiananmen Square, which, unlike most uprisings across the world during that great 'wave of democratisation', had been crushed. On the mainland she had never seen images of those events, and there was something stunning about looking at them for the first time. But these books still upheld the state-sanctioned side of things: instead of photos of civilians killed by soldiers, they had pictures of government soldiers purportedly murdered by the demonstrators. Next to the photos other readers had scribbled, 'Lies!' The difference between Hong Kong and China, thought Wu, was that in Hong Kong the authorities had to go so far as to create books that showed their version of what happened in 1989, while on the mainland the story was silenced.

This was in 2008, and the Chinese blogosphere was blooming. But Wu found herself irked by how political identities had been categorised, both by the regime and by its opponents. One category was known as 'right-wing', which meant being 'pro-freedom', pro-West, seeing the state as the root of all evil, and was bundled together with everything from human rights through to the most radical of free-market economics. The opposing position was described as 'left-wing', which saw state involvement in the economy as vital and supported the Chinese government in everything apart from its cultural opening up to the West. Wu felt both categories were irrelevant to her personal experience: what if one believed in human rights, for example, but wasn't so sure about libertarian economics?[5]

When she moved on to a PhD programme in media, technology and communication at Northwestern University in the US, Wu found that American analysis of China could fall into another cliché, imagining some sort of innately freedom-loving Internet user silenced by an oppressive state, ready to jump into the arms of an American-style democracy the moment they could escape censorship.

Wu wanted to work out what really defined political identity in China. She started by analysing the issues that actually defined groups on the Chinese Internet. She found that economic issues, despite what the terms 'left-wing' and 'right-wing' would imply, were not actually particularly divisive; most people were pretty hazy when it came to economics generally. Neither was censorship something that divided people: both pro- and anti-government voices could want less of it. Instead, the divide lay in what Wu calls the 'China as a superpower ideology': a militarist, territorially obsessed nationalism intent on dominating others and which saw China as surrounded by enemies weaving conspiracies against her, which harped on the humiliations China suffered at the hands of European colonial powers in the nineteenth century, humiliations that the party claimed it could relieve by restoring past greatness. There were people who embraced this position, and others who didn't.

Rather than an alternative, China seemed to provide another variant of what I had encountered in the US and Russia, peddling a nostalgia for a greatness before the 'century of humiliations', much like Putin promised to 'bring Russia off its knees' and Trump to 'Make America Great Again'. The Chinese government even invoked colour revolutions as a threat.

After she had defined the party line, Wu wanted to understand more about those who were opposed to it. Her petri dish was a blogging site called Bullog, home to opposition writers, publicists and poets. She had spent years as a dedicated Bullog follower herself. She wanted to know more about the people who visited the site. What did they have in common?

She travelled all across the country, to many towns and cities she'd never visited before. Bullog readers, it turned out, came from all sorts of backgrounds: from civil servants in the interior to fashion-conscious students in the coastal mega-cities; from self-made business people to housewives. They didn't share much of a coherent ideology when it came to things like economics, but after conducting twenty-seven interviews Wu started to detect a pattern. Many had been voracious readers from a young age:[6] not factual material necessarily, but fiction, plays and poetry. This fitted in with previous studies Wu had come across, where the more creative the literature you read, the more you would be able to imagine a different reality to the one around you.

As they grew up, her fellow Bullogers moved from books to other media, and all shared a deeply emotional bond with it.

One man told her how he had cried when the first television had arrived in his rural village – it was his first link with the outer world. Others talked about how they preferred the company of blogging sites and newspapers to their friends and family.

This intense relationship with media in turn led to an awareness of the extent to which their world view and personalities were formed by it. Then would come a moment when they realised how duplicitous the Chinese state media was. For many it was in the aftermath of national catastrophes, earthquakes or train crashes, which the government had attempted to hush up. This provoked a sense that they had been 'brainwashed' by the regime and needed to 'purge' themselves of the information they had been consuming all their lives.[7]

And so began a journey of what they called 'leaping over the wall', a reference to the Great Firewall, which censors material on the Chinese Internet. Finding ways to leap the wall, through the use of various computer programs, became a whole subculture, with its own manuals and slang.

When they leapt the wall, however, the Internet escapees didn't feel they found 'reality' or stable ground elsewhere. There were Chinese anti-regime sites, but many of them indulged in their own disinformation. And the West barely represented a place driven by informed factuality. And so they carried on further and found themselves in a process of always trying to outstrip their own identities, endlessly leaping over walls.

Wu told me she hadn't been totally happy with the results of her research. It hadn't given her the clarity she had been hoping for. She now focused on analysing big data, and the results were more solid. It was, however, the very lack of a fixed end point which I found beguiling. It reminded me of how, at the European School, being 'European' didn't mean a new supra-identity, but the ability to move between different ones and wear them lightly. Or of Rashad's work, where he encouraged those drawn into extremism to unpick the patterns that had closed their attitudes so they could be both Muslim and British, Asian and from Yorkshire.

For the Bullogers, it was their relationship with media, with televisions, radios, books, blogs, which helped them to re-imagine themselves over and over.

That sticky day in Beijing, stuck in traffic on a flyover, with the 'cranked loop structure' of the CGTN building in the distance, I found myself turning back to Igor's first novella, *Reading Faulkner*. It seemed oddly relevant again, not so much about the Cold War – or maybe it was the Cold War that needed to be redefined. In the novella the author is constantly writing and rewriting his own life and his descriptions of his home town of Chernivtsi in different styles and genres influenced by his favourite author William Faulkner's book *The Sound and the Fury*. It was a novella that was in part about one's relationship with media, full of the sound of typewriters, radio, poetry (and for my parents, shoeboxes of samizdat, radio broadcasts, poems had literally been the things on which their lives had turned).

Early in the story the author is trying to work out where his sense of self begins, referencing Faulkner's writing, which constantly explores where awareness emerges. Does identity, Igor asks, begin with politics?

I am in a room of music and smoke. My father's taut back. The awfulness of newspaper editorials; what ponderous words father has to juggle. Machine and Tractor Stations, Party Directive . . . Did Faulkner begin with this? No.

Are religion and creed, then, where identity begins?

Midday, helmets of cupolas, steep steps, we're in T-shirts, six years old, in the cool close air of the church. From above a voice and a pock-marked face grunts: 'Out, Jewish runt.' Did Faulkner begin like this? No.

And so Igor reaches for somewhere beyond these, to a place where, if I understand him correctly, identity only appears when it recognises the presence of someone else.

A girl, on the shore of you. How high the sky. How deep the kiss. We do not say 'you' to each other but 'I'. I swim far out into you: past – buoys, past – horizons; glancing back could not see the rim of the shore and was glad. Remember how ten Julys ago you went into the breath-taking Black Sea and were a warm current in it? But does Faulkner have anything to do with this? He does. He does!

Lines that I find impossible to read without thinking that he would be arrested by the KGB when emerging from a real swim in the same sea soon after.

Chernivtsi/Czernowitz

During his decades away from Chernivtsi Igor had learnt to see his home town afresh.

Growing up he had been dimly aware that it had formerly been a distant province of Austro-Hungary, but he had no idea about the literary riches it had once yielded. It was only during conversations in Kiev, Austria, Israel that he learnt that before the Holocaust, the war and the arrival of the Soviet army, it had been home to renowned German and Austrian poets and writers (Paul Celan, Rose Ausländer, Gregor von Rezzori), legendary rabbis and Israeli novelists (Aharon Appelfeld), Romanian classics and all manner of great, late Austro-Hungarian tenors, economists and biochemists, who had all emerged in one great burst of early-twentieth-century energy and tragedy from this tiny town. Their memory had been suppressed in the Soviet Union, and it was only when he arrived in the West that Igor would meet people who would suddenly become animated when he mentioned where he had been raised: 'You are from Chernivtsi? A city of geniuses!'

And before the Austro-Hungarian era the town had another life as a distant outpost of the Ottoman Empire. This little place had so many histories, each with little knowledge of the others: Turk and Viennese, Romanian, Soviet, Ukrainian. It had different names too: Chernivtsi, Czernowitz, Черновцы, Cernăuți, Czerniowce, Csernovic, Chern. Away from the town, Igor was even inspired by its prison, which was built at the start of the nineteenth century. The square it stands in was called Criminal Square, then Soviet

Square, now Cathedral Square. How many layers of curses, verses, promises were scratched onto the walls of its cells in how many languages, raging at how many different overlords?

For decades Igor had tried to construct a world in the airwaves and in books that would interlace different cultures and could thus be home, when all the time he had the material of Chernivtsi to work with, a whole lost history to surface, like the computer scientists who raise unknown interconnections from the dark pools of data.

'Growing up,' Igor wrote, 'we were little barbarians. We couldn't feel solid ground under our feet. We had no idea what priceless ruins we walked over. Barbarism is the absence of memory.'

In 2009 Igor started going back to Chernivtsi. He began to organise a poetry festival in the town. Poets came from across the world, drawn to see the forgotten home of their literary heroes, and the faded lecture halls, libraries and cafes, which had long forgotten their own polyphonic ancestry, were suddenly full of readings in German and Yiddish, Hebrew, Romanian, Ukrainian, Russian, Polish, as well English, Flemish, French, Spanish . . .

Igor's aim was to awaken the memory of the town, not because the past can be recoverable, but because it can give an impetus for how Chernivtsi and Ukraine can understand themselves tomorrow, beyond the dead ends of information war.

Igor and Lina currently live in Prague, the city that Soviet tanks entered in 1968 in an invasion that did so much to turn Igor against the Soviet regime. This is where Radio Free Europe is now based, invited in 1995 by then president Václav Havel as a sign of thanks for the support of the Western 'voices' in the Cold War. Havel is now dead, those who still trumpet his ideals of 'living in truth' often scorned as naive 'Haveloids'. RFE lives in a strange

limbo, still dedicated to a set of ideals which the US may not con-
tinue to even pretend to support in the future. Indeed, calling it
'Radio' is already a misnomer, as it tries to straddle television,
podcasts, texts. 'Europe' is barely the right word either: most of
the language sections are now from Central Asia and the Middle
East. The majority of the Central and Eastern European services
were disbanded after those countries began to enter the EU. Since
then Hungary and Poland have slipped back into flirtations with
authoritarianism, led by nationalist politicians who were once
anti-Soviet dissidents, but for whom 'national rights' turned out to
be not the same as 'human rights'; being 'anti-Communist' turned
out to be not much of a political identity in and of itself.

Tomorrow morning Igor will head to work. He is the last Cold
War veteran at the 'Radio'. When students are brought round
on tours, he is pointed out like some sort of museum piece. He
still dreams of a radio of the future that can 'fuse the soul of
mankind', that can find the echoes and interconnections between
stories in Manila and St Petersburg, Mexico and Tallinn. In one
of his later books Igor came up with a tragicomic alter ego who
works at an international radio station and has become obsessed
with the idea that he can resurrect people through the power of
radio – a story that captures the strange mix of megalomania
and actual power bestowed on those who work in the media. The
idea had first come to Igor when he recalled how, when Cold War
political prisoners managed to get information about their cases
broadcast by Western media, it felt as if they had secured a few
minutes' liberty, or at least been given the possibility of exercising
in the open air – a second life on the airwaves, when the secret
police had squeezed their first. Now his alter ego stretched that
feeling further:

I have released thousands of voices into the cosmos.
According to the laws of physics,
these voices will live forever.
Who would have thought it: some drudge
goes to the office every day,
records somebody and then . . .
yes, then grants them immortality!

It is half-term and I am visiting my mother and father with my nine-year-old twin boys. They want to know if the world now was the same in Lina's youth. She tries to explain Kiev in the 1970s. Much sounds wild to them ('Igor was arrested for reading books? How? Why?' they ask). Other things can sound familiar.

'I had the sense that all the big, official words around us didn't mean anything any more,' says Lina. 'They were like old linen blowing in the wind, empty.'

And then she quotes a line from a poem: 'Dead words smell foul.'

I am surrounded by dead words. Or, to be more precise, the association of words and images, stories and meanings that I inherited have lost their power. The sight of a statue of a dictator being pulled down is still important to those people who lived under him, but I don't instantly connect to a story of ever greater freedom any more. Millions of people out in the streets of a city à la 1989 don't immediately signify a happy future. Perhaps it's not a coincidence that social media's favourite genre is memes: pictures that can be defaced by people with new phrases that change the meaning of the image, symptoms of a time when sense is ceaselessly unstable. So that one might take a picture of a pipe and write beneath it: 'This is not a pipe.'

The old associations were imperfect, often false. But they also held within them the memory of why they had mattered in the first place. Certain images and language were taboo because they acted like little knots tying in a notion of the unacceptable. Now these little knots are coming loose. In 2018, in Hungary, you could see government posters accusing Jewish financiers of undermining the nation, in visual motifs reminiscent of the 1930s, but at the time they didn't stop an ever-closer alliance between the Hungarian president and the Israeli prime minister, as if the latter no longer cared whether he was friends with someone who drew on Nazi codes. In the US, when criticism of the president is labelled 'McCarthyism' or Russia's trolls are compared to 9/11 or Pearl Harbor, the references are so shorn of context one imagines the wreckage from a plane crash in a desert, with commentators wandering around beating jet engines with spanners to make a spectacular sound that has no relation to the thing they're beating. In Britain the best-selling newspaper accuses independent judges of being Enemies of the People, calls for the crushing of saboteurs who oppose the government, in language popularised in the Soviet Union to validate mass murder, and whose use today only serves to debase the memory of those misdeeds.

When I began working on the passages about my parents in this book, I started off looking at how much has changed between the centuries, how the calcified words 'freedom', 'democracy', 'Europe', even whole genres of art have had their meaning stripped or hacked. Instead, I found myself awakening to the experiences which gave those words their power, which opens up the possibility for their regeneration in the future.

In a week's time we will be heading home to London, and I will be walking the boys up the hill to school. It's a Victorian

pile, and when you walk in there are flags of all the nationali-
ties of the children who attend. It looks like the UN, and I don't
know half the flags. What reconfigurations of identity will play
on this? Will there be ever more intense iterations of 'people'
and 'non-people'? I keep on waiting for the questions from the
twins to start. Are we English or Russian? Jewish? European?
Ukrainian? What do any of those words mean? Already I am
worrying about what to answer.

'The real you will emerge in the collisions between them!
Consider Chernivtsi!'

I wonder if they will understand if I quote Igor to them? Or has
something been passed on already?

The other day the twins were in a playground in the local park.
Another child came up to them and began asking, 'What are you?
Who are you? Tell me.'

There was a pause. What would the twins answer? Which
nation, creed, tribe, 'in' or 'out' group would they claim as theirs?
What clue would it give us for the future?

The twins considered the question seriously. Then they turned
and said, in unison, 'I'm Superman.'

The other boy answered, 'And I'm Batman.'

Acknowledgements

This book draws on essays published in *Granta*, the *Guardian*, *American Interest* magazine and the *London Review of Books*. I would like to thank my editors there for giving me the opportunity to develop my ideas. None of this would have been possible without the support and advice of Sigrid Rausing, Luke Neima, Pru Rowlandson, Jonathan Shainin, Damir Marusic, Daniel Soar, Mary-Kay Wilmers and Thomas Jones.

Zinovy Zinik, Frank Williams, Seva Novgorodtsev, Peter Udell, Masha Karp and Diran Meghreblian provided extensive and insightful background on the history of the BBC's Russian Service. Sergey Danilochkin and Arch Puddington did likewise for Radio Free Europe. Martin Dewhurst has been a source of many gems over the years. Michael Zantovsky advised on Václav Havel; Mario Corti on the *Chronicle of Current Events.*

Chloe Colliver and Melanie Smith have been most kind in helping me understand the basics of data analysis and 'the space'. Nick Cull has been a fount of knowledge about the history of propaganda. Thanks also to Leonard Bernardo and Chris Walker.

Ant Adeane was my excellent producer for the BBC Radio 4 *Analysis* programmes mentioned: 'British Politics: A Russian View' (broadcast 9 July 2018) and 'The War for Normal' (broadcast 28 January 2019). He, Anne Applebaum, Daniel Soar and Ben Williams have provided vital editorial support. Carolina Stern has been a terrific colleague at the LSE, helping me with numerous translations.

I owe a huge debt of gratitude to Paul Copeland and my parents for all their time, patience, multiple rereads and improvements. My aunt Sasha has been unstinting in her support, while my wife and children have been exceedingly understanding.

Igor Pomerantsev extracts: *Reading Faulkner*, translated by Frank Williams, with adaptations by Peter Pomerantsev; 'KGB Lyrics', translated by Frank Williams; 'Eye and a Tear', translated by Peter Pomerantsev (*Sintaksis*, 1979); 'Right to Read', translated by Marta Zakhaykevich (*Partisan Review*, vol. 49, no. 1, 1982); 'Radio Times', translated by Frank Williams.

Lina Pomerantsev documentaries: *Tripping with Zhirinovsky*, directed by Paweł Pawlikowski, released 1995; *The Betrayed*, directed by Clive Gordon, released 1995; *Mother Russia's Children*, directed by Tom Roberts, released 1992.

Radio programme referenced in the text: 'Reading Faulkner', narrated by Ronald Pickup, broadcast on BBC Radio 3, 2 August 1984.

Notes

I have intentionally changed one name and omitted some surnames to protect the contributors to this book.

PART 1

1 McCoy, Alfred, 'Dark Legacy: Human Rights under the Marcos Regime', *World History* archives, 20 September 1999. http://www.hartford-hwp. com/archives/54a/062.html.

2 Beck, H. P., S. Levinson and G. Irons, 'Finding Little Albert: A Journey to John B. Watson's Infant Laboratory', *American Psychologist*, 64(7), 605–14 (2009). http://dx.doi.org/10.1037/a0017234.

3 Ong, Jonathan Corpus and Jason Vincent A. Cabañes, 'Architects of Networked Disinformation', University of Leeds (2018); https:// newtontechfordev.com/wp-content/uploads/2018/02/ARCHITECTS-OF-NETWORKED-DISINFORMATION-FULL-REPORT.pdf.

4 Amnesty International, 'Detained Duterte Critic Must Be Freed Immediately' (23 February 2018); https://www.amnesty.org/en/latest/ news/2018/02/philippines-detained-duterte-critic-must-be-freed-immediately/.

5 Ressa, Maria A., *From Bin Laden to Facebook: 10 Days of Abduction, 10 Years of Terrorism* (London: Imperial College Press, 2013).

6 BBC News, 'Philippine President Duterte Calls God "Stupid"', 26 June 2018; https://www.bbc.com/news/world-asia-44610872.

7 Forrest, Adam, 'Jair Bolsonaro: The Worst Quotes from Brazil's Far-Right Presidential Frontrunner', *Independent*, 8 October 2018; https://www. independent.co.uk/news/world/americas/jair-bolsonaro-who-is-quotes-brazil-president-election-run-off-latest-a8573901.html.

8 Bakhtin, Mikhail Mikhailovich, *Rabelais and His World* (Bloomington, IN: Indiana University Press, 1984).

9 Ressa, Maria A., 'Propaganda War: Weaponizing the Internet', Rappler, 3 October 2016, updated 7 February 2019; https://www.rappler.com/ nation/148007-propaganda-war-weaponizing-internet.
Hofileña, Chay F., 'Fake Accounts, Manufactured Reality on Social Media', Rappler, 9 October 2016, updated 6 February 2019; https:// www.rappler.com/newsbreak/investigative/148347-fake-accounts-manufactured-reality-social-media.
Ressa, Maria A., 'How Facebook Algorithms Impact Democracy', Rappler, 8 October 2016, updated 6 February 2019; https://www.rappler. com/newsbreak/148536-facebook-algorithms-impact-democracy.

10 McCoy, Alfred W., *A Question of Torture: CIA Interrogation, from the Cold War to the War on Terror* (New York: Owl Books, 2006), pp. 79–80.

11 Conde, Carlos H., 'Aquino's Last Chance on Human Rights', Human Rights Watch, 27 July 2015; https://www.hrw.org/news/2015/07/27/aquinos-last-chance-human-rights.
Mydan, Seth, 'Aquino Said to Condone Human Rights Abuses', *New York Times*, 18 June 1988; https://www.nytimes.com/1988/06/18/world/aquino-said-to-condone-human-rights-abuses.html.

12 Gutierrez, Nataysha, 'Bots, Assange, an Alliance: Has Russian Propaganda Infiltrated the Philippines?' Rappler, 26 February 2018. https://www.rappler.com/newsbreak/in-depth/196576-russia-propaganda-influence-interference-philippines.

13 Lister, Tim, Jim Sciutto and Mary Ilyushina, 'Exclusive: Putin's "Chef," the Man Behind the Troll Factory', CNN, 18 October 2017; https://edition.cnn.com/2017/10/17/politics/russian-oligarch-putin-chef-troll-factory/index.html.

14 Howard, Philip, Bharath Ganesh et al., 'The IRA, Social Media and Political Polarization in the United States, 2012–2018' (Oxford, UK: Computational Propaganda Research Project, 2019); https://comprop.oii.ox.ac.uk/wp-content/uploads/sites/93/2018/12/The-IRA-Social-Media-and-Political-Polarization.pdf.

15 Cave, Andrew, 'Deal that Undid Bell Pottinger: Inside Story of the South Africa Scandal', *Guardian*, 5 September 2017; https://www.theguardian.com/media/2017/sep/05/bell-pottingersouth-africa-pr-firm.
Fielding, Nick and Ian Cobain, 'Revealed: US Spy Operation That Manipulates Social Media', *Guardian*, 17 March 2011; https://www.theguardian.com/technology/2011/mar/17/us-spy-operation-social-networks.

16 DiResta, Renee, Kris Shaffer, Becky Ruppel, David Sullivan, Robert Matney, Ryan Fox, Jonathan Albright and Ben Johnson, 'The Tactics & Tropes of the Internet Research Agency' (Austin, TX: New Knowledge, 2018); https://disinformationreport.blob.core.windows.net/disinformation-report/NewKnowledge-Disinformation-Report-Whitepaper.pdf.

17 Monaco, Nicholas and Carly Nyst, 'State-Sponsored Trolling: How Governments Are Deploying Disinformation as Part of Broader Digital Harassment Campaigns' (Palo Alto, CA: Institute for the Future, 2018); http://www.iftf.org/fileadmin/user_upload/images/DigIntel/IFTF_State_sponsored_trolling_report.pdf.

18 Wu, Tim, 'Is the First Amendment Obsolete?' Knight First Amendment Institute, Columbia University, September 2017. https://knightcolumbia.org/content/tim-wu-first-amendment-obsolete.

19 Gavilan, Jodesz, 'Maria Ressa's Arrest Part of Broader Gov't Campaign, Say Rights Groups', Rappler, 14 February 2019, updated 15 February

Notes

2019; https://www.rappler.com/nation/223457-human-rights-groups-statements-maria-ressa-arrest.

20 International Center for Journalists, 'Maria Ressa Accepts the 2018 Knight International Journalism Award', 2018; https://www.icfj.org/maria-ressa-accepts-2018-knight-international-journalism-award.

PART 2

1 Đondović, Jelena, 'Turci Optužili Bivšeg Otporaša: Srđa Popović ruši vlade!' *Alo!*, 25 August 2017; https://www.alo.rs/vesti/aktuelno/srda-popovic-rusi-vlade/120133/vest.

2 Popović, Srdja and Matthew Miller, *Blueprint for Revolution: How to Use Rice Pudding, Lego Men, and Other Nonviolent Techniques to Galvanize Communities, Overthrow Dictators, or Simply Change the World* (New York: Spiegel & Grau, 2015).

3 'Democracy Continues Its Disturbing Retreat', *The Economist*, 31 January 2018; https://www.economist.com/graphic-detail/2018/01/31/democracy-continues-its-disturbing-retreat.

4 Karnitschnig, Matthew, 'Aleksandar Vučić: Let's Not Go Back to the '90s', *POLITICO*, 14 April 2016; https://www.politico.eu/article/aleksandar-vucic-interview-serbia-balkans-migration-kosovo-bosnia/.

5 'Serbian Media Coalition Letter to the International Community', 22 October 2018; http://safejournalists.net/serbian-media-coalition-alerts-international-community/.
Trevisan, Matteo, 'How Media Freedom in Serbia Is Under Attack', *EUobserver*, 2 November 2018; https://euobserver.com/opinion/143268.
Reporters Without Borders, 'Who Owns the Media in Serbia?', 21 June 2017; https://rsf.org/en/news/who-owns-media-serbia.

6 Karnitschnig, Matthew, 'Serbia's Latest Would-Be Savior Is a Modernizer, a Strongman – or Both', *POLITICO*, 14 April 2016, updated 21 April 2016; https://www.politico.eu/article/aleksandar-vucic-serbias-latest-savior-is-a-modernizer-or-strongman-or-both/.

7 Mercea, D. and M. T. Bastos, 'Being a Serial Transnational Activist', *Journal of Computer-Mediated Communication*, 21(2), 140–55 (2016); http://openaccess.city.ac.uk/13151/7/Being%20a%20serial%20transnational%20activist_prepublication.pdf.

8 'Liberación de datasets sobre #YaMeCansé y Ayotzinapa'; https://loquesigue.tv/liberacion-de-datasets-sobre-yamecanse-y-ayotzinapa/.

9 Finley, Klint, 'Pro-Government Twitter Bots Try to Hush Mexican Activists', *Wired*, 23 August 2015; https://www.wired.com/2015/08/pro-government-twitter-bots-try-hush-mexican-activists/.

10 Olver, Dulce, 'El 81.3% de los ataques de bots en Edomex fueron contra Delfina, confirma otro análisis técnico', 1 June 2017; https://www.sinembargo.mx/01-06-2017/3230408.
Gallagher, Eric, 'Manipulating Trends & Gaming Twitter', *Medium*,18

December 2016; https://medium.com/@erin_gallagher/manipulating-trends-gaming-twitter-6fd31714c06c.

11 Woolley, Samuel C. and Douglas R. Guilbeault, 'Computational Propaganda in the United States of America: Manufacturing Consensus Online', Samuel Woolley and Philip N. Howard (Eds), Working Paper 2017.5 (Oxford, UK: Computational Propaganda Research Project); http://blogs.oii.ox.ac.uk/politicalbots/wp-content/uploads/sites/89/2017/06/Comprop-USA.pdf.

12 Griffin, Em, *A First Look at Communication Theory*, 7th edn (New York: McGraw-Hill, 2008); http://www.afirstlook.com/docs/spiral.pdf.

13 Noelle-Neumann, Elisabeth, *The Spiral of Silence: Public Opinion – Our Social Skin*, 2nd edn (Chicago, IL: University of Chicago Press, 1993).

14 Ibid., p. 218.

15 Kosachev, Konstantin, 'Neftegazovaia Diplomatia kak Ugroza Marginalizatsii', *Nezavisimaya Gazeta*, 28 December 2004; http://www.ng.ru/world/2004-12-28/5_uspeh.html (last accessed on 7 July 2009).

16 McGuinness, Damien, 'How a Cyber Attack Transformed Estonia', BBC News, 27 April 2017; https://www.bbc.com/news/39655415.

17 For background, see *The Humanitarian Dimension of Russian Foreign Policy Toward Georgia, Moldova, Ukraine, and the Baltic States*, Centre for East European Policy Studies, International Centre for Defence Studies, Centre for Geopolitical Studies, School for Policy Analysis at the National University of Kyiv-Mohyla Academy, Foreign Policy Association of Moldova, International Centre for Geopolitical Studies (2010, Gatis Pelnens, Ed.).
The Security Police of the Republic of Estonia, *Annual Review 2003*, p. 12.

18 Estonia was accused of rehabilitating fascist and Nazi ideology, revering Nazi symbols, glorifying SS veterans, brutally discriminating against the Russian-speaking population, denying the Holocaust, and Hitlerism. After the riots of 26–28 April 2007, direct threats against Estonia and insults targeting Estonians became widespread in the Russian press. Distorted versions of the names of the state and nation – e.g. 'eSStonia' and 'eSStonians' – appeared in the press, on the Internet and at demonstrations organised by pro-Kremlin forces. Some examples of typical accusations:
Interfax, 26 April – Moscow mayor Yuri Luzhkov: 'Estonian leaders have started to condone Fascism and to collaborate with Fascists. They have no right to rewrite history! They identify with the people against whom the entire Europe fought.'
Interfax, 26 April – Speaker of the State Duma, Boris Gryzlov: 'What is happening in Estonia is pure madness. What the Nazis did not manage to do to the living, the Estonian government is now trying to do to the dead.'
Ria Novosti, Oslo, 26 April – Sergey Lavrov: 'The situation

surrounding the Bronze Soldier is despicable. It cannot be justified. It will have serious consequences for Russia–NATO and Russia–EU relations because these organisations have welcomed a new member state that has trampled on all the values that form the foundation of the EU, European culture, and democracy.'

Interfax, 26 April – Chairman of the State Duma Committee on Foreign Affairs Konstantin Kosachev: 'In essence, Estonian authorities have taken a stand against the international public – against everyone who still remembers the price that was paid for victory. The actions of the Estonian leadership stimulate neo-Nazi and revanchist attitudes. As a result, Estonia is in opposition to modern European civilisation, to the entire civilised world. Estonia is undermining its relations with all the states that hold dear the memory of victory over Nazis.'

27 April – Statement by the Russian Communist Party: 'At a time when sixty years have passed since the end of the war, Fascism is reborn in Estonia! The removal of the memorial statue is a Fascist orgy. The first public battle with Fascism in the twenty-first century was held in Estonia.'

Strana.ru, 2 May – Russian representative Boris Malakhov's speech to the UN Committee on Information: 'Why are memorial statues to Soviet liberators removed? This raises the issue of whether these acts constitute attempts to rehabilitate Nazi crimes. Neo-Nazism is on the rise all over the world, as is demonstrated by the removal of memorial statues dedicated to soldiers/liberators.'

Interfax, 8 May – Chairman of the Federation Council Sergey Mironov: 'What was done by the Estonian leadership shows that Fascism and Nazism are reborn in Estonia.'

19 DiResta, Renee et al., 'The Tactics & Tropes of the Internet Research Agency'.

20 Associated Press, 'US Secretly Created "Cuban Twitter" to Stir Unrest and Undermine Government', *Guardian*, 3 April 2014; https://www.theguardian.com/world/2014/apr/03/us-cuban-twitter-zunzuneo-stir-unrest.

21 International Center for Journalists, 'Maria Ressa Accepts the 2018 Knight International Journalism Award'; https://www.icfj.org/maria-ressa-accepts-2018-knight-international-journalism-award.

22 Hosenball, Mark, 'British Authorities Ban Three Foreign Right-Wing Activists', Reuters, 12 March 2018; https://uk.reuters.com/article/uk-britain-security-deportations/british-authorities-ban-three-foreign-right-wing-activists-idUKKCN1GO2LO.

23 Ebner, Julia and Jacob Davey, *The Fringe Insurgency: Connectivity and Convergence of the Extreme-Right* (Institute for Strategic Dialogue, 2018); https://www.isdglobal.org/wp-content/uploads/2017/10/The-Fringe-Insurgency-221017.pdf.

24 'Text of Sakharov Letter to Carter on Human Rights', *New York Times*, 29 January 1977; https://www.nytimes.com/1977/01/29/archives/text-of-sakharov-letter-to-carter-on-human-rights.html.

25 'What Price a Soviet Jew?' *New York Times*, 22 February 1981; https://www.nytimes.com/1981/02/22/opinion/what-price-a-soviet-jew.html.

26 Saunders, Frances Stonor, *The Cultural Cold War: The CIA and the World of Arts and Letters* (New York: New Press, 2000).

27 Seaton, Jean, *Pinkoes and Traitors: The BBC and the Nation, 1974–1987* (London, UK: Profile Books, 2015).

28 'Ricin and the Umbrella Murder', CNN.com, 23 October 2003; http://edition.cnn.com/2003/WORLD/europe/01/07/terror.poison.bulgarian/.

PART 3

1 Panarin, Igor, *The First Information World War. Collapse of the USSR* (Piter, 2010). See also: Yablokov, Ilya, *Fortress Russia: Conspiracy Theories in the Post-Soviet World*, Chapter 3 (Cambridge, UK; Medford, MA: Polity, 2018); Lischkin, Shelepin, 'The Third Information-Psychological World War', *Moskva* (1999); Rastorguev, Sergey, 'Information War', *Radio and Communications* (1999).

2 Interview with Igor Ashmanov, 'I Packed My Gun with Data', *Rossiijskaja Gazeta*, 23 May 2013; https://rg.ru/2013/05/23/ashmanov.html.

3 Ibid.

4 @znak_com, 'Власть не может поверить, что люди добровольно вышли против пенсионной реформы. На митинги их согнал ужасный твиттер, который подсовывает Навального', Twitter, 14 September 2018, 5.53 a.m.; https://twitter.com/i/web/status/1040584225236373504.
'Igor Ashmanov: Freedom of Speech Is an Illusion That Is Part of the Information War', 5 June 2013; http://z-filez.info/story/igor-ashmanov-%E2%80%9Csvoboda-slova-%E2%80%93-eto-takaya-illyuziya-kotoraya-yavlyaetsya-chastyu-informatsionn.

5 'И Ашманов Свобода слова как инструмент', YouTube, uploaded by Khnar Film, 25 December 2018; https://www.youtube.com/watch?v=cb6fqc02vt0.
Interview with Igor Ashmanov, 'I Packed My Gun with Data'.

6 Interview with Igor Ashmanov, ibid.

7 Foot, Rosemary, 'The Cold War and Human Rights', in Melvyn P. Leffler and Odd Arne Westad (Eds), *The Cambridge History of the Cold War, Vol. III* (Cambridge, UK: Cambridge University Press, 2010), pp. 445–8.

8 Lakoff, George, *Don't Think of an Elephant* (Hartford, VT: Chelsea Green, 2014).

9 Atlantic Council – Digital Forensic Research Lab, 'Question That: RT's Military Mission', *Medium*, 8 January 2017; https://medium.com/dfrlab/question-that-rts-military-mission-4c4bd9f72c88.

10 Kofman, Michael, 'The Moscow School of Hard Knocks: Key Pillars of Russian Strategy', *War on the Rocks*, 27 January 2017; https://warontherocks.com/2017/01/the-moscow-school-of-hard-knocks-key-pillars-of-russian-strategy/.

11 Bērziņš, Jānis, 'Russia's New Generation Warfare in Ukraine: Implications for Latvian Defense Policy', National Defense Academy of Latvia, Center for Security and Strategic Research (2014).

12 A good resource for Kremlin influence campaigns in Ukraine is https://www.stopfake.org/en/news/.

13 'Disinfo News: The Kremlin's Many Versions of the MH17 Story', *StopFake*, 29 May 2018; https://www.stopfake.org/en/disinfo-news-the-kremlin-s-many-versions-of-the-mh17-story/.

14 Hill, Thomas M., 'Is the U.S. Serious about Countering Russia's Information War on Democracies?', 21 November 2017; https://www.brookings.edu/blog/order-from-chaos/2017/11/21/is-the-u-s-serious-about-countering-russias-information-war-on-democracies/.

15 Website of Andrey Shtal: https://www.stihi.ru/avtor/shtal.

16 Amos, Howard, '"There Was Heroism and Cruelty on Both Sides": The Truth Behind One of Ukraine's Deadliest Days', *Guardian*, 30 April 2015; https://www.theguardian.com/world/2015/apr/30/there-was-heroism-and-cruelty-on-both-sides-the-truth-behind-one-of-ukraines-deadliest-days.

17 Ennis, Stephen, 'Vladimir Danchev: The Broadcaster Who Defied Moscow', BBC Monitoring, 8 March 2014; http://www.bbc.co.uk/news/magazine-26472906 (last accessed 25 August 2017).

18 'A Nuclear Disaster That Brought Down an Empire', *The Economist*, 26 April 2016; https://www.economist.com/europe/2016/04/26/a-nuclear-disaster-that-brought-down-an-empire.

19 Radio interview for BBC Russian Service, Margaret Thatcher Foundation, 11 July 1988; https://www.margaretthatcher.org/document/107072.

20 Ibid.

PART 4

1 PolitiFact, 'Donald Trump's File', www.politifact.com/personalities/donald-trump (accessed 20 July 2016); PolitiFact, 'Hillary Clinton's File', www.politifact.com/personalities/hillary-clinton (accessed 20 July 2016).

2 BBC Breadth of Opinion Review; http://downloads.bbc.co.uk/bbctrust/assets/files/pdf/our_work/breadth_opinion/content_analysis.pdf.

3 BBC News, 'Kremlin's Chief Propagandist Accuses Western Media of Bias', 23 June 2016; http://www.bbc.co.uk/news/world-europe-36551391.

4 Yaffa, Joshua, 'Dmitry Kiselev Is Redefining the Art of Russian Propaganda', *New Republic*, 1 July 2014; https://newrepublic.com/article/118438/dmitry-kiselev-putins-favorite-tv-host-russias-top-propogandist.

5   Balmforth, Tom, 'Gene Warfare? Russia Raises Eyebrows', Radio
    Free Europe/Radio Liberty, 3 November 2017; https://www.rferl.
    org/a/russia-biological-warfare-accusations-raise-eyebrows-
    lawsuit/28834069.html.
    Lomsadze, Giorgi, 'Does the US Have a Secret Germ Warfare Lab on
    Russia's Doorstep?', *Coda Story*, 19 April 2018; https://codastory.com/
    disinformation/information-war/does-the-us-have-a-secret-germ-
    warfare-lab-on-russias-doorstep/.
    See also EU Versus Disinfo website, which tracks disinformation and
    has an archive of stories: https://euvsdisinfo.eu. For example, https://
    euvsdisinfo.eu/report/ukraine-asked-the-united-states-to-spread-the-
    ebola-virus/; https://euvsdisinfo.eu/report/there-is-a-secret-laboratory-
    near-kharkiv-where-ukrainians-with/.
6   Ferraris, Maurizio, *Introduction to New Realism* (London, UK:
    Bloomsbury, 2014).
7   Roy, Deb, 'The Spread of True and False Information Online', MIT Media
    Lab; https://www.media.mit.edu/projects/the-spread-of-false-and-true-
    info-online/overview/.
8   Lewis, Paul, '"Fiction Is Outperforming Reality": How YouTube's
    Algorithm Distorts Truth', *Guardian*, 2 February 2018; https://www.
    theguardian.com/technology/2018/feb/02/how-youtubes-algorithm-
    distorts-truth.
9   Zollo, F., P. K. Novak et al., 'Emotional Dynamics in the Age of
    Misinformation', *PLoS ONE*, 10(9): e0138740 (2015); https://doi.
    org/10.1371/journal.pone.0138740.
10 Brodsky, Joseph, 'A Commencement Address', *New York Review of Books*,
    16 August 1984; https://www.nybooks.com/articles/1984/08/16/a-
    commencement-address/.
11 Judt, Tony, 'From Military Disaster to Moral High Ground', *New
    York Times*, 7 October 2007; https://www.nytimes.com/2007/10/07/
    opinion/07judt.html.
12 Schmidt, Brian C. and Michael C. Williams, 'The Bush Doctrine and
    the Iraq War: Neoconservatives Versus Realists', *Security Studies*,
    17(2), pp. 191–220 (2008); https://www.tandfonline.com/doi/
    full/10.1080/09636410802098990.
    'In Bush's Words: "Iraqi Democracy Will Succeed"', *New York Times*,
    6 November 2003; https://www.nytimes.com/2003/11/06/politics/in-
    bushs-words-iraqi-democracy-will-succeed.html.
13 Boym, Svetlana, *Nostalgia and Its Discontents*, https://agora8.org/
    SvetlanaBoym_Nostalgia/.
14 Tarabay, Jamie, 'For Many Syrians, the Story of the War Began
    with Graffiti in Dara'a', CNN, 15 March 2018; https://edition.cnn.
    com/2018/03/15/middleeast/daraa-syria-seven-years-on-intl/index.html.
15 For more on language in Assad's Syria, see Lisa Wedeen's great

book *Ambiguities of Domination: Politics, Rhetoric and Symbols in Contemporary Syria* (Chicago, IL: University of Chicago Press, 1999).

16 Associated Press, 'A Look at Key Events in Syria's Aleppo since 2016', 14 December 2016; https://apnews.com/300da72a31284420810e1ba9ebef2052.

17 Amnesty International, 'Death Everywhere: War Crimes and Human Rights Abuses in Aleppo, Syria', 2015; https://www.amnesty.org.uk/files/mde2413702015english.pdf?R9pyrgEmq_XcKpQAqW_t2G8oKziKBO0h=.

18 Barnard, Anne and Somini Sengupta, 'Syria and Russia Appear Ready to Scorch Aleppo', *New York Times*, 25 September 2016; https://www.nytimes.com/2016/09/26/world/middleeast/syria-un-security-council.html?smid=tw-share&_r=0&module=inline.

19 Atlantic Council, 'Breaking Aleppo', 2017; http://www.publications.atlanticcouncil.org/breakingaleppo/attacks-overview/.

20 For background on the use of barrel bombs and attacks on medical facilities, see: Boghani, Priyanka, 'A Staggering New Death Toll for Syria's War – 470,000', PBS, 11 February 2016; https://www.pbs.org/wgbh/frontline/article/a-staggering-new-death-toll-for-syrias-war-470000/; Barnard, Anne, 'Death Toll from War in Syria Now 470,000, Group Finds', *New York Times*, 11 February 2016; https://www.nytimes.com/2016/02/12/world/middleeast/death-toll-from-war-in-syria-now-470000-group-finds.html; Physicians for Human Rights, '2015 Marks Worst Year for Attacks on Hospitals in Syria', 18 December 2015; https://phr.org/news/2015-marks-worst-year-for-attacks-on-hospitals-in-syria/; International Committee of the Red Cross, 'Syria: Aid Stepped Up Amidst Heavy Fighting in Aleppo Province', 10 February 2016; https://www.icrc.org/en/document/syria-fighting-conflict-aleppo.

21 Physicians for Human Rights, 'UN Security Council Calls for End to Attacks on Doctors, Hospitals', 3 May 2016; https://phr.org/news/un-security-council-calls-for-end-to-attacks-on-doctors-hospitals/.

22 Syrian American Medical Society, 'The Failure of UN Security Council Resolution 2286', January 2017; https://www.sams-usa.net/wp-content/uploads/2017/03/UN-fail-report-07-3.pdf.

23 McKernan, Bethan, 'Aleppo Attack: Syrian Army to Invade City with Ground Troops', *Independent*, 23 September 2016; https://www.independent.co.uk/news/world/middle-east/aleppo-syria-war-assad-troops-to-invade-city-under-siege-rebels-a7326266.html.

24 Atlantic Council, 'Breaking Aleppo'.

25 BBC News, 'Syria Conflict: US Accuses Russia of Barbarsim in Aleppo', 26 September 2016; https://www.bbc.co.uk/news/world-middle-east-37468080.

26 Atlantic Council, 'Breaking Aleppo'.

27 Osborne, Samuel, 'Donald Trump Wins: All the Lies, Mistruths and

Scare Stories He Told During the US Election Campaign', *Independent*, 9 November 2016; https://www.independent.co.uk/news/world/americas/donald-trump-president-lies-and-mistruths-during-us-election-campaign-a7406821.html.

28 Graham, David, 'The Wrong Side of the Right Side of History', *The Atlantic*, 21 December 2015; https://www.theatlantic.com/politics/archive/2015/12/obama-right-side-of-history/420462/.

29 Shaheen, Kareem, '"Hell Itself": Aleppo Reels from Alleged Use of Bunker-Buster Bombs', *Guardian*, 26 September 2016; https://www.theguardian.com/world/2016/sep/26/hell-itself-aleppo-reels-from-alleged-use-of-bunker-buster-bombs.

30 Violations Documentation Centre: http://www.vdc-sy.info. http://www.vdc-sy.info/index.php/en/martyrs/1/c29yd GJ5PWEua2lsbGVkX2RhdGV8c29ydGRpcj1ERVNDfGFFwcHJvdmVkP XZpc2libGV8ZXh0cmFkaXNwbGGF5PTB8cHJvdmmluY2U9NnxzdGFydE RhdGU9MjAxMi0wNy0xOXxlbmREYXRlPTIwMTYtMTItMjJ8. See also: Guha-Sapir, Debarati, Benjamin Schlüter et al., 'Patterns of Civilian and Child Deaths Due to War-Related Violence in Syria', *The Lancet, Global Health*, 6 December 2017; https://www.thelancet.com/journals/langlo/article/PIIS2214-109X(17)30469-2/fulltext.

31 Syrian Network for Human Rights: http://sn4hr.org/.

32 Specia, Megan, 'Death Toll in Syria: Numbers Blurred in Fog of War', *Irish Times*, 14 April 2018.
Boghani, Priyanka, 'A Staggering New Death Toll for Syria's War – 470,000'.
Barnard, Anne, 'Death Toll from War in Syria Now 470,000, Group Finds'.
Physicians for Human Rights, '2015 Marks Worst Year for Attacks on Hospitals in Syria'.

33 Dove, Steve, '*The White Helmets* Is the 2017 Oscar Winner for Documentary (Short Subject)', ABC, 27 February 2017; https://oscar.go.com/news/winners/the-white-helmets-is-the-2017-oscar-winner-for-documentary-short-subject.

34 Solon, Olivia, 'How Syria's White Helmets Became Victims of an Online Propaganda Machine', *Guardian*, 18 December 2017; https://www.theguardian.com/world/2017/dec/18/syria-white-helmets-conspiracy-theories.

35 Buncombe, Andrew, 'Trump Suggests "Vicious World" Should Be Blamed for Khashoggi Murder While Disputing Saudi Responsibility', *Independent*, 22 November 2018; https://www.independent.co.uk/news/world/americas/us-politics/trump-khashoggi-murder-blame-vicious-world-saudi-journalist-a8647701.html.

36 Miliband, David, 'America Is Fueling Our Age of Impunity. Just Look at Yemen', *Guardian*, 5 April 2019.

37 Cruickshank, Michael, 'A Saudi War-Crime in Yemen? Analysing the Dahyan Bombing', *Bellingcat*, 18 August 2018; https://www.bellingcat.com/news/mena/2018/08/18/19432/.

38 Safi, Michael and Amantha Perera, 'Sri Lanka Blocks Social Media as Deadly Violence Continues', *Guardian*, 7 March 2018; https://www.theguardian.com/world/2018/mar/07/sri-lanka-blocks-social-media-as-deadly-violence-continues-buddhist-temple-anti-muslim-riots-kandy.

39 Hall, Eleanor, 'Syrian War Crimes Evidence Strongest Since Nuremberg Trials', ABC News, 3 December 2018; https://www.abc.net.au/radio/programs/worldtoday/these-are-crimes-the-world-wont-forget-stephen-rapp-on-syria/10577142.

40 Puddington, Arch, *Broadcasting Freedom: The Cold War Triumph of Radio Free Europe and Radio Liberty* (Lexington, KY: University Press of Kentucky, 2015).

41 Parta, Eugene, *Discovering the Hidden Listener: An Empirical Assessment of Radio Liberty and Western Broadcasting to the USSR in the Cold War* (Stanford, CA: Hoover Institution Press, 2007).

42 Zinik, Zinovy, 'Soviet Paradise Lost', *Carnegie International*, Vol. 1 (Carnegie Museum of Art, Pittsburgh, PA; Rizzoli, New York, 1991).

43 Groys, Boris, *History Becomes Form* (Cambridge, MA: MIT Press, 2010).

PART 5

1 al-Nabahani, Sheikh Taqiuddin, *The Islamic Personality*, Vol. 1 (2005); http://www.hizb-australia.org/wp-content/uploads/2012/03/Shakhsiyya-I.pdf.

2 Central Intelligence Agency, 'Release of Abbottabad Compound Material', November 2017; https://www.cia.gov/library/abbottabad-compound/index.html.

3 Institute for Economics & Peace, *Positive Peace Report 2018: Analysing the Factors That Sustain Peace*, Sydney, October 2018; http://visionofhumanity.org/app/uploads/2018/11/Positive-Peace-Report-2018.pdf.

4 Institute for Strategic Dialogue, '"I Left to Be Closer to Allah": Learning about Foreign Fighters from Family and Friends', 2018; http://www.isdglobal.org/wp-content/uploads/2018/05/Families_Report.pdf.

5 National Public Radio, 'Study: No One Issue Clearly Unites 5 Groups of Trump Voters', 2 July 2017; http://www.npr.org/2017/07/02/535240706/study-no-one-issue-clearly-unites-5-groups-of-trump-voters. Bowman, Carlyn, 'Who Were Donald Trump's Voters? Now We Know', *Forbes*, 23 June 2017; https://www.forbes.com/sites/bowmanmarsico/2017/06/23/who-were-donald-trumps-voters-now-we-know/#bdc19a138942.

6 Mouffe, Chantal, 'The Affects of Democracy', *Eurozine*, 23 November 2018; https://www.eurozine.com/the-affects-of-democracy/.

7 Krastev, Ivan, *Experimental Motherland. A Conversation with Gleb Pavlovsky* (Europa, 2018).

8 Yablokov, Ilya, *Fortress Russia: Conspiracy Theories in the Post-Soviet World* (Cambridge, UK; Medford, MA: Polity, 2018), p. 30.

PART 6

1 Committee for Culture, Media and Sport, 'Disinformation and "Fake News"', 18 February 2019; https://publications.parliament.uk/pa/cm201719/cmselect/cmcumeds/1791/179102.htm.
Gyldensted, Cathrine, *From Mirrors to Movers: Five Elements of Constructive Journalism* (GGroup Publishing, 2015).
Ghosh, Dipayan and Ben Scott, 'The Technologies Behind Precision Propaganda on the Internet', *New America,* 23 January 2018; https://www.newamerica.org/public-interest-technology/policy-papers/digitaldeceit/.

2 King, Gary, Jennifer Pan and Margaret E. Roberts, 'How Censorship in China Allows Government Criticism but Silences Collective Expression', *American Political Science Review*, 107(2) (2013), pp. 1–18; https://gking.harvard.edu/publications/how-censorship-china-allows-government-criticism-silences-collective-expression.
MacKinnon, Rebecca, 'Liberation Technology: China's "Networked Authoritarianism"', *Journal of Democracy*, 22(2) (2011); https://muse.jhu.edu/article/427159.

3 Roy, Eleanor, 'I'm Being Watched: Anne-Mary Brady, the China Critic Living in Fear of Beijing', *Guardian*, 23 January 2019; https://www.theguardian.com/world/2019/jan/23/im-being-watched-anne-marie-brady-the-china-critic-living-in-fear-of-beijing.

4 Halper, Stefan et al., 'China: The Three Warfares', prepared for Office of Net Assessment, US Department of Defense (2013).

5 Wu, Angela, 'Ideological Polarization Over a China-As-Superpower Mindset: An Exploratory Charting of Belief Systems Among Chinese Internet Users, 2008–2011', *International Journal of Communication*, 8 (2014), pp. 2,243–72.

6 Wu, Angela, 'The Shared Pasts of Solitary Readers in China: Connecting Web Use and Changing Political Understanding through Reading Histories', *Media, Culture & Society*, 36(8) (2014), pp. 1,168–85.

7 Wu, Angela, 'Brainwashing Paranoia and Lay Media Theories in China: The Phenomenological Dimension of Media Use (and the Self) in Digital Environments', *Media, Culture & Society*, 40(6) (2018), pp. 909–26.